Reconstructing Church

Reconstructing Church

Tools for Turning Your Congregation Around

Todd Grant Yonkman

An Alban Institute Book

ROWMAN & LITTLEFIELD
Lanham • Boulder • New York • London

Published by Rowman & Littlefield
4501 Forbes Boulevard, Suite 200, Lanham, Maryland 20706
www.rowman.com

10 Thornbury Road, Plymouth PL6 7PP, United Kingdom

British Library Cataloguing in Publication Information Available

Library of Congress Cataloging-in-Publication Data

Yonkman, Todd Grant, 1970–
Reconstructing church : tools for turning your congregation around / Todd Grant Yonkman.
pages cm
"An Alban Institute book."
Includes bibliographical references.
ISBN 978-1-56699-762-1 (cloth : alk. paper) — ISBN 978-1-56699-721-8 (pbk. : alk. paper) — ISBN 978-1-56699-715-7 (electronic)
1. Church renewal. I. Title.
BV600.3.Y66 2014
254—dc23
2014016084

Printed in the United States of America

Contents

Preface

When my wife, Nicole, and I were first dating, I took her backpacking in the Big South Fork National River and Recreation Area near Oneida, Tennessee. My brother and I had gone backpacking there a couple of times during our college spring breaks. We had had good experiences exploring new territory, bonding, and enjoying the great outdoors. Nicole also enjoyed backpacking, so I was hopeful that this would be a nice opportunity for the two of us to share some time together away from divinity school. We had been dating for six months or so. Things were going well. She had met my family. I had met hers. We shared a passion for ministry and scholarship. It was time to take things to the next level—or so I thought. And what better way than eating macaroni and cheese from a camp stove and sleeping on the ground? We planned the trip for our spring break. We would spend four days and three nights on the trail, which left us a day for travel from Chicago to Oneida and back on either end of the trip. For the first three and a half days on the trail, everything went well. The weather was nice. The trail was as I remembered it. I showed Nicole the good camping spots, the scenic overlooks, the swimming hole underneath a waterfall. We had packed just the right amount of food and gear. Then, on the last leg of our journey—just a mile or two from the trailhead, our car, and hot showers—we took a wrong turn, or rather, I did.

We were standing at a fork in the trail. One direction invited us to ford the river and continue into the woods on the other bank. The other direction would take us along the riverbank on which we stood. I remember the stress building as I stood on the riverbank, the wrinkled, trail-stained map in my hand. I wiped sweat from my eyes as I tried to figure out where we went wrong. "We should have gotten there by now," I said to Nicole. We had eaten the last of our food hours ago, and it was now past lunchtime. Nicole was getting irritated. This was the first time I learned what I now have come to accept as a fact of my existence: when Nicole says she needs to eat, she needs to eat—like, now. In any case, we had nothing to eat.

We started to argue about which way to go, whether we were lost (we were), and whose fault it was (mine, of course), which turned the stress level up a notch higher. Finally, in a fit of frustration, Nicole decided to follow the trail across the river. Normally, she would take her boots off first to keep them dry, but getting to the car was so urgent, she left her boots on, and her feet got soaked. Nicole's instincts about direction were correct—though her wet feet made her even more miserable. We were about a fifteen-minute walk from our car, some snacks, and a hot shower. Today—after seventeen years of marriage, two kids, and five churches—this is an adventure story we tell and retell as a little snapshot of our emotional-spiritual DNA as a couple and ministry team.

Writing a preface is a little like inviting you, the reader, on an adventure through territory that I, the writer, have already explored. But that certainly doesn't mean I know everything about it, that there aren't many more interesting discoveries for us to make, or that there won't be any perplexing moments when we'll have to stop, check the map, and get back on track. As the above story illustrates, even with a map, one can still get turned around, because, as philosopher Alfred Korzybski famously wrote, "The map is not the territory."[1] And even in this era of Google Earth, territory—especially theological territory, which is what this book is about—tends to change faster than maps do. Keeping this in mind will be helpful to us as we develop together a map or maps (which I call *ministry models*) of church redevelopment in postmodern contexts.

If this is true for adventures in unfamiliar territories, it can also—even especially—be true in walking familiar paths. One function of postmodern thought is to destabilize received certainties and thereby raise awareness of unconsciously held assumptions—a calling into question of what German theologian-philosopher G. W. F. Hegel called the "familiarly known."[2] Almost two centuries ago, Hegel warned that *received* truths were not necessarily *known* truths—that knowing truth was a process that had to be engaged again and again, sometimes starting all over from the beginning. For Hegel, the truth is the *whole* and the whole truth includes both the proposition and all the reasoning that leads to the proposition. The destination and journey can't be separated. Memorizing a map is no substitute for walking the path.

If you've picked up this book, it may be that you thought you knew how to do church. After being raised in the church, attending Christian schools from kindergarten through college, studying theology in Germany, and graduating from three years of divinity school, I certainly thought I did. Or perhaps you're attempting to lead a congregation of people for whom the truths of church life are entirely obvious to themselves and completely opaque to everyone else. This is how we can get lost even in familiar territory: the landscape has changed, but our maps have not. That's the situation in which Beneficent Church found itself four years ago when Nicole and I were called to serve as senior co-ministers there.

Perhaps you are a pastor who found the title of this book interesting, or maybe you find yourself leading a dying church and are desperately looking for answers. Perhaps you're a lay leader who has dedicated years of your life and a significant chunk of your hard-earned money to an organization that now finds its future in question. Perhaps you're a denominational leader who is noticing that too many of your congregations are either stagnant or declining. Perhaps you're a seminary student who has been warned about congregational decline, and you're wondering if anything can be done about it. If you're ready for an adventure in the strangely familiar territory of the (once) mainline Protestant church in America, this book is for you. It is an attempt to write a practical theology of church redevelopment in a postmodern mode. The approach I am taking is a close examination—a close reading, if you will—of a congregation (namely, Beneficent Church) that I hope will seem in some ways familiar to you. The postmodern practice of close reading of the familiarly known, which opens up new possibilities for life and fresh perspectives for practice, grounds the approach to this practical theology.

The following is a study of one congregation—Beneficent Church, Providence, Rhode Island—that has undergone a successful and faithful process of redevelopment over a period of four years.[3] The congregation has been successful in an institutional sense in that we now have enough human and financial resources that we no longer feel the threat of imminent demise. The church has been faithful in that a key to our new life as a congregation has been an authentic connection to our spiritual heritage—what scholar Diana Butler Bass might call *religio*: experiencing the divine in community. As reader and writer, you and I will not have the time or space to examine every aspect of the congregation's history and context. We will not be able to examine in detail every decision, every conversation, or every contribution that brought Beneficent Church to where it is today. To make meaning, we have to make decisions, and—though I've had a lot of help with, critique of, and conversation about these topics—I take responsibility for the decisions that have yielded this text.

Instead of imagining this study as complete, perfected, and comprehensive, I invite you to imagine it not only as a journey through (un)familiar territory, which may have both familiar and unfamiliar aspects, but also as a microscope through which we will examine a small slice of congregational life. A microscope is a powerful tool for helping us see something familiar from an *other* perspective. I remember the first time I looked at a tissue sample through an electron microscope in college. I was disoriented at first because I had a sense of not knowing what I was looking at anymore. A familiar, often overlooked object was suddenly rendered strange. Perhaps this feeling of disorientation, discomfort, or *dis-ease* is a small taste of how a person suffering Parkinson's disease regards his hand: that over which he once had mastery now feels out of control—a frightening prospect that demands incredible spiritual fortitude.[4] Interrogating the obvious and unmasking mastery are a couple of things postmodern thinkers love to do and a couple of the reasons why postmodern thought is useful for the practice of church redevelopment. One key to successful and faithful redevelopment at Beneficent Church was Nicole's and my willingness (for me, it was a *grudging* willingness) to let things be (to a certain extent) out of control and our willingness relearn (to a certain extent) how to be pastors for this particular context.[5]

Mainline Protestant churches—particularly the historic, urban churches to whom this book is primarily addressed—could be thought of as the back of America's hands: so familiar as to be overlooked, and yet, on closer examination, increasingly foreign to the culture to which it gave birth. Churches were among the first institutions established by early settlers of North America, and they played a decisive role in shaping the history and values of civic life and culture in the United States. Although what are now known as mainline Protestant churches were not de jure the established religion of the land, they were de facto the moral arbiters of culture. This situation has been rapidly changing over the past fifty years, or, in some cases—like the one described in this study—even longer. The church built 250 years ago on the green at the center of town in many cases is no longer the center of town life.

Mainline Protestant churches are becoming disestablished relative to their standing among other institutions in American culture. For some congregations, this has meant a new lease on life. No longer burdened with the responsibilities of being chaplains to political and economic power, they have reinvented themselves in myriad ways that allow them to carry their gospel heritage into new mission fields. Having grown dependent on the tacit support of the wider culture, many other congregations now find themselves foundering as that support is slowly withdrawn. They suffer dis-ease at the loss of cultural privilege and all the institutional benefits that attend this elevated status. These congregations may or may not have the resources and willingness to engage in the work of church redevelopment, which I define as imagining and actualizing new life in dying churches.

Church redevelopment cannot be done alone. Either it is done together as a community or it is not done at all. In a similar way, this book is the result of a community effort. I would like to thank and acknowledge the many good folks who have contributed to it, including all at Beneficent Church, and particularly the thirteen co-researchers who participated in the qualitative interview portion of this study. Thank you to Paul Nickerson, our redevelopment coach, without whose guidance and support the new life at Beneficent Church likely would not have emerged. I would also like to thank the editors with Alban Institute—Richard Bass, Fritz Gutwein, and Andrea Lee—for guiding this manuscript to publication. I thank my beautiful daughters, Fiona and Olivia, for supporting my writing by doing "homework club" with me at the kitchen table. Most of all, I thank my wife and co-pastor, Nicole Grant Yonkman, without whose unfailing support and skillful shared leadership neither the redevelopment at Beneficent Church nor this book about the congregation's redevelopment would have been possible.

I would also like to extend my gratitude and respect to the thinkers—scholars, philosophers, theologians, sociologists, historians, pastors, educators, consultants—who provide the broader context and framework for this study. The hope is that this selected assemblage will result in a productive and mutually influencing *multidisciplinary transformative conversation*. In a lecture on postmodern theology and spirituality, theologian Shelly Rambo described herself as an "interloper" in postmodern conversations. She warned the class that we would be trespassing into philosophical and theological territories that were not *ours*, in which others might have greater expertise, and which have been constructed with great care. I imagine this book in a similar way. Born in 1970, I consider myself a postmodern native.

Nevertheless, my area of expertise is as a religious practitioner—a practical theologian unafraid and unashamed to beg, steal (not without attributing the source, of course!), or borrow from any resource that will help me more effectively and faithfully help people connect to God. In fact, one key of successful and faithful church redevelopment is getting help wherever you can find it from whomever God has brought into your life. Theologian Catherine Keller invites us to be open to "new and stranger coalitions" as we walk this creative edge.[6] As we step off the edge of the map into this strangely familiar territory, we humbly thank our unlikely allies—trailblazers, traveling companions, teachers, and friends who will help make this impossible journey possible.

One such strange ally to this study is twentieth-century philosopher Jacques Derrida. Derrida (1930–2004) was an Algerian Jew who lived and worked in France. Of himself, he said he "could rightly pass for an atheist"; yet he wrote extensively—even lovingly—about religion, theology, God, Judaism, and Christianity.[7] Toward the end of his life, he spoke movingly about his personal practice of prayer, saying, "If you knew my experience of prayers, you would know everything."[8] This led one Christian philosopher John D. Caputo to dub Derrida (with a touch of irony) "St. Jacques." Derrida's writing contains ideas to unsettle thinking across the religious, philosophical, theological, and political spectrum. It would be naïve for anyone—secular, religious, atheist, believer, liberal, conservative—to assume Derrida is one of us. Nevertheless, I will approach his work as a potential friend whose practice of deconstruction and attention to difference continually point toward the undeconstructible or the "indescribable undestructible"[9]—what Derrida terms the call to justice, the yes, the Messiah, the "to come."[10]

The map for ministry in postmodern contexts will borrow heavily from what's gone before. The exciting thing about postmodernity for some traditionalists is that what's gone before and perhaps disappeared from view—what Derrida (following philosopher Emmanuel Levinas) calls the "ancient"—reappears. But before you long-timers get too excited about a return to the past, let me warn you that traditions frequently reappear in strange and transfigured forms. After all, much of postmodern thought centers on repurposing.

Derrida calls his work "bricolage." *Bricolage* is a French term referring to "(1) a piece of artwork assembled from a diverse range of things that happen to be available, (2) a skill that involves using bits of whatever is to be found and recombining them to create something new, and (3) a very skilful professional DIY [do it yourself] expert."[11] Derrida describes the work of *decon-struction*—a key term for this book—as bricolage.[12] In this study, bricolage is simply meant to emphasize the style of this text as an assemblage of carefully chosen and more or less close-at-hand heterogeneous voices and perspectives. It also suggests that the kind of theology we are doing here has an aesthetic quality that is not entirely accidental. That aesthetic notions of beauty, harmony, pattern, form, design, and the like play a role in this post-modern practical theology mirrors responses gathered in the interviews I conducted for the study, many of which mentioned the beauty of the worship space or the quality of the music or other aesthetic elements of the church as factors in the redevelopment process. The image below shows a detail from a bricolage by Gary Jackson to help illustrate the metaphor of bricolage for both the form and the method of this book.[13]

Bricolage resonates not only with the form of this study and the process for constructing it but also with the process of church redevelopment itself in at least two ways. First, creative use of the tools and materials at hand—whatever they may be—is key to successful and faithful church redevelop-ment in a postmodern context. In my experience, you're never going to have

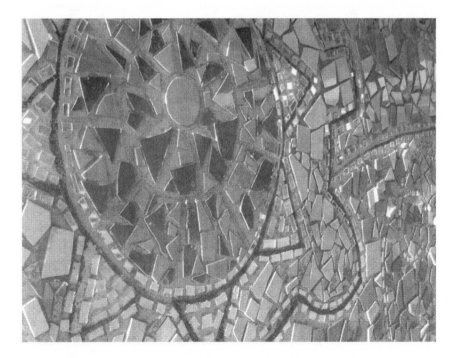

all the resources, training, and so forth that you need to get the job done as you envision it. Improvisation and making do are givens. Volunteers aren't going to have all the gifts and graces needed for the congregation's programs. I've served churches with millions of dollars in endowments and churches that use a pay-as-you-go budgeting process: in both "rich" and "poor" churches there is never enough money to do everything you want to do in the way you want to do it. I was not perfectly trained or prepared for redevelopment work when my ministry context demanded it. I only slowly gained the skills and knowledge needed as I experimented with different approaches, tried different strategies, succeeded, and failed.

Second, bricolage resonates with theologian Diana Butler Bass's practice of *retraditioning*, which is simply taking inherited religious resources—symbols, theologies, traditions, practices, stories, histories, and so forth—and putting them to new uses in new contexts.[14] In the process, both resources and contexts are transformed. What was once so familiar as to be overlooked suddenly becomes strange, new, and perhaps even revelatory. Throughout this study, we will observe a number of instances of retraditioning at Beneficent Church.

Finally, I want to offer a word of love and respect to the LGBTQ members of Beneficent Church. After an initial failed attempt, in 2001 Beneficent Church voted to become a denominationally designated congregation that is "Open and Affirming" to LGBTQ individuals.[15] The contributions of gays and lesbians to the success and faithfulness of the redevelopment work this book documents have been significant. Not long after voting to become Open and Affirming, the congregation became the home of the Providence Gay Men's Chorus (PGMC). Through our ministry partnership with PGMC, both organizations have grown. We are one of the first, and probably the largest presence, among the religious groups at the annual Providence Pride Fest, and Beneficent members helped found the annual Providence Interfaith Pride Service. In 2013, when the same-sex marriage bill that ultimately was passed into Rhode Island law was first making its way through the state senate, Nicole and I had the honor of testifying on behalf of Beneficent Church in favor of the bill. Our LGBTQ members are some of the strongest leaders, best evangelists, and biggest financial contributors in the congregation. Gay and lesbian folks were among the people who contributed to the interview study that informs this book (explained in detail in the introduction). Because the study doesn't specifically highlight the contributions of the LGBTQ community to Beneficent's redevelopment, I want to acknowledge them here.

Years after my adventure in Big South Fork with Nicole, our ministry of church redevelopment led me to work as a substitute teacher in a poor, rural high school in northern Maine (it's a long story). One of the hallway walls in the school displayed a handmade poster with a quotation from novelist Marcel Proust: "The voyage of discovery is not in seeking new landscapes but in having new eyes." My hope is that this study of one local congregation experiencing new life after many years of decline will inspire you in the work of redevelopment, that it will help you see your context with "new eyes," and that by courageously facing your situation, you will come to know that while new life for congregations is not guaranteed, it is nevertheless possible.[16]

KEYS FOR REDEVELOPMENT

A willingness to let things be out of control, to a certain extent.

A willingness to relearn, to a certain extent, how to be pastors for this particular context.

Getting help wherever you can find it from whomever God has brought into your life.

Creatively using the tools and materials at hand, whatever they may be.

Introduction

To think and act practically in fresh and innovative ways may be the most complex thing that humans ever attempt. [1]
—Don S. Browning, *A Fundamental Practical Theology*

The following is a story of the redevelopment process under way at Beneficent Church, an urban, mainline Protestant, multiracial, multicultural, Open and Affirming, peace with justice congregation located in Providence, Rhode Island. [2] Church redevelopment is the work of imagining and realizing new life in dying congregations. This is a story of how God in partnership with a small group of people is creating new life in a congregation left for dead. And though it's a story, it's not just any story. It's a special kind of story genre called practical theology.

DECONSTRUCTION AND DIFFERENCE

Practical theology as described in this book is an attempt to tell a story about God, a congregation, and its leaders in a particular place at a particular point in history. It's about God's call and the things a people did in response—in other words, their *practices*. Hence, *practical theology*. And while writing practical theology can take a number of different forms—including the traditional *applied theology* method in which systematic theology is *applied* to a practical ministry situation in a way analogous to applying theoretical physics to an engineering problem—the approach I am using in this book takes the view that God speaks authoritatively not only through academic theologians but also through faithful laypeople and practicing clergy as they give

1

testimony to the work of God in their lives. So this practical theology has the form of testimony, a concept to which we will return in chapter 6. The hope is that the story of a particular congregation's redevelopment practices—those things Beneficent Church did to partner with God in creating new life—will inspire you to do your own practical theology in your own particular context.

A number of stories and histories of Beneficent Church have been written, told, and passed on throughout the centuries. Some of these accounts have been written and published by previous pastors of Beneficent Church itself: Arthur Wilson and James Vose, to name two. Others stories, articles, and journals have been written by journalists, laypeople, historians, and the like. These form a veritable mountain of sources dutifully archived at the church, the Rhode Island Historical Library, the Congregational Library in Boston, and other places. I will refer to a selection of these sources in this retelling, which is also a rereading woven from a number of different threads and told from a number of different perspectives in a number of different voices. It's a story woven of stories. I will try to gather these perspectives, hear these voices, and center this narrative around two key concepts: deconstruction and difference.

Deconstruction will take several forms throughout this story, but, briefly defined, deconstruction is the awareness that any creative process in which we seek to organize our experience or generate knowledge—that is, every system of meaning, whether it's a story, theology, a congregation, a denomination, a song, a nation, and so forth—is constituted and maintained through acts of exclusion. Something invariably gets left out.[3] There is always a remainder. We simply can't include everything. Human beings—and even God, if we take the biblical testimony seriously—have to make decisions. Deconstruction is the fruit of decision.

Deconstruction's accomplice, *difference*, is the notion that the play of distinguishing marks—whether the succession of words on a page, the timed variations of musical pitches in the air, or that something (or things) that allows me to distinguish, for example, between this congregation and another—generates meaning. Difference is also the mark of the *other*: that which is excluded from or more often *exceeds* the meaning and coherence we try to create for our lives. The other is that unassimilated, incomprehensible something that continually threatens to disrupt our dearly held certainties. Think of God, for example, who is described as "beyond all knowledge and all thought" in Horatius Bonar's hymn "O Love of God, How Strong, How

True." God may be the ultimate other, or, as theologian Karl Barth famously wrote, the wholly other.[4]

Deconstruction and difference at work produce a surprising result for church redevelopment: Beneficent Church has discovered that redevelopment work is justice work. Church redevelopment is a deconstructive-reconstructive movement that happens inside people individually and communally as differences are respected, entrenched power is called into question, and systems of equity are created in which the voices of marginalized others can be heard and have influence on congregational culture.

Deconstruction and *difference* may be unfamiliar terms to you. Perhaps you have heard them in connection to the word *postmodern*. For the time being, I invite you simply to welcome them into this conversation, trusting that they will become more familiar and perhaps even friendly as this practical theology unfolds.

Beneficent Congregational Church was founded in 1743 during the First Great Awakening—a revival movement that reshaped the religious landscape of colonial America and gave birth to much of what we now know as evangelical Christianity in the United States. We will pick up this thread in chapter 1. Beneficent is located in downtown Providence, Rhode Island, on the campus of Johnson and Wales University, two blocks from the largest homeless shelter in the state, two blocks from the Providence Performing Arts Center, four blocks from City Hall, half a mile from the Rhode Island School of Design and Brown University, and half a mile from the State House. Beneficent Church has a large meetinghouse built in 1809, which is on the National Register of Historic Places. The church also owns a small park next to the meetinghouse, a 180-unit apartment building, and a historic home known as the Palmer House.

Beneficent was once the largest congregation in the state. In 1930 it boasted a membership of almost 1,000—enormous for the time. The church outgrew its 1809 meetinghouse, which seats about 750, so in the late nineteenth century an additional chapel—known as the Round Top Center—was constructed, complete with its own pipe organ. Beneficent reached its peak membership in the 1930s as the population of Providence reached its peak. Precisely at that point, both the church and the city began a long, slow decline. While Providence began something of a turnaround in the 1990s, Beneficent found itself foundering in a very different downtown from the one it helped build many decades earlier.

By the time my co-pastor, Nicole, and I arrived in 2009, Beneficent had an average Sunday worship attendance of thirty-five and an active membership of about fifty. A cycle of anxiety and significant conflict was disrupting the congregation's conversation about its long-term viability. Over the next four and a half years, redevelopment work at Beneficent Church would ease the cycle of anxiety and conflict, increase average weekly worship attendance to about 150, weekly children's Sunday school participation from five in 2009 to thirty-five in 2014, and add 114 (and counting) new members to the church. About 75 percent of today's active members have come to Beneficent in the last three years. Financial pressures remain but have lessened considerably. Beneficent Church has a history of religious, cultural, ethnic, racial, and economic diversity, but redevelopment has brought this aspect of the church to the fore. The once majority European American congregation is now about 50 percent white, 50 percent people of color, which better reflects the racial and ethnic composition of our downtown neighborhood.

Beneficent today—a diverse gathering of spiritual seekers—is not the church it once was—namely, a beacon of establishment values and power. I remember the church the longtimers still talk about—or something like it. The church of my childhood was suburban, racially homogenous, a grand brick building set on several acres that fronted the main thoroughfare, was filled every Sunday (with chairs set up in the narthex on Easter), offered cradle-to-grave programming, and was led by a respected pastor. That church was a place to see and be seen, where prominent and not-so-prominent families gathered to share their common culture and express their common faith. It was healthy, stable, good, and powerful—or so it seemed to my young eyes.

SPIRITUAL JOURNEY

I now realize that I was living on a religious and cultural island. Suburban Grand Rapids, Michigan, was slower in feeling the effects of the cultural changes going on around the United States in the second half of the twentieth century. For example, Beneficent Church was already four decades into its decline when I was a child sitting in Ridgewood Christian Reformed Church's long wooden pews eating peppermints and taking notes on the pastor's sermon. My Dutch immigrant family had been members of the Christian Reformed Church (CRC) since my great-grandparents settled in the Midwest in the early twentieth century. I grew up going to Christian schools and, after graduating from Unity Christian High School, went on to Calvin College—the college of the CRC located in Grand Rapids. All my friends were CRC, as was all my family. Though we did some traveling on family vacations, which exposed me to other ways of life, differing cultural influences on my childhood were relatively limited. Looking back, I can see that the CRC's cultural and religious dominance—or at least prominence—in Grand Rapids created a social space where parents and community could more easily and successfully protect their children from *outside* influences. I grew up thinking every good and safe and healthy community was more or less like my community (or was aspiring to be so).

The suburban, Dutch Calvinist church, school, family, and community bubble that I grew up in was good, safe, and healthy in many ways. There was an outward appearance of stability and tranquility. Children were protected and cared for. Economic and social differences were mitigated by a common commitment to advancing the welfare of the community. Parents and grandparents took seriously their job of passing on community values, beliefs, and traditions to the next generation. Both clergy and laypeople studied the Bible and theology with great care. People were committed to attending worship, giving sacrificially of their time and finances, doing ministries of justice and compassion, and vigorously sharing the good news of God's love in Jesus with their neighbors at home and abroad. The CRC planted a faith in me that has withstood difficult personal, family, and career trials. For this I am grateful. What we weren't good at was talking about differences.

I am not aware of explicit efforts on the part of any individuals or organizations to create a more or less racially, ethnically, culturally, and religiously homogenous community. It may simply have emerged out of the tendency of immigrant groups to create and seek out places where their beliefs, values, and cultures are affirmed, where people speak a common language and share a set of assumptions, where folks don't have to be continually explaining themselves and spelling their surnames, where people can feel "comfortable." It may have emerged out of genuine pride in a culture and heritage that was a source of stability and meaning for vulnerable people. It may have emerged out of an evangelism model that equated conversion with conformity and unity with uniformity. Regardless, the result was a beautiful, kind, earnest ethnic-religious-cultural box that offered generous support to those who fit. But for a family like mine that couldn't keep up the appearance of conformity, it was a different story.

Things began unraveling for my family and me while I was in high school. My mom left the CRC to pursue a call to ordained ministry in the Reformed Church in America. In the CRC at the time, women becoming pastors was simply not an option. The church based its policy on selected biblical texts that were interpreted as excluding women from ordained ministry. As a young adult, I engaged in these biblical and theological debates over women's ordination. The result was that I began to question the beliefs and values that had shaped my identity. Several years later, while I was in college, my dad came out as a gay man. This also was not an option in the CRC.

Dad told me that he had known he was gay from the time he was young. While he was attending Calvin College, he finally got up the courage to ask a trusted psychology professor what to do about his orientation. According to Dad, the professor told him to "get married and 'it' will go away," which, of course, "it" didn't. Compounding the shock and pain of discovering my dad's double life was the revelation that he had AIDS, a disease that would take his life in 2012 after a twenty-six-year battle. Soon after my dad came out, my parents' twenty-year marriage ended in divorce, and my dad sought out a church that would affirm his identity—in this case, a Presbyterian church.

I took the disruption of my family and faith as I had known it pretty hard. My church—reinforced by my extended family, my school, and the cultural assumptions of my wider community—had taught me that both preserving certain gender roles and prohibiting gay relationships were key components of being a good Christian. It seemed that I was being confronted with a choice. Either I would no longer identify as a Christian or I would need to find a new way of being a Christian. Either way, I felt like I needed to learn more about this cultural force that had so profoundly shaped me. What I couldn't understand was how the church could, on the one hand, be such a source of comfort, inspiration, stability, and hope and, on the other, such a source of suffering, exclusion, pain, and injustice.

After I had graduated from Calvin College, I spent a year studying theology in Marburg, Germany. From there I went to University of Chicago Divinity School. While in Chicago, I learned of the United Church of Christ (UCC) and its motto taken from John 17:21: "That they may all be one." It seemed to me that, if nothing else, the UCC offered an opportunity to seek out a new way of being Christian that could bring healing to my family and my heart.

I began my ministry career in 1996 as a hospital chaplain. In 1999 I was ordained in the UCC. From there I went on to serve UCC congregations in Illinois, Indiana, Ohio, Maine, and Rhode Island. My wife, Nicole Grant, whom I met in divinity school, is also a UCC minister. We have served churches separately in various roles and together as co-pastors. Though at times sharing a call to ministry, a church, and a family can be stressful, on balance it has been a blessing. In fact, this study argues that a partnership ministry model was key to Beneficent Church's redevelopment success.

Though I saw in the UCC an opportunity to construct a new way of being Christian that would avoid the gender and sexual orientation exclusions that had led to my painful leave-taking of the church I had been raised in, I soon discovered that exclusions, marginalizing, and painful breaks were a part of church life in the UCC as well. As a denomination, the UCC had removed policy barriers to women's ordination and the affirmation of LGBTQ identity. I was and am grateful that the UCC as a denomination has made these choices and, for the most part, is moving on to other important theological and ecclesiological conversations. However, the UCC vision for a multiracial, multicultural, Open and Affirming, peace-with-justice church that is accessible to all is something toward which the denomination is still working. The church I encountered on local, judicatory, and seminary levels was declining, distressed, and conflicted. My divinity school training had not fully prepared me for the leadership challenges I would face. The healthy, stable, full, and active church of my youth was the exception rather than the rule. I soon learned that I had left an evangelical tradition on the upswing only to join a mainline tradition in decline. I had left a strong and prominent community in which I was known only to become an unknown in a new and strange community struggling with the harsh reality of becoming marginalized relative to the wider culture.

Though I had never encountered the concept of church redevelopment in any of my training, I found myself doing redevelopment work beginning with my first call to pastor a church. When I arrived the church was in a financial and membership crisis. The small, German, neighborhood church had been founded more than one hundred years earlier when the neighborhood was filled with German immigrants. By the start of my tenure, the neighborhood was more than three-quarters Latino. The neighborhood elementary school provided fully bilingual Spanish and English instruction for all students. My response to this situation was to do what made sense to me: to build relationships among the new immigrants in this neighborhood and to invite willing church members to join me in what this study further develops as *impossible* hospitality. By the time I finished my first call, the church had begun several initiatives that connected it to its neighborhood, including sharing its building with a Latino new church start, hosting an early Head Start program, starting a clothing pantry, establishing a safe Halloween program for neighborhood families, and initiating a vacation Bible school program. Accompanying these changes in mission and program was a change in lay leadership at the church. Early on, I learned that key pieces of responding to church decline included reaching out to marginalized people—both inside and outside the church—and building new leadership within the church.

Subsequent calls confirmed and built on these early lessons of my ministry. Though I continued to search for a call to a healthy, stable, vibrant church, it was simply nowhere to be found. Instead, almost every church I encountered was in some state of decline and distress. I began to notice that everywhere I served, distress and decline were accompanied by related dynamics of entrenched power, anxiety, marginalization, and shame. I began to search for language and concepts that could help me put what I was experiencing into a wider framework. I found the language of church redevelopment and revitalization in literature from the Alban Institute. I discovered resources for leadership in systems theory and in Ronald Heifetz's work on adaptive change. Brian McLaren made a connection between Christianity and postmodern thought that was revelatory for me. Finally, liberation theology, with its claim of God's preferential option for the poor—and, by extension, all those marginalized by operations of power—gave me a theological warrant for looking at issues of social justice as they relate to how churches organize themselves. This study is an attempt to weave these different theoretical and theological strands together with the concrete, lived experiences of redeveloping churches so as to create a practical theology for church redevelopment.

I share this brief account of my spiritual and ministry journey to let you know where I'm coming from. Along the way, clergy coaches, teachers, mentors, colleagues, and a few key books from people who have "been there" have been important sources of comfort, instruction, and inspiration for my work. My hope is that the following pages can be that for you. Ministry can be fun, amazing, joyful, and meaningful, but at times it can also be difficult, painful, confusing, impossible, and seemingly pointless. If these ups and downs resonate with your church experiences; if you are looking for an example of a congregation that has faced the challenges of disestablishment, decline, dis-ease, and the threat of death; if you find encouragement in the testimonies of clergy and lay leaders who are working together to create new, vital models for ministry; and if you like a story of a dying church finding new life, this book is for you.

A GUIDING QUESTION

The following chapters present the results of a 2011 qualitative interview study that I led with thirteen co-researchers from Beneficent's staff and lay leaders. I have used pseudonyms for the co-researchers except for Pastor Nicole Grant Yonkman. Together we explored a strategic practical theological question as it related to our shared experience of redevelopment at Beneficent Church: What does it take to do successful and faithful church redevelopment in a postmodern context? The answer that emerged had to do with a complex series of shifts in theology and practice that I will attempt to categorize as shifts from a modern-patronage ministry model to a postmodern-plural ministry model. For reasons that will become clear as Beneficent Church's story unfolds, these shifts are not a matter of repealing and replacing one model with another. Rather, they indicate a process of infecting and disrupting a closed, paralyzed system of domination and control. A deeper, fully practical theological question that haunts the pages of this study is this: How is God active in the deconstructive-reconstructive process?[5] The set of strategies, awakenings, and testimonies that I will provisionally call postmodern-plural does not arrive on clouds like the Son of Man with his angels to eradicate opposition—though moments of judgment and decision will be inherent in the experience. Rather, its process is more like leaven in the loaf that catalyzes the rising dough or the mustard seed that sprouts and takes over the garden.

I will take time to describe and construct the operations of these models. As I do so, let your own picture emerge. As a preliminary sketch, I will note a few things.

First, these are local models. You will have to decide their credibility and relevance to your context. Rather than provide hard and fast answers, they are meant to stimulate your own thinking about what ministry models might be operating your particular context and whether redevelopment might entail a shift in models. Nevertheless, if something in this story resonates with you, if you sense a strategy might work in your particular context, if some tool developed at Beneficent could be adapted to your situation, by all means experiment with the approaches developed at Beneficent. I want to encourage you to become a *bricoleur*. Pull this book apart, rearrange it, discuss it with your group, recombine its insights with those of other authors. Create something new. Create something amazing.

Second, as an attempt at making sense of the great mountain of information shared and decisions made—from the minute to the momentous—in the process of redeveloping Beneficent Church, this narrative arc is itself subject to deconstruction. That is, this book is just one reading—one interpretation—of what was and is happening at Beneficent Church. Though a variety of perspectives are included here, not all of them are. In other words, this text cannot avoid the very exclusion that it seeks to call attention to.

Third, in describing and constructing ministry models, I have employed a certain exaggeration of contrasts for effect. It's not like folks at Beneficent Church sit in our meetings and say, "Now we are operating out of a modern-patronage model" or "This follows the postmodern-plural model." In reality, we read the Bible, worship, pray, and seek to discern God's will in community just as Christians have for millennia. The description of models simply tries to bring to light some of the assumptions the members of Beneficent Church carry with us as we approach embodiment of the gospel in the world—the theological word for which is *incarnation*.

Fourth, this is a description *after the fact*. Nicole and I didn't begin our ministry at Beneficent with the idea that we needed to shift from a modern-patronage to a postmodern-plural model; we just jumped into a situation *already in progress* and made decisions that made sense in the moment—much like my first ministry experience in West Chicago. Only with a backward look do the broader arcs of the story emerge. This is a story of the creative work of the Spirit of God in a particular context—a Spirit that "blows where it chooses" (John 3:8). We are simply followers. The Spirit is always out there, ahead, preceding and exceeding. We are simply following the trace of a movement that has already moved on.

Finally, we will pin our hopes to a claim made by educator and social justice advocate Denis Goulet in his introduction to Paulo Freire's *Education for a Critical Consciousness* that "genuine theory can only be derived from some *praxis* rooted in historical struggles."[6] The ministry models described here and the strategic shifts in practice are rooted in the historical struggles of Beneficent Church to stay relevant in a changing culture. They correspond to the genuine experience of real people, and I hope they will ring true for you.

With these caveats in mind, I can briefly introduce the ministry models hypothesized here.

The *modern-patronage ministry model* that I am hypothesizing here corresponds to a culturally established Protestant Christianity in the United States. This culturally established Protestant Christianity closely equates American cultural values with Christian values. In other words, to be a good American is to be a good Christian and vice versa. It is the *civic faith* described by pastor and author Anthony Robinson and others.[7] Theologian Darrell Guder, among others, traces this identification of Christianity and Western cultural values all the way back to the time of Constantine, who ended the Roman persecution of Christianity with the Edict of Milan in 313 CE (which, of course, stretches the story back well beyond modernity all the way to ancient times). Christianity went from being a tiny, persecuted sect to a world-dominating religion in a matter of centuries. Along the way, the complex process of intertwining religion and culture resulted in what Guder calls "gospel reductionism"—that is, reducing the gospel to Western cultural values of what constitutes good government, good families, good music, good education, and the like.[8] The intertwining of the gospel and Western culture evolved into a certain approach to Christian ministry that tended to equate conversion with cultural conformity and unity with institutional uniformity.[9] It is the Christianity of empire.[10]

Postmodern-plural ministry models are emerging out of the aftermath of modernity's triumphs and failures. Cultural critic Frederic Jameson links the term *postmodern* with a general sense of fragmentation, disintegration, and endings. In the mainline Protestant world, one gets this sense in titles like the latest from Diana Butler Bass, *Christianity after Religion: The End of the Church and the Birth of a New Spiritual Awakening*, in which she argues that Western culture currently finds itself at the "end of the beginning" of a fourth Great Awakening. A less hopeful view of the breakup of the American cultural-religious establishment is taken by journalist Ross Douthat, who, in his book *Bad Religion: How We Became a Nation of Heretics*, documents the decline of the American religious establishment and the rise of three broadly outlined "heresies": the prosperity gospel, self-help spirituality, and "save the world for democracy" American messianism. The postmodern-plural ministry model outlined in this study takes a position somewhere between Bass and Douthat. It sees the postmodern moment as simply the reality that we as a local congregation face, which contains both threats we hope to avoid and opportunities we hope to make the most out of.

The Western cultural project was incredibly successful in spreading modern ways of life around the world through colonization and trade. Side by side with the conquistadors, merchants, and explorers, Christian missionaries spread the gospel and planted churches. Missionaries also sought to alleviate hunger, disease, and poverty through Western medicine and technology. They started schools to educate indigenous peoples in Western knowledge. Their successes were such that by the end of the nineteenth century, mainline Protestant leaders would declare the twentieth century to be the "Christian century" and announce their anticipated universal triumph by giving their new ecumenical magazine that very name. With science doing the work of discovering universal natural laws and liberal Christianity doing the work of discovering universal ethical laws, human progress, and perhaps even perfectibility, was virtually guaranteed—or so some thought. Enlightenment modernity in the West promised universal peace and prosperity through universal reason.

When violence and destruction on an unprecedented scale erupted in the twentieth century in the heart of Western culture in the form of two world wars, the modern project began to lose credibility. After reaching their zenith in the mid-twentieth century, mainline Protestant churches, which had been at the vanguard of Western culture, began losing credibility as well. The dream of the Christian century did not come true. Voices of the formerly colonized and marginalized began to be heard as they called Western cultural assumptions into question. Some in the church started noticing that the quest to establish worldwide dominance of Christianity carried within it assumptions that discredited the very gospel they were trying to promote. The diverse strategies, discourses, and movements that have emerged out of the breakup of this particular form of Western cultural hegemony are called postmodern, which theologian Gregory Mobley defines as a tool "for getting closer to the truth. It is a weed-eater specially designed to cut down the overgrown jungle of modernity."[11] In this study, the postmodern-plural ministry model takes shape around strategies that borrow language from postmodern thought.

WHAT IS CHURCH REDEVELOPMENT?

We will explore the modern-patronage ministry model and the postmodern-plural ministry model in the context of church redevelopment. Church redevelopment is the creative, faithful work of imagining and actualizing new life in dying churches. Church consultant Alice Mann, in her helpful resource *Can Our Church Live? Redeveloping Congregations in Decline*, argues that congregations are social organisms, which—like biological organisms—are subject to a life cycle of birth, formation, stability, decline, and death.[12] The graph of the church life cycle is drawn as a bell curve, with *birth* and *formation* on the upward slope—moving left to right—*stability* at the top of the curve, *decline* on the downward slope, and *death* at the end of the line. Mann describes three different interventions for "imagining and actualizing new life," depending on where a particular congregation finds itself on the life cycle bell curve. All of them, if they are successful, involve revisiting the three formation questions: Who are we? What are we here for? Who is our neighbor?[13] *Ongoing renewal* is a revival or self-study process for "stable" churches threatened by stagnation. *Revitalization* is a process for congregations in the early stages of decline that might involve a "hard look at the facts," "new learning," and perhaps hiring a new pastor. *Redevelopment* is a process for churches that have experienced steady decline for years and have had significant losses of "people, energy, flexibility, and funds."[14] This "difficult path" involves

- recognizing the death of the congregation's previous identity and purpose;
- reallocating the bulk of the congregation's resources to discovering and living out a new identity and purpose;
- finding and empowering leaders who can, in effect, start a new congregation on an existing site; and
- caring for the remaining members of the previous congregation—sometimes by providing a separate chaplaincy ministry as long as it may be needed.[15]

What distinguishes redevelopment from the processes of ongoing renewal and revitalization in Mann's scheme is that redeveloping congregations find "*substantially* new answers to the three formation questions" (italics mine).[16]

Mann's sketch of redevelopment has been influential in my work and is a good starting point for our discussion. As our exploration here progresses, you will see that even after more than four years of doing redevelopment, members of Beneficent Church have a range of understandings about what, exactly, it is. Some see it more along the lines of ongoing renewal, and others see it as a distinct stage closer to Mann's definition of redevelopment. We will discover that in Beneficent Church's context redevelopment involves

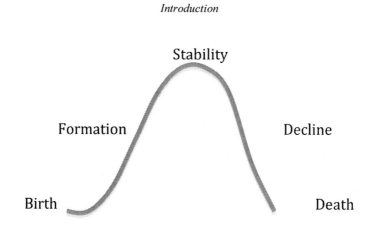

both maintaining continuity and managing change. The definition being developed here is broader than Mann's so as to accommodate the range of understandings discovered in the congregation's study. We have experienced unprecedented moments involving the death of previous identities and purposes, as well as the sense that spirits of those who have gone before are energizing the changes. Redevelopment as defined in this study could be applied to churches anywhere along the downward slope of the bell curve, though where a church finds itself on that slope will significantly affect how redevelopment is approached and to what degree redevelopment effects new life (read "change") in the church.

Mann seems to take the term *redevelopment* from the developmental arc of congregational birth, formation, stability, decline, and death described above;[17] however, a number of others terms are used in the literature to describe the dynamics we are focusing on in this study, including *congregational transformation, congregational renewal, church revitalization,* and *church growth*. A variety of terms have been constructed, developed, put forward, and offered to describe a range of responses to the disestablishment, marginalization, and decline of mainline Protestant churches in America. The specific term is less important to this study than the actual work of inviting people into life-giving, life-changing relationships with God and God's creation. *Redevelopment*—as opposed to *renewal, revitalization,* or *transformation*—for me includes connotations of the latter terms, including aspects that focus life, energy, new behaviors and attitudes, new organizational forms, and the like. But redevelopment also includes the intentional and constructed nature of a congregation as both an institution and a social organism. Redevelopment involves removing obstacles that are blocking the natural and organic development of the congregation and also carefully constructing new structures, patterns, and norms. The redevelopment process described here is a hybrid: both organic and constructed; it both emerges and is built. With all these considerations, the deconstructive-reconstructive dynamic is key. Theologian Don Browning writes, "Religious communities go from moments of consolidated practice to moments of deconstruction to new, tentative reconstructions and consolidations. Then a new crisis emerges and the community must launch into the entire process once more."[18] Regardless of the particular term used in this study, I am referring to the deconstructive-reconstructive, life-giving, life-changing dynamic implied in all the terms.

The guiding question for this study—what does it take to do *successful and faithful* church redevelopment?—begs the question of redevelopment criteria. How do we know that redevelopment is happening? I use the word *successful* to indicate that the work is inescapably institutional, and that institutions have needs for people and money. While individual spiritual transformation is a key piece of redevelopment work, individual psychotherapy or pastoral counseling or spiritual direction is not the individual transformation to which I'm referring. If change happens only at an individual level without those individuals being connected to a wider community, then we probably do not have redevelopment going on. For this reason, while numbers are not everything, they are something when it comes to redevelopment—increased numbers in worship attendance, membership (however that is defined), program participation, financial contributions, and the like. These are the sorts of things that lead to institutional "success." I also use the word *faithful* in recognition that sometimes redevelopment might not look like institutional success and that we do not want a congregation's success to come at a cost to faithfulness to God's call for that congregation. Faithfulness as a congregation can take many forms and should be measured not by numbers, but rather by the fruit of the Spirit: "love, joy, peace, patience, kindness, generosity, faithfulness, gentleness, and self-control" (Gal. 5:22–23); by the Great Commandment: "You shall love the Lord your God with all your heart, and with all your soul, and with all your mind" and "You shall love your neighbor as yourself" (Matt. 22:37–39); and by the Great Commission: "Go therefore and make disciples of all nations" (Matt. 28:19). A redeveloping church may get bigger, but it may at some point in the process downsize—selling its building or losing longtime members who are resistant to God's call for the church. The point of redevelopment is to manage this oscillation between continuity and change while handing on a legacy of Christian faith to a new generation of believers. At this point, success and faithfulness converge: the point is to hand on a faith legacy in some form, even if it means that some part of this particular congregation's life is coming to a close.

WHY DO CHURCH REDEVELOPMENT?

Why do church redevelopment? This is perhaps the most compelling question. Indeed, why bother? Why intervene? Why not let nature take its course with churches in decline? There are a number of reasons to do church redevelopment. Some are better than others. The mainline decline story in its multiple tellings and retellings assumes that the decline of established mainline Protestant churches in America is a problem. The implied answer to the question "Why do church redevelopment?" is that if we do not, our churches will die. When congregations die, denominations shrink, financial support for judicatory structures diminishes, and anxiety about the future of the wider church increases, all of which are motivating forces leading to denominational concern for church redevelopment. Why do church redevelopment? Simple answer: institutional survival.

Institutional survival can be a legitimate motivator for church redevelopment. In fact, most congregations will engage the redevelopment process only when the pain of not changing outweighs the fear of change. One co-researcher for this study recalls thinking at the beginning of Beneficent's redevelopment, "Redevelopment? I don't know what that is, but it can't be any worse than this." This study also extends respect to those longtimers who kept the lights on at the church long enough so that a new generation of leaders might emerge to carry the church's legacy forward. There's one caveat, however: a key to successful and faithful redevelopment is that the congregation must unflinchingly and courageously face the threat of its death. Beneficent Church calls this the "To Be or Not to Be" question. To transition from survival to growth, the congregation had to honestly ask, "Is there a reason to be here?"

Another survival-related motivator emerges when pastors (or judicatory staff or denominational leaders), whose livelihoods depend on their congregations' health and vitality, look to redevelopment to save their jobs. While employment is good and a paycheck is a powerful incentive (trust me, I know!), waiting until your church's future is in doubt to engage in questions of mission and identity is not usually a strategy for success. I don't want to be too negative. After all, we serve a God of miracles. But every successful turnaround I have witnessed began with new pastoral leadership. It seems that engaging the level of change and resetting the norms of the pastor-congregation relationship once a solo or senior pastor has been in place for a number of years is very difficult. Redevelopment needs to be the ministry agenda from the beginning.

Even further, some might understand the implied answer to be something along the lines of "We do church redevelopment so that we mainline churches can reestablish our dominance or regain our central place in American civic life." But some might respond, "So what? Perhaps the world is better without assuming the privilege of mainline churches." The mainline decline story has multiple strategic aims: to diagnose, to comfort, to grieve, to challenge; however, it is almost always told from the perspective of someone or some group that has a previous investment in the institutions. It is told from a perspective of religious privilege.[19] When considered from the perspective of a growing number of unchurched and dechurched Americans, responses to the question "Why church redevelopment?" might range from "Who cares?" to—as one of my Facebook friends once put it—"Religion is evil." This study argues that new life for congregations can be found when we intentionally *disestablish* ourselves with regard to the wider culture so that we might reengage our communities from a stronger sense of our distinctive religious identity.

I'm sure other reasons for and motivators of church redevelopment work exist. For now, I will share why I do church redevelopment in mainline Protestant churches. First, I do church redevelopment because I was called to the work. We will return to this issue of call in the chapter on leadership. Let me just say at this point that call, though a mysterious (and, to some extent, ineffable) experience, is absolutely critical to the work. Unless one is called to it, neither pastor nor congregation should do church redevelopment, because there will be days when the call may be the only thing to keep a person going. Second, I do church redevelopment because churches embodying mainline Protestant religious experiences, stories, and practices are worthy of attention and care. Though the history of mainline Protestant churches in the United States is a mixture of triumphs and failures, many of these churches have done, and continue to do, work that is absolutely critical to the lives of their communities. Third, I do redevelopment because there is a need. This is related to the mainline decline narrative above. See, for example, the 2008 Trinity College *American Religious Identification Survey*: "Historic Mainline churches and denominations have experienced the steepest declines."[20] Fourth, I do redevelopment because people keep showing up. Despite the data that tell us that the fastest growing religious identity in the United States is "none," week after week, year after year, people keep showing up for worship, programs, and events—people seeking something that they are hoping the church can give them: connection, purpose, meaning, hope, healing, spiritual support and direction. Finally, I have found that mainline churches, as they engage in the work of redevelopment, reach people whom other kinds of churches do not reach.

OVERVIEW

With these purposes and models for church redevelopment in mind, our exploration continues as we consider the following topics. Chapter 1, "(Re)reading a Redevelopment Context" is an examination of Beneficent Church's history and spiritual DNA.[21] Chapter 2, "Sharing Leadership," tells the stories of Nicole's and my call to Beneficent Church and how we began to redefine leadership in ways that created the opportunity for redevelopment to emerge. Chapter 3, "Conflict and Conversation," tells the story of the dark days that preceded our arrival and how we engaged conflict in ways that reduced anxiety, increased hope, and created space for new voices to be heard. Chapter 4, "Shifting Power," tells the stories of leadership transitions in two key ministry teams at Beneficent Church and how they modeled a new way of exercising power in the church. Chapter 5, "Extending Welcome," develops the concept of impossible hospitality through the stories of transitions in leadership in the deacons and in the music program. Chapter 6, "Becoming Church," tells the story of a change in atmosphere at Beneficent Church and sketches possible theological trajectories for successful and faithful church redevelopment in postmodern contexts.

KEY TERMS

Practical theology is an attempt to tell a story about God, a congregation, and its leaders in a particular place at a particular point in history.

Deconstruction is the awareness that any creative process in which we seek to organize our experience or generate knowledge is constituted and maintained through acts of exclusion.

Difference is the notion that the play of distinguishing marks generates meaning. Difference is also the mark of the other.

The other is that unassimilated, incomprehensible something that continually threatens to disrupt our dearly held certainties.

The *modern-patronage ministry model* corresponds to a culturally established Protestant Christianity in the United States that closely equates American cultural values with Christian values.

Postmodern-plural ministry models are (1) diverse strategies, discourses, and movements that have emerged out of the breakup of Western cultural hegemony and (2) tools for getting closer to the truth.

Church redevelopment is the creative, faithful work of imagining and actualizing new life in dying churches.

Chapter One

(Re)reading a Redevelopment Context

You have to understand the institution—its culture, its history, and its malaise.
(Response to the interview question "What does it take to do successful and
faithful church redevelopment?")
                                    —Andrew, inactive member of Beneficent Church

The founding document of Beneficent Congregational Church dates from the
year 1743—not with a covenant or constitution but with "a narrative of the
proceedings of the Congregational Church of Christ in Providence against
the Rev. Mr. Josiah Cotton who was their minister; who appeared to them
manifestly unworthy of that office and did depose him and clearly loose him
from the office."[1] The lengthy title itself tells the reader a lot about the story
and its sharp perspective, which animates Beneficent Church to this day—
namely, that what was to become Beneficent Church was *the* (first and true)
Congregational church in Providence and that the work of founding the
church should be characterized as "deposing" an "unworthy" pastor. This
might lead one to the question: What kind of church begins with the *removal*
of a pastor? Clearly, there must be another way to understand the history of
Beneficent Church. And there is.

In his 1836 *Discourses Comprising a History of the First Congregational
Church in Providence*, Edward B. Hall, pastor of First Congregational—now
First Unitarian—Church in Providence, calls the movement that gave birth to
Beneficent "the only schism that this church has ever experienced."[2] So what
happened? Did a congregation depose its unworthy pastor, or did a significant but still minority group in the congregation create a schism by breaking
away and forming a new church? The Beneficent narrative is clearly one

21

sided, defensive, and self-justifying. Hall's retelling of the church's history some ninety-three years later, though couched in the patronizingly magnanimous language of an aggrieved parent, is no less sharply condemnatory of the other side.

Though Beneficent's founding story states that a group claiming the name Congregational Church of Christ in Providence deposed its pastor, in fact the pastor in question remained at his post another four years following the events recounted in the narrative. Instead of installing a more suitable pastor to their pulpit, the group claiming to have deposed its pastor ended up forming a new congregation, Second Congregational Church, which later came to be known as Beneficent Church. (We will get to the story of the name change in what follows.) The "deposed" pastor, Josiah Cotton, continued to minister to his remaining parishioners under the name First Congregational Church in Providence. It would seem, then, that the group that became Beneficent did not in fact depose their pastor. It would appear they lost the church fight. Though the Beneficent narrative may be history told from the losing side, the stories from both sides confirm that the split was incredibly painful and left each congregation diminished for many years. Though slow in coming, it eventually brought Cotton's ministry at First Congregational Church to an end. Nevertheless, both First and Second churches continued to claim to be the "true" and "original" Congregational church in Providence. On what basis were these claims made?

First Congregational Church (a.k.a. "the Cotton party") had the clearer claim to be the true and original church. They had the meetinghouse, and they had the pastor. Neither side, however, was content with institutional symbols when it came to establishing its claim to legitimacy. Both appealed to Scripture and covenant. The dispute, then, came to be over the notion of what constituted the covenant. Whoever could win the argument over what exactly the covenant was could then make the claim to legitimacy.

The way the Beneficent narrative tells it, Cotton was "offended with a particular brother" and "did not follow the rule of the gospel." In this case, the "rule of the gospel" seems to come from a specific piece of Scripture—namely, Matthew 18, which contains an ancient Christian process for dispute resolution. The nature of the offence on the part of the brother against Cotton is not clarified. The narrative claims that Cotton "publicly complained about this brother without first going to him privately"—a clear violation of the Matthew 18 process, which states, "If another member of the church sins against you, go and point out the fault when the two of you are alone" (Matt.

18:15). Imagine how ashamed and powerless this "brother" must have felt when his pastor publicly complained about him.

Creating an impression of innocence, the narrative describes the behavior of the unnamed "brother"—who made a countercomplaint against Rev. Cotton—following Matthew 18 to the letter. He first approached Cotton in private. When that conversation didn't bring resolution, he brought with him two "brothers" to confront Cotton. The content of the complaints on either side is never divulged. The final step of the Matthew 18 process is to bring the complaint to the congregation. If the one against whom the complaint is brought will not be reconciled, Scripture instructs, "let such a one be to you as a Gentile and a tax collector" (v. 17). That is, excommunicate him. The stakes for both sides were high! The lay brother made several attempts to bring public complaint against Cotton, but "Mr. Cotton would stamp the floor and command silence." In a final attempt, a congregational meeting was called to hear the complaint, but "Mr. Cotton in a dreadful heat of Spirit said the Holy Ghost had made him moderator, and he would magnify his office." He adjourned the meeting and left. The congregation remained in silence. After that incident, the separation—led by Deacon Joseph Snow—began in earnest. Nevertheless, it would take two full years of appeals to other Congregational churches, reconciliation attempts, and other maneuvers before the separation was complete. The narrative seems to indicate that from the beginning Beneficent Church has defined a faithful Christian community by its use of a biblical process of reconciling differences and by congregation members' right to call leadership into question.

Second Congregational based its claim to legitimacy on the story of the unnamed lay brother who—in contrast to Cotton—had tried to resolve his differences with his pastor privately, thereby following Scripture and keeping the covenant. Thus, though Beneficent's founding document is not itself a covenant, as was expected for congregational churches—the formal covenant would come later and even then it would take its own unique form—its argument assumes a covenant, one whose rupture resulted in a chaotic dislocation in the congregation. Out of that chaos and dislocation, Beneficent Church was born, and a certain element of chaos and dislocation came to be a permanent feature of Beneficent Church. In other words, a certain unsettled and unsettling quality—a tendency to self-deconstruct—seems to be a part of Beneficent's spiritual DNA.[3]

In addition—as we will see in Hall's account of the split—the people who followed Joseph Snow had gained through the Great Awakening a new understanding of conversion that did *not* equate it with conformity to established congregational practice, but rather to testimony, emotional connection, and *change* in practice. The value of unity defined by uniform allegiance to denominationally authorized and educated leadership was disrupted and redefined in the direction a congregationally defined mission of revival.

Not surprising, Hall's perspective on the conflict is very different. Instead of locating the germ of the dispute in an undefined offense that had been mishandled by the pastor, Hall places the blame squarely with what he calls "the pernicious effects of the great Whitefield revival." The picture Hall paints is of a group of people who have lost their faculties of reason and have been overcome by "enthusiasm," which produced in them a "different sentiment." Josiah Cotton, a "rational and charitable" man whose character was "highly exemplary and irreproachable,"[4] was the victim of this movement and its "excesses." Nothing is said of foot stamping or a dreadful heat of Spirit on his part. According to Hall, Snow and his party publicly denounced Cotton, calling him "an opposer of the work of God's spirit, a preacher of damnable good works or doctrines, a hypocrite, etc." When Cotton attempted reconciliation, Snow's leaders alleged that Cotton came "not in the spirit of God, but in the spirit of the devil," and that he was leading his followers "right down to hell." Snow and his followers called those in the church who didn't agree with them "Babylon, Egypt, and Anti-Christ whom God would destroy." Of the leadership, they said, "Their priests were hirelings and wolves in sheep's clothing." Hall documents one specific charge—namely, Cotton was "not being evangelical enough."[5]

Hall's defense of Cotton and the congregation that remained loyal to him is made on several levels that tell us a lot about the values that were coming into conflict. First, the covenant that bound Snow, Cotton, and the rest congregation together was, in Hall's assessment, "decidedly Trinitarian and moderately Calvinistic but not harsh or at all exclusive . . . in the common language of the day . . . its temper . . . more than commonly humble and charitable." In other words, First Congregational Church of Providence was just a regular old Congregational church with a conventional covenant undeserving of the attacks made against it. Second, Cotton was "reasonable and charitable," whereas Snow and his followers were "out of their wits." Third, Cotton loyalists "patiently examined thirteen 'articles of grievance,' brought against [Cotton] and found them wholly without reason." Fourth, the Separates—as they called themselves, according to Hall—believed themselves to be the majority of the church and thus had a right to dictate policy, but it was proved, in fact, that they were not. Finally, because Snow's party was unreasonable, aggressive, in the minority, and obstinate in response to repeated attempts at reconciliation, they could be blamed for breaking covenant, creating schism, and bringing "great dishonor to the cause." The picture Hall paints of the aftermath is that of a greatly weakened congregation and of Cotton's ministry as irreparably damaged. Ninety-three years later, the grief is still palpable in Hall's writing.[6]

Attempting to maintain the credibility of the claims for charitability on the part of the author and his congregation, Hall allows that "Mr. Snow is believed to have been a perfectly upright and pious man, of a benevolent disposition and some strong traits of character." The cause of the rift is blamed on his lack of education that allowed the "excitements of the day" to produce a zeal "not according to knowledge" in his "uneducated and undisciplined mind."[7] Indeed, whereas to this day Beneficent declares with pride that its first pastor, Joseph Snow Jr., son of Deacon Joseph Snow, was the "son of a carpenter" (in obvious allusion to Jesus), Hall refers to Snow as "the son of a carpenter" in a derogatory fashion. Hall makes sure to note that while the 1743 conflict was the only schism in First Congregational Church's history, in 1793 Snow and some followers broke away from the church he had founded fifty years earlier to start yet another "first and true" Congregational church in Providence. What are we to make of these beginnings, and how are they related to the redevelopment process under way at Beneficent Church today?

CONTINUITY AND CHANGE

The first and key piece of what it takes to do successful and faithful church redevelopment in postmodern contexts is an adequate rereading of the redevelopment context. This includes the church, its history, its culture, and its malaise; the church's neighborhood; and the wider communities. The metaphor of *spiritual DNA* will help us reread these contexts. Spiritual DNA is a development of Alice Mann's notion that congregations are social organisms that follow a process of birth, growth, maturity, decline, and death and church consultant William M. Easum's argument that the most appropriate model for congregational life in a postmodern context is as the "Body of Christ."[8]

What defines the redevelopment process and its particular shape in a given community? DNA—deoxyribonucleic acid—is a nucleic acid containing the genetic instructions used in the development and functioning of all known living organisms. DNA can be understood as a blueprint that defines potentials and limitations of an organism, that regulates the functioning of an organism, and that contains information necessary for reproduction.[9] One way of rereading a redevelopment context is doing a spiritual DNA analysis. An analysis of Beneficent Church helped us identify a number of genes in our spiritual DNA that both held promise for successful redevelopment and posed threats to those same efforts. Promising genes included the congregation's beginnings as a spirit-led, multicultural revival movement. Threatening genes included its beginnings in congregational conflict.

Spiritual DNA is a metaphor for how information gets passed down from one generation to the next in a congregation. It tries to account for both continuity and change in the redevelopment process. *Working the tensions* of continuity and change is a key aspect of leadership in a redeveloping church.[10] This study tries to describe and account for change as a hybrid deconstructive, reconstructive, and organic process. The theological correlates to change as deconstruction and reconstruction are *death, chaos, void,* or *loss,* on the one hand, and *new life, abundant life, new creation,* or *resurrection,* on the other. Redevelopment happens precisely at this dizzying, heartbreaking, liminal space—the creative edge, if you will—between life and death, continuity and change, promise and threat, strength and weakness. Clarity about this dynamic is incredibly important, because a congregation's two most destructive illusions are "the fantasy that growth can occur without change" and "the fantasy that change can occur without conflict."[11] In other words, there is no new life, no reproduction of a new generation, without eruptive birth pains.[12] The theological word for this work is *eschatology*— the study of ends (and new beginnings).

Change can be an emotionally charged aspect of congregational life. The above story shows how a change in "sentiment" resulted in a highly emotional "schism" at the Congregational Church of Christ in Providence. Change in itself is not necessarily a problem. Predictable change that maintains the status quo tends to be welcomed and expected. This is the modern Industrial Age incremental change of Newtonian physics, out of which the mainline Protestant establishment was born.[13] Change paired with loss—particularly diminished power—is often not welcomed by established leadership. In the above story, Josiah Cotton and a group of loyal lay leaders clearly did not welcome the challenge to his leadership brought by Deacon Snow.

The change we will be dealing with in this study is not the predictable and incremental kind. It is akin to leadership author Robert Quinn's "deep change," which is "major in scope, discontinuous with the past and generally irreversible."[14] That is, change itself has changed.[15] Some writers associate this type of change with quantum physics.[16] Easum's quantum change disrupts the power of those he calls "controllers"—those official and unofficial congregational power brokers who "want to control everything that happens."[17] Quinn's deep change not only similarly disrupts entrenched power but also relates institutional change to the personal change of key leaders. Deep change and quantum change also resonate with educator Ron Heifetz's "adaptive change," which inextricably links the personal change of leaders and followers with institutional change at all levels. Deep, adaptive, quantum change is the kind of system-level change that characterizes redevelopment.

Deep change could be used to describe the process that the people of Israel underwent when they escaped Egyptian slavery. It disrupted their previous way of life, and despite their longings to return, there was no going back to Egypt. Despite discontinuity with their previous lives, God's people were able to reconstruct a new life, a new covenant, and a new future that reconnected them with their history precisely because they found that reconnecting power in the God of their ancestors Abraham, Isaac, and Jacob. How can continuity be maintained if deep change is by definition discontinuous? Only through God's re-creative power. In this postmodern model, working the tensions of continuity and change no longer means maintaining congregational culture in an unbroken line. It is not *addition*. Rather, it is a process of disrupting established culture, noticing the differences always already in operation, and reconstructing a new cultural configuration from the fragments. I have noticed this fantasy of change by addition in other congregations. For example, I remember a conversation with a lay leader of a previous congregation that was experiencing birth pains. The birth pains were the result of rapid growth after the launch of a new contemporary worship service. I explained to this leader what I had been saying all along: that redevelopment meant change in church culture at all levels—including how he exercised his leadership in the congregation. He responded, "Oh, we don't want to change our culture. We just want to add a new one." Needless to say, that redevelopment project failed.

Spiritual DNA is a metaphor for congregational culture. Church redevelopment involves deep changes in congregational culture. This involves theological work, emotional work, relational transformation, a retelling of the congregation's story, engagement with power and conflict, and reimagining of institutional practices in a way that narrows the gap between what the congregation claims to value and what it in fact does. One way of passing on genetic information from one generation to the next is cloning, which produces an exact replica of the parent. Rabbi and educator Edwin Friedman writes about cloning in a congregational context as a process whereby leaders use a kind of emotional coercion to try to control their followers by equating conversion with conformity—that is, an emotional fusion in which differences in perspective are effaced. This anxious dynamic that tends to take extreme positions in relation to the *other* could be seen in the story of Snow and Cotton. What is damnation and excommunication if not a failed attempt at emotional-spiritual coercion? Friedman argues that congregational systems characterized by cloning tend to be unhealthy and unable to adapt to changing circumstances.[18]

By contrast, sexual reproduction produces genetic recombinations and mutations that allow for both the passing on of genetic information and the emergence of new forms that can adapt to and survive in a changing environment. Friedman's healthy, well-differentiated congregations reproduce themselves in ways analogous to this latter process, but not without periodic disruptions in which paralyzed or fossilized cultural forms are deconstructed and recombined in surprising and adaptive ways.

At Beneficent Church we have seen evidence for the operation of both kinds of reproductive processes. We have noted a tendency toward cloning in anxious, conflicted times. But Beneficent's spiritual DNA also has an openness toward new movements of God's Spirit that it has inherited from the Great Awakening. In a sermon delivered in 1918 on the 175th anniversary of Beneficent Church, the church's pastor, Rev. Dr. Asbury Krom, identified three qualities that have allowed Beneficent Church to endure: stability, adaptability, and catholicity. Paradoxically, it is precisely Beneficent's ability to change and adapt—to self-deconstruct and reinvent itself—that gives the congregation a sense of stability and continuity. Beneficent's openness to reproducing itself through cross-fertilizing with *other* cultural forms has allowed it to continue to worship God on the same location for the past 269 years. This "sexual"—as opposed to cloning—reproduction produces continuities as well as discontinuities across generations.

For example, those early generations of worshipers at Beneficent under the leadership of Joseph Snow Jr. expressed the spirit of the Great Awakening movement by valuing simplicity and humility. These values informed their worship practices and led them to sing without hymnbooks or instrumental accompaniment. Generations later, Beneficent had become the largest congregation in Rhode Island. The congregation and culture had changed, and organ music was expected for a quality music program; therefore, Beneficent added a magnificent organ, which does not reflect simplicity and humility, but rather an established mainline Protestant ethos. In recent years the congregation and culture changed once again, and our music program is adapting accordingly. Today, in addition to organ and European-style hymnody, our worship is accompanied by a full worship band and a range of music styles—from gospel to rap to contemporary Christian, Native American, and Latin American—that reflect the diversity of cultures in our congregation and community. Musically, things are different from what they were before, but there is continuity with what has gone before—namely, a value for music that speaks to the heart and connects with the changing cultures of the congregation's wider communities.

Just like physical DNA provides a concrete physical link to the past, spiritual DNA is the thin thread of continuity that informs a congregation. Henry, a Beneficent interview study respondent, described this thin thread as "the spirit of the whole congregation from 1743 forward pulling in a direction that sort of says, 'Don't let us fade.'" But here's the thing about DNA: it doesn't get passed from one generation to the next unchanged. Parents' genes mix together to produce children who are both similar to and entirely different from their parents. Genes undergo beneficial mutations that can help individuals adapt to new environments. We now know that the interactions between genes and our environment are extremely complex. Environmental factors can switch certain genes on or turn others off. DNA isn't so much an unalterable destiny as it is a range of possibilities that can become realities depending on our circumstances. The same applies to spiritual DNA—the stories we tell and the things we do—as it doesn't so much determine our future as offer us a fund of possibilities out of which we can shape our future together with God. Imagined in this way, church redevelopment is like a genetic reengineering of switching off unhelpful genes and activating dormant ones. In other words, not only does our past shape us, but in our telling and retelling of the past we also can (and do) reshape it.

CONFLICT, CULTURE, AND CONGREGATIONAL MODELS

The spiritual DNA analysis that we are doing in this study as author and reader is a form of *descriptive theology*, which is a moment in the larger practical theological work we are doing here. To get at the theology that is being incarnated at Beneficent Church, I need to begin by describing the congregation's culture and the history that informs it. All description is an interpretive exercise, and spiritual DNA analysis is no different. To guide our interpretation, we need a set of interpretive keys. These are theoretical frameworks that help a faith community tell its story and make decisions about what to include in the telling. One of those keys is Friedman's systems theory, which understands congregations as emotional systems whose unspoken norms for relationships are encoded among the members at the big bang of their initial formation and then passed down from one generation to the next. This emotional system produces a congregational culture. Spiritual DNA is a metaphor for this culture that is passed down. This study borrows another interpretive tool from sociologist Penny Edgell Becker to help us further analyze the culture at Beneficent Church.

In her book *Congregations in Conflict: Cultural Models of Local Religious Life*, Becker identifies four cultural models for congregational life: House of Worship Model, Family Model, Community Model, and Leader Model. In addition, a fifth category that Becker calls "Mixed Congregations" are ones in which two (or possibly more) cultural models are active in the life of the congregation.[19] Becker demonstrates that each of these cultural models represents a distinct set of values and a distinct way of addressing conflict in the congregation. For Becker, each model represents a different congregational response to two identity questions: Who are we? How do we do things here? (See table 1.1.)

House of Worship Model churches focus their identities on providing worship and Christian education for parishioners. They get stuff done through staff people who provide those religious services. The Family Model focuses its identity on meaningful and supportive relationships and gets stuff done with the approval of matriarchs and patriarchs who govern the congregational family. The Community Model is a gathering of individuals who work to define and express their shared values and get stuff done through inclusive decision-making processes. Leader Model congregations see themselves as leaders in their denominations and communities and get stuff done through the leadership pastors and staff who demonstrate expertise in the

Table 1.1.

Model	*Who Are We?*	*How Do We Do Things Here?*
House of Worship	We provide worship and religious education so that people can connect to God.	Staff provide religious services to the community.
Family	We are a family that provides meaningful relationships and support for each other.	Matriarchs/patriarchs direct, discipline, and care for the faith family.
Community	We are a gathering of individuals who work together to define and express our values.	Pastors and staff work with lay leaders to develop and lead just and inclusive decision-making processes.
Leader	We are leaders in our denomination, community, and world. Our job is to advance our inherited values in order to change the world.	Pastors and staff lead our congregation through their expertise in our denomination's traditions and values.

denomination's traditions and values. One model is not better than the other. Each one has unique gifts and graces that the others do not. [20]

The identity questions of Becker's congregational models are similar to the formation questions (Who are we? What are we here for? Who is our neighbor?) identified by Alice Mann. Depending on the cultural model or models at work in a congregation's life, pastors and lay leaders will need to adjust their approach to church redevelopment. Being clear about *who we are* and *how we do things as a congregation* is key.

Becker's second key insight into congregational conflict is that some of the more serious conflicts she encountered were conflicts over identity. [21] Borrowing concepts from Elaine Tyler May, Becker suggests that the conflicts in the churches she studied could be categorized into "within-frame" conflicts, which result from a violation of shared expectations, and "between-frame" conflicts, which result from the clash of two fundamentally different sets of expectations. [22] *Within-frame conflicts* are those in which the cultural model of the congregation is not seriously called into question. The conflict is resolved simply by applying the answers to the identity questions to the situation at hand. Within-frame conflicts may or may not pose an adaptive challenge to the congregation, depending on the nature of the problem. An adaptive challenge—as opposed to a technical challenge—is one in which both defining problems and reaching solutions require learning on the part of the leaders and the congregation. A technical challenge is one in which the problem as well as the solution is defined within the community's known frameworks.[23] We will discuss these concepts further in chapter 2. Within-frame conflicts are not primarily conflicts over identity and tend to be more technical in nature. Becker found that the conflict was simply over how, given the church's identity, the congregation should respond to a particular situation.

Between-frame conflicts focus squarely on the identity question. Between-frame conflicts could arise in two ways: (1) the cultural model of the congregation is directly challenged, or (2) stresses in congregational life upset the balance of the cultural models active in the life of the church, which results in conflict until a new, more stable mix of models can be achieved. Between-frame conflicts are always adaptive challenges because they call the fundamental assumptions of the congregation's life into question. Inasmuch as between-frame conflicts are always about identity, they can be particularly challenging because "identity conflicts involve both power and symbols."[24] Power and symbols generate enormous amounts of emotional energy because they are understood to be salvific. They also are not amenable to compromise. Given these two factors, between-frame conflicts easily degenerate into win-lose contests in which one faction feels it must subordinate or destroy the other.

Becker connects identity directly to power issues. For Becker, power has two faces: one having to do with setting agendas and distributing resources—official or formal power[25]—and a second, more diffuse face that has to do with "structuring what can be legitimately said in the different contexts of public life."[26] Identity, for Becker, also has two faces. First, it involves the congregation's "public culture"—that is, a core bundle of tasks that the church feels good about and that serve as the church's public face (certain programs, a style of worship, building and properties, and the like). Identity's other face involves sometimes unspoken norms and expectations about how people relate to the congregation and each other, and the level of personal investment people have in the church: Whether the church is warm and welcoming or formal and dignified, do people have close friends and family at the church, or do they keep their personal lives separate from church life? Do people stay a long time with the church or tend to stop in and pass on? The connection between power and identity becomes most apparent during conflict. "Conflicts over identity are conflicts over power in both of its faces."[27] Which core tasks will get priority for funding and attention and therefore shape the public identity of the congregation? Whose vision and values of how the church feels its atmosphere and the kind of people we are hold sway? Who "has the ability to shape the rules for the public arena of discourse?"[28] This intersection of power, identity, and conflict is an interpretive key for this (re)reading of Beneficent Church.

The Snow-Cotton conflict that gave birth to Beneficent Church was a between-frame conflict. It wasn't a disagreement about the application of established norms to a particular situation. It was a fight for the covenant itself. The essence of the conflict was a battle for the soul of the congregation. It involved power on both formal and informal levels: factions were formed, formal accusations brought, ecclesiastical councils called, documents created. The symbols over which this battle was waged included Scripture, ecclesiastical authority, the meetinghouse, and the burial ground. In chapter 3 of this study, we will examine another between-frame conflict at Beneficent Church. It had some characteristics of the Snow-Cotton big bang—most notably, it was in large part a conflict over pastoral authority— but instead of resulting in a new church institution with a new name, a new constitution, a new building, and a new pastor, this contemporary between-frame conflict created an opening for new life in a dying church. Given these realities, another key issue for leaders engaged in redevelopment is to identify whether a conflict is within frame or between frame.

THE BENEFICENT SOCIETY:
CHURCH STRUCTURE IN TENSION

The congregation that now calls itself Beneficent was formerly known as Second Congregational Church. The church changed its name in the late eighteenth century following the formation of the Beneficent Society. Today, the origins and purpose of the society are mysterious and confusing to many in the congregation. As an example, in 2010 about twenty church members participated in a conversation facilitated by a consultant from the Brookfield Institute on the topic of Beneficent Church and Beneficent Society. In this discussion about half of the church members expressed confusion and doubt as to the origins and purpose of the society. Space does not allow for a detailed account of the Beneficent Congregational Society, but I can begin the sketch with some verifiable facts. In October 1785, the Beneficent Con-

gregational Society was founded by an Act of Incorporation by the Rhode
Island state legislature "for the purpose of raising a fund, by free and voluntary subscriptions, contributions, legacies, and donations, for the support of
public worship in the Congregational Society in the town of Providence
aforesaid, of which Rev. Joseph Snow is the present pastor."[29] The names of
eighty-five petitioners are listed, including Rev. Joseph Snow Jr., which, as
far as I can tell, correspond to all the male members of the church at that
time. In other words, in the beginning (and, as far as I know, to this day), the
church and the society were legally coterminus. Even here, however, we can
see how easily confusion could develop, since the church is referred to as
"the Congregational Society." Several years later, Second Congregational
Church took the name of its society and became Beneficent Congregational
Church. These are the facts. Beyond this, we move into the realm of conjec-
ture.

One current story of the society's origin and purpose is that the society
was formed because in colonial Rhode Island churches were not allowed to
own property, so a separate legal entity needed to be created to hold the
property. This story seems unlikely, since the church (a.k.a. Congregational
Society) owned land and a meetinghouse for forty-two years without any
problem before the Beneficent Society was formed. Perhaps the confusion
lies in the comparison of Beneficent Society with Congregational Societies in
Massachusetts and Connecticut, where the Congregational Church was the
legally established church of the colony. This was, of course, not the case in
Rhode Island. My understanding is that in Massachusetts and Connecticut,
societies were established to facilitate that relationship between the colony
and its established church by collecting church taxes and the like. (Notice the
emphasis on "free and voluntary" contributions in the Beneficent Society
charter.) As far as I can tell, the Beneficent Society was not a legal necessity
for the Congregational Church as it was in the other colonies. So why a
society? For the rest of this discussion, I rely on oral histories passed on by
church members.

After the "church couldn't hold property" story, the second theory of the
origins of the society is that it was formed either to protect the church's
assets against a spendthrift pastor or because the church could not be trusted
to manage its own money, thereby building a legal wall between the church
and its assets. While this may describe the current functioning of the society,
it does not describe its original purpose, since, as I have outlined above, the
original charter included "all" (voting—that is, male) church members, as

well as the pastor. Today, while one can nominate oneself to the society, all church members are not also automatically members of the society. Though the Beneficent Society may have been used at times throughout the centuries for political purposes to put pressure on the congregation or the pastor, the only hard data we have to go on for the purpose of the society is simply what is stated in the original charter: its purpose was and is to raise money for the support of public worship at Beneficent Church. This little exercise illustrates a point worth noting: Sometimes what lay leaders remember to be the church's history is not based in documented fact and may not be entirely accurate. A key to redevelopment is doing some historical research into primary sources where possible in order to ground your (re)reading in reality.

Beneficent comes from Latin, meaning "doing good." The signal achievement of the Beneficent Society was constructing the current 750-seat, Greek Revival–style meetinghouse in 1809. In addition, the society holds Abbott Park, a property adjacent to the meetinghouse, and some $5 million in endowments that generate income, a portion of which supports Beneficent Church's budget. Some years before the arrival of Nicole and me, the society adopted a fiscal policy focused on growing its endowments. As expenses related to maintaining the meetinghouse and other church-related properties increased, the society's contributions did not keep pace, resulting in the church reaching into its endowments to make up the difference. Not surprising, this resulted in chronic, low-intensity conflict that flared up in 2009 and created an opening for redevelopment to take root. We will pick up this thread of the story in chapter 3.

Viewed through the metaphor of spiritual DNA, the continued existence of Beneficent Society along with two other separately incorporated entities— the Women's Guild and the 180-unit affordable housing complex, Beneficent House (in addition, of course, to Beneficent Church)—could be read as a persistent tendency toward fragmentation encoded at the time of the church's big bang. Over the years each entity has developed distinct subcultures and even mission orientations. They could be read as expressing different congregational models. Read in this way, it seems that *between-frame* conflict has been encoded into Beneficent's spiritual DNA, which means that Beneficent's congregational identity is under continuous negotiation.

As it turns out, Beneficent's complex and fragmented structure in some ways supported redevelopment. As we will see, it was precisely the society's willingness to take a hard line on the issue of financial responsibility that created an opening for redevelopment to take root. Nevertheless, it was an extremely risky approach to creating an opening for redevelopment, and in this postmodern, post-Christendom moment, when the supports of established culture are rapidly being taken away, can Beneficent Church really afford this level of organizational complexity?

EXODUS AND COVENANT

Spiritual DNA expresses itself in congregational practices, and what a congregation actually *does* reflects its theology much more accurately that what it says. The model for practical theology underlying this study is based on theologian Don S. Browning's "practice-theory-practice" approach. Simply put, we describe the congregation's practices with an *interpretive sociology* and then bring those practices into conversation with normative texts—including the Bible and theological texts—with the view to "think and act practically in fresh and innovative ways." Browning sees calling practices into question as a part of a larger congregational deconstructive-reconstructive dynamic that comes to the fore particularly when things aren't working—such as in a time of institutional decline. The decline and disestablishment of mainline Protestant churches has generated a lot of questioning and a lot of searching of Scripture. Taking cues from pastor and consultant Gil Rendle's book *Journey in the Wilderness: New Life for Mainline Churches* and theologian Catherine Keller's "theology of becoming," in this study I bring Beneficent Church's practices into conversation with the biblical exodus narrative as a story of God's re-creating God's people.

We will enter the exodus story in what is perhaps a surprising place: the episode of the golden, or molten, calf (Exod. 32–34). Beneficent's creation story features the disruption of covenant and a resulting emotional and social explosion. Following the spiritual DNA metaphor, the golden calf story gives us further clues into the dynamics of continuity and change and the key role of leadership. Continuity has to do with the impossible situation of standing in the breach—of reconstituting covenant when covenant has been disrupted, of reinventing identity when differences have been erased, of reconfiguring operations of power, of destroying idols and restoring faith. Continuity involves the work of confession, repentance, forgiveness, and reconciliation.

While Moses spent forty days and nights "dillydallying" with God at the top of Mount Sinai, God's people, who were camped at the foot of the mountain, grew anxious in their leader's absence. In response to the anxiety and shame of being left alone, this newly created people, unused to living within the bounds of God's covenant, responded to their situation by creating, together with Moses's brother, Aaron, a new god in the form of a golden calf. When God hears the revelry of the people worshiping the golden calf, God becomes furious and threatens to destroy the people and start over with Moses. Moses stands in the face of God and argues God down:

> Turn from your fierce wrath; change your mind and do not bring disaster on your people. Remember Abraham, Isaac, and Israel, your servants, how you swore to them by your own self, saying to them, "I will multiply your descendants like the stars of heaven, and all this land that I have promised I will give to your descendants, and they shall inherit it forever." (Exod. 32:12b–13)

Then Moses takes action with the people to restore the covenant.

One key role of the leader-prophet—expressed in the above texts—is to work with emotions of anger, grief, shame, and confusion that result from covenantal rupture and to negotiate the terms of a renewed covenantal relationship. Moses can "stand" (*yatzab*, Exod. 33:21, 34:2, 34:5) in the face of the people's anxiety and of God's anger and escape mortal harm. God's people are feeling vulnerable and exposed in the wilderness. They are either not willing or not able to exercise the self-control needed to remain faithful to God's covenant and to make the journey through the wilderness. In a moving image of the pain, confusion, and shame that erupts through the breach of covenant, God's reactive anger threatens to doom the whole project, mirroring, to a certain extent, the people's lack of self-control. God seems to need Moses almost as much as God's people do. To use biblical scholar Yochanan Muffs's words, Moses "stands in the breach."[30]

Moses addresses the broken covenant first by "standing" courageously in the face of God's anger to mitigate it. Moses "entreated before" (*khalah*) or "soothed the face of the Lord his God" (Exod. 32:11, trans. mine). He calms God down. In doing so, Moses also resists what Bible scholar Everett Fox calls "a dictator's dream."[31] When God offers to wipe Israel off the face of the earth and start over with Moses, Moses refuses. Moses directs God back to God's chosen people. No more starting over, like when God sent the flood and started over with Noah and his family in Genesis 6–9. Moses argues that even if these people have broken the Sinai covenant, they are still children of Abraham, and God is still obligated to honor his promise to Abraham, who was faithful (Exod. 32:13): "Yes, they are a stiff-necked people, but you chose them, God, not they you."

This is a poignant scene and a turning point in God's relationship to God's world. From here on out, the biblical story will be one of God and Israel—for better and for worse. Moses ends up working out a renewed covenant between God and God's people. Unlike in the time of Noah, when God decided to wipe the slate clean and start over with a faithful patriarch and his family, this time, because of Moses's intervention, God and God's people manage to stay together. This sets the pattern for the rest of the Bible. The rest of the story is one of covenantal rupture and renewal that in time becomes the basis for the renewal movement led by Jesus of Nazareth. Exodus 32 is testimony to how one person with the courage and skill to stand in the face of God's anger and a people's unfaithfulness can change the course of history. In the case of Beneficent Church, we used a shared leadership model, which meant that it wasn't a lone hero standing in the breach, but rather a coalition of called and equipped leaders who were willing to hold each other accountable to a vision of new life and renewed covenant for the congregation.

God listens to Moses's arguments and relents, but note that following the golden calf incident, the relationships among God, Israel, and Moses are not simply restored to what they once were. Things have changed. For one thing, Moses returns from the mountain to order the deaths of a significant number of the people. Numerically, the people are diminished. In addition, the remaining people are stripped of the ornaments they had plundered from the Egyptians. Financially, the people are diminished. After Moses smashes the first set of Law tablets, God writes another, but this time only Moses is allowed to meet God on the mountain. It seems God no longer has a desire to deal with the people directly. In fact, God wants to desist from leading the people altogether and instead put God's messenger in charge, but Moses convinces God to back off from this proposal.

All this is to say that when I relate this spiritual reality to my experience of church redevelopment, I recognize that the covenant that once was between God and God's mainline churches in the United States will not be restored to a previous state. One way we say this is that no time machine exists that will bring the United States and its mainline churches back to the 1950s—which for many churches were the glory years. Declining churches can be restored to a life-giving, life-changing relationship with God, but the relationship will not look and feel the same as it did before. The same was true back in 1743 for the Congregational Church of Christ in Providence— once one people, now two.

In a moving conclusion to his story of the "schism" or "removal of an unworthy pastor"—depending on your perspective—Hall writes about the disposition of the burial ground, which contained ancestors of both the Snow group and the Cotton group. According to Hall—and confirmed by the current historians of Beneficent Church—First Congregational Church and Second (or Beneficent) Congregational Church continued to jointly own and administer the burial ground, even though—again according to Hall—Snow's group had "forfeited all legal claim by their separation."[32] Hall understands this as an extension of First Congregational's generosity and forbearance toward their estranged spiritual kin. Beneficent's historians report that part of the role of the Beneficent Society may have been to administer the burial ground with their First Congregational counterpart, the Benevolent Society, which is no longer in existence.

Hall draws a moral lesson from this powerful symbol of continued—I would say miraculous—connection in the face of the abyss that difference opened between the groups. He calls it "the fellowship of the grave." In this case, individual physical death—whose spiritual counterpart in Hall's *Discourses* was congregational schism and abrogation of covenant—has a way of mitigating conflict arising from differences, opening a space for grace, and exposing "the utter vanity of human pride and prejudice." "Let the living listen to the dead," he admonishes, "and when you are tempted to strife or uncharitableness . . . look forward and see your own bodies laid low there." He calls his readers to remember "the pure and gracious Savior who died to reconcile us to one another and to God."[33] Here Hall is drawing on that ancient Christian claim that Jesus is the new Moses who stands in the breach to reconcile God and people.

The burial ground connection shows that despite each side's willingness to engage the conflict and separation, something about the reality of death—the sheer unspeakable otherness of it—confounded them. In the words of the current First Congregational (now First Unitarian) Church historian, "There were certain things they just wouldn't mess with."[34] It was as if this symbol of death were an abyss that limited the abyss that had opened up between the groups in their conflict. In any case, even though Hall allows that, with so much fault, there must have been some on both sides, he doesn't give any evidence of fault on the part of Cotton's people, which seems to weight his "solemn warning" of the grave toward Snow's people, implying that, had they made different choices, this all might have been avoided.

With the benefit of today's perspective, which no longer understands the Great Awakening simply as a divisive movement of uneducated people who had lost their minds but as a legitimate religious-social movement that produced one of America's greatest theologians—Jonathan Edwards—and brought significant religious and social gains to American religious life, I have to wonder if something else wasn't going on. Yes, people on either side could have made different choices, but would they have changed the outcome? Would they have been able to turn the tide of emotional, social, and spiritual forces beyond any one person or group's control? How is God implicated in all this? Hall says that God brought "good out of evil" in that First Congregational/Unitarian was able to define itself as "wholly independent and liberal" following the separation.[35] Is it that simple? Was the suffering and diminishment of both sides only the result of offenses against God and covenant, or could the rupture be understood as a power struggle over identity among groups who were operating out of different cultural models for connecting with God and constructing community? A key to redevelopment is a willingness and spiritual fortitude to hold these deep theological questions open, to be willing to face the mystery of God and hold judgment in reserve, realizing that ministry engages ancient and powerful forces that are larger than any of us.

A key to successful and faithful redevelopment at Beneficent Church is engaging this past that is always present (another way of understanding spiritual DNA). It is an interesting fact that the first clergyperson to welcome Nicole and me to Providence was the pastor currently serving First Unitarian Church of Providence. In his note he mentioned the shared history of our two congregations. Part of the redevelopment process at Beneficent has been rebuilding a relationship between the two congregations. Over the years Rev. Ford has become a friend and colleague. We have done pulpit exchanges. Our congregations have built a ministry partnership that includes a feeding program that our social justice teams developed together called Y'all Come Community Lunch. We now have an annual tradition of worshiping together on Memorial Day weekend—the first worship services the congregations have shared in 269 years.

NEW LIGHTS AND OLD LIGHTS

Church splits like the one that gave rise to Beneficent Church were numerous throughout New England. Those congregations that supported the Great

Awakening movement came to be known as "New Lights," and those opposed were "Old Lights." These New Light–Old Light splits tended to follow discernable patterns that shape congregations to this day. Old Light churches tend to be wealthier, establishment churches. New Light churches tend to draw people from a broader range of economic classes and to be more evangelical in their piety. This dynamic is easy to see in comparing Beneficent Church with its mother church. We have already noted the different understandings at First Congregational and Second/Beneficent of what it meant that Beneficent's founder was the son of a carpenter, as opposed to Josiah Cotton, who was Harvard educated.

Speaking in a series of lectures in 1893 on the occasion of the 150th anniversary of Beneficent Church, Rev. James Vose, who served Beneficent from 1866 to 1901, concurs with Hall that the impetus for the congregations' separation was the Great Awakening movement. From Vose's perspective, Josiah Cotton and his Congregational mission to Providence were viewed as a bit pompous and presumptuous from the start. Vose writes with ironic hyperbole that Congregationalism came to Providence "with a flourish of trumpets." Writing in the mid-twentieth century, Beneficent pastor Arthur Wilson cites historical documents that describe Cotton's ordination to First Congregational Church as "the grandest in North America." In other words, Cotton's mission to Providence was, in part, to teach the Baptists and Quakers of Providence, who for almost one hundred years conducted their religious life without "regular"—meaning "paid"—clergy and without a formally designated meetinghouse, how to do church in the "correct," colonial establishment way.

In our reading, admittedly anachronistically, through the lens of Becker's congregational models, we might sense some resonances between Becker's leader model and the cultural assumptions of Cotton's congregation—namely, that (1) being leaders in our denomination, community, and world, the job of Beneficent Church is to advance our inherited values in order to change the world, and (2) pastors and staff lead our congregation through their expertise in our denomination's traditions and values. In Beneficent, however, the Great Awakening may have created a kind of genetic mutation in which call to individual repentance, conversion, and piety gave rise to a congregational model akin to Becker's community model, which operates under the assumptions that (1) we are a gathering of individuals who work together to define and express our values, and (2) pastors and staff work with lay leaders to develop and lead just and inclusive decision-making processes.

In any case, it is my analysis that when Beneficent split off from its parent, it took with it bits of both establishment-leader and movement-community cultures that continue to operate today.

We can also see how bits of a patronizing, cloning, assimilating gene got spliced onto the leadership model and how a more diverse, individualistic, plural gene got spliced onto the community model in what would ultimately become the Beneficent mix.[36] This being said, both the establishment, reason-based Congregational religiosity and the experience-based, Great Awakening reform movement were solidly rooted in assumptions about "true knowledge" located within the horizon of modern Enlightenment thought. This is not surprising. Derrida argues that deconstruction is something that happens, and it happens within—in other words, it "operates necessarily from the inside."[37] The approach to redevelopment being described here is also to a large extent an *inside job*. That is, the process of exposing underlying assumptions is done using tools borrowed from the very thought system being called into question. Mobley's "weed-eater" is a *bricolage* of parts borrowed from modernity itself. These genetic clues give us hints of the modern-patronage and postmodern-plural models that will begin to emerge in the following chapters.

KEYS FOR REDEVELOPMENT

An adequate (re)reading of the redevelopment context.

Working the tensions of continuity and change.

Clearly answering the identity questions "Who are we?" and "How do we do things here?"

Identifying whether conflict is within frame or between frame.

Doing historical research into primary sources where possible in order to ground your (re)reading in reality.

Working with emotions of anger, grief, shame, and confusion that result from covenantal rupture and negotiating the terms of a renewed covenantal relationship.

Being willing to face the mystery of God and hold judgment in reserve, realizing that ministry engages ancient and powerful forces that are larger than any of us.

Engaging this past that is always present (another way of understanding spiritual DNA).

Chapter Two

Sharing Leadership

Leadership that is willing to lead and a congregation that is willing to follow. (Response to the interview question "What does it take to do successful and faithful church redevelopment?")
—Steve, Beneficent Church member for fifteen years

Our initial contact with Beneficent Church happened while my wife, Nicole, our two daughters, and I were living in Nicole's grandparents' house in Washington County, Maine. We had moved there mere months earlier after our new church start project in Fishers, Indiana, came to an abrupt and unexpected end during the Great Recession of 2008. Nicole and I had shared a call to be church planters for the Indiana-Kentucky Conference of the UCC. When our denominational funding dried up, we were left without adequate means of supporting ourselves. Not having any better options, we packed up, moved to Maine, and worked as substitute teachers while we each looked for a new call.

Our previous experiences with the search and call process had taught us a number of things: (1) there are a lot of dying and desperate churches out there looking for someone to save them; (2) some churches have more potential for redevelopment than others; (3) therefore, it was important that, as candidates, we have our own process of assessing redevelopment potential in the churches with whom we interviewed; and (4) our clear and consistent communication of a vision for redevelopment beginning with the candidate's profile and throughout the interview process greatly increased the chances of successful and faithful church redevelopment. In other words, in some significant ways, the redevelopment process at Beneficent Church began with calling a new senior minister. In our case, it turned out to be senior co-ministers. The interview study bore this out: time after time respondents identified the arrival of Nicole and me with the beginning of redevelopment.

Looking back, however, I can see that years of preparation had led to this particular call to redevelopment at Beneficent Church. For me, it began with a call to help people connect to God—particularly those who have been marginalized or overlooked by established church cultures—that had developed over a number of years from my initial decision to study theology as a graduate student through a series of experiences serving dying churches. For Beneficent Church, it began with a long, slow decline starting in the 1930s, which paralleled an overall population decline in the city of Providence. This decline continued gradually but steadily until 2006, when a series of conflicts led to the departure of a settled pastor. The shock of this departure caused an initial drop in membership and worship attendance; however, by the time the church fired its interim minister fewer than two years later, membership and attendance had dropped to such alarmingly low levels that the remaining members feared for the congregation's continued existence. A second interim minister managed to restore enough calm for Beneficent to complete its search process for a settled minister. It was during this second interim that Nicole and I made our initial contact with the church.

A key to successful and faithful church redevelopment in a postmodern context is leaders—clergy and lay—who are willing to lead and a congregation that is willing to follow. Every one of the thirteen congregation members interviewed for this book mentioned leadership as decisive for the redevelopment process at Beneficent Church. The initial contact between the candidates for senior minister—Nicole and I—and the Beneficent Church search committee determined everything that followed. Much in the same way that the initial conditions—the big bang—that gave rise to Beneficent Church back in 1743 encoded a spiritual DNA and therefore decisively shaped both the possibilities and the limitations of the congregation, so, too, the initial encounter between pastors and congregations decisively defines the possibilities and limitations of that relationship going forward. A key to the redevelopment success at Beneficent Church was that the co-pastors and a critical mass of the lay leaders were able from the beginning to define their mission together as redevelopment.

Defining our relationship with Beneficent Church began with writing the candidate's profile, which is an important tool in our denomination's call process. Though I did not use the term *redevelopment* in my profile, I did show that every church I had served had seen a significant increase in membership, worship attendance, and program development. I included self-appraisal sentences such as the following: "I have a strong sense of call to ministry in the church as a missional pastor. I love the work of embedding myself in a community and building healthy, respectful, and fruitful relationships with the people I meet there. There is nothing more rewarding than helping both churchgoers and unchurched people connect to the gospel message. I have strong leadership skills that I have developed and sharpened through the experience of leading churches through periods of change, growth, and transition. I will not let fear and anxiety prevent me from following God's call. I am able to move into God's future in trust and humility, and I invite others to do so as well." In my "Statement on Ministry" I described my vision for a church that communicates "the good news of God's love in Jesus in life-giving, life-changing ways." The UCC search process begins with an exchange of profiles on the parts of candidates and churches. Different denominations will have different processes. Pastors and congregations should use whatever tools their denomination gives them to self-define a vision for redevelopment work.

From the perspective of a pastor looking to do redevelopment work, success begins with defining your ministry as redevelopment. This contributes to success for a number of reasons: (1) It may self-select some (though not all) churches out as unready for redevelopment work. (2) Being clear and consistent with one's message reduces anxiety in the congregation and builds trust. It gives a measure of authority. Declining congregations tend to be chaotic, anxious, and distrustful. People will be attracted to a direction, even if they are not entirely clear on what it means. (3) Talking about redevelopment and casting a vision for it from the beginning of your ministry becomes a resource for allies in the congregation who, when people begin complaining about the changes happening in the congregation, can point to your call to do redevelopment and say, "This was the will of the congregation. The pastors are only doing what we asked them to do."

From the perspective of a congregation looking for a redevelopment pastor, chances of success are greatly increased by using whatever tools the denomination's call process makes available to define the congregation's vision for redevelopment. This should be a process that engages the entire congregation and prepares them for the work to come. Ideally, an interim minister would lead the congregation through a searching and honest inventory of the church's history of decline, its resources for redevelopment, and its willingness to engage the redevelopment process. This does not usually happen. In my fifteen years of ministry, I have interviewed one congregation—First Congregational Church of Dunbarton, New Hampshire—where the interim minister was able to adequately prepare the church for redevelopment. The key to that success was the congregation taking responsibility for its own decline. In almost every other instance I have encountered, declining congregations find a scapegoat for their situation—the previous pastor(s), Sunday morning soccer practice, "young people," and so forth. Applying insights from family systems theory to congregational dynamics, author, educator, and rabbi Edwin Friedman calls this dynamic "blame displacement," which is "an emotional state in which family members focus on forces that have victimized them rather than taking responsibility for their own being and destiny."[1] Educator and leadership theorist Ronald Heifetz would identify it as "work avoidance."[2]

Taking responsibility does not mean wallowing in shame and placing blame on the congregation. We will address how to deal with those issues in chapter 3. It simply means achieving a level of self-awareness that allows the congregation to see how its decisions have contributed to its decline so that it can make different decisions moving forward. Many declining congregations recognize the need for what they call a change in leadership, but what they mean by that is a change in pastor. While it is true that without a change in pastoral leadership, redevelopment probably will not happen, a change in pastor is not enough. The model of shared leadership means when a change in pastor occurs, the lay leaders need to share in the change as well. If this can be recognized in the interim process, redevelopment will really have a leg up. Unfortunately, this is often the exception rather than the rule. Though a few key leaders at Beneficent Church recognized the need for their own transformation, this was not a widely held awareness. Some expected the new pastors to save them; others expected the pastors to do as they were told. Few were ready for full partnership in ministry.

LEADERSHIP AS PARTNERSHIP

Because Beneficent Church called my wife and me as senior co-ministers, we were able to define and embody our shared leadership model from the start. Nicole and I have found that sharing a career in ministry while helpful in some ways—for example, having a spouse who understands the peculiar demands of ministry, having ready access to a trusted colleague—can also be extremely difficult and complex.

After graduation from divinity school, Nicole and I married, had a couple of children, and served separately in a variety of ministry contexts. Our children were twelve months old and four years old when I began a search for a new call. That search led us to a dying congregation in southwest Ohio. This church had a day care center in its building that could take both our children. They were also searching to fill two staff positions—a full-time senior pastor and a half-time director of Christian education. They asked if we would be willing to work with them in reconfiguring the two positions into one and a half positions' worth of co-pastor. We had heard horror stories about serving as co-pastors from other clergy couples but were willing to take the risk.

The call to Ohio did not turn out as we had hoped. The church grew rapidly at first, the stress of which blew the lid off past issues that the congregation had not dealt with effectively, including a previous clergy misconduct that had been covered up. Though Nicole and I ended up leaving at a time when the congregation was focusing the bulk of its energy on avoiding coming to terms with its past, we both knew that we could work together as a team.

By the time of the search that led to our call to Beneficent, Nicole and I had a much clearer idea of the costs and benefits of co-ministry. We discovered that co-ministry is not right for every congregation. We were also much clearer about how we co-ministered together. We approached the search open to either serving as co-ministers or not, depending on our assessment of what would be best for the congregation and our family.

Beneficent was searching for one full-time senior minister. Both Nicole and I applied for the job. In an initial telephone conversation with the search committee we explained our approach to the search process. They were interested in exploring the idea of having senior co-ministers. We shared with the committee an information sheet that outlined our model for co-ministry. (See appendix B.) We also assessed the church's readiness for co-ministry and whether it would be appropriate in this particular context. In the end, we agreed that Nicole and I would share one position as senior co-ministers with the understanding that, together with the congregation, we would undertake a redevelopment process to grow the church. After three years of redevelopment, we would then reevaluate the pastoral needs of the congregation and work toward increasing our position to two full-time senior co-ministers. At the time of this writing, we have been increased to three-quarters time each.

Several interview study respondents reported the significance of the co-pastor model for the success of redevelopment at Beneficent Church. In our interview, Nicole helpfully summarized what several people identified as key to the success of the co-pastor model at Beneficent Church:

> [It was] that we were willing to take it on and work more than what we are being contracted to do—meaning [more than what] we're getting paid for. So putting more time in and also refusing to fall into any of those previous patterns—to create something new—put people enough off balance that they weren't able to do their sneaky, backhanded [sabotaging]. They haven't been able to follow through with any of these tactics to undermine leadership in the church—that includes us and it includes other lay leaders.

In the following paragraphs I will unpack Nicole's observations.

For some Beneficent leaders, the decision to call co-pastors was based primarily on financial reasons. "Two for the price of one," they said. Though we consistently responded to comments like these by reminding them that we were sharing one position and, therefore, would be limiting our hours to the number appropriate to one senior minister, in reality, each of us worked far more than half time. In effect, we donated innumerable hours of work to the church with the understanding that after three years the congregation would engage in a process of full ministry evaluation, including staffing needs. This was both a gamble and a sacrifice on our part as pastors. Nevertheless, our decision to meet the need regardless of the cost demonstrated our commitment to redevelopment and our personal willingness to put it all on the line for the future of this church. Shared leadership means shared sacrifice and shared risk. As pastors, we needed to take the lead in this with the hope that others would follow.

Nicole and I decided to make significant sacrifices on behalf of redevelopment at Beneficent Church because we believe in the work and we believe in the church. But faith wasn't the only motivation. In fact, much of the time we were just trying to survive the extremely high level of conflict and institutional chaos present at the church at the beginning of our ministry. When talking about the ways in which some in the congregation continually tried to undermine and sabotage pastoral leadership, one respondent, Henry, said of Nicole and me that "you couldn't corner one against the other." In other words, we always had each other's back. Henry also identified complementary skill sets as important: Nicole has an "admin touch," and I have a "pastoral touch." Finally, the emotional, spiritual, and sheer time demands of the congregation would have, in Henry's words, "crushed" a lone pastor. In his view, some leaders were "dragging out" meetings unnecessarily in order to wear us down, thereby destroying the vision for redevelopment before it had a chance to take root and grow.

Nicole noted that insofar as the co-pastor model has succeeded, it is in part because this was not our first time co-pastoring together. She warned that not every church can handle co-pastoring. Beneficent had never had co-pastors before, so trying the co-pastoring model was a risk for everyone. Nevertheless, the precipitous decline of the congregation had created a "leadership vacuum." That vacuum, combined with Beneficent's very "liberal and open" theological perspective—along with the more-staff-for-less-money reasoning—created receptivity to a new pastoral leadership model.

Like Henry, Nicole pointed to different but complementary leadership skills and styles as a key to making the partnership work. Sexism, while still operative, was not quite as present at Beneficent Church as in previous ministry contexts, and that also helped. According to Nicole, at Beneficent "there was the question of who's really in charge, but they were open to it being me, so there was not that gender thing in general."

A key piece of the effectiveness was that the co-pastor model disrupted the congregation's unhealthy patterns of relating to their pastors, which had led to so many power struggles and bad pastor-congregation breakups over the years. Above, Henry noted how the co-pastor model broke up the pattern of cornering one pastor against the other. Nicole agreed that "there was a probably a deep-seated communication pattern or the way they deal with their pastor that they tried to use with us, and it never really worked." Just calling ourselves co-pastors, however, was not enough. What disrupted the unhealthy patterns was that she and I had already experienced people trying to put us into "those boxes"—that is, preconceived notions of the pastor's proper place and role in the congregation. Both Henry and Nicole were specifically referring to the unhealthy use of emotional triangles, a concept developed by Friedman that describes how two people, A and B, reduce anxiety in their relationship by triangling in a third, C, and dumping the anxiety on that person. The trouble is that this practice provides only short-term relief. It tends to build anxiety in the larger system until A and B can speak directly to each other and resolve their differences.[3] Our congregational relational covenant (see appendix C), whose development will be described in chapter 3, allowed us to reappropriate the Matthew 18 covenant implied in the congregation's founding documents in a public and explicit way. It also helped us teach and institutionalize healthier communication patterns. But using the co-pastor leadership model as a tool to embody and practice those patterns at the highest levels—what Friedman would call the "head" of the congregational "body"—allowed us to affect changes in how members related to leaders and each other.

Nicole raised another interesting aspect of the co-pastor model that relates to the postmodern theme of difference—that is, the co-pastor model means that differentiation is built into the pastoral office itself. The pastoral office in a co-pastor model always includes an *other* perspective and an *other* way that demands continual negotiation. This builds flexibility and strength into the pastoral office, because when it comes to pastoral leadership, there is always an *other* way.

In our interview, Nicole quoted Pastor Michael Piazza, church consultant and founder of Cathedral of Hope in Dallas, Texas, who once said in a church planting and redevelopment conference, "You can always have your own way as long as you have more than one way." Nicole went on to explain, "I think actually the co-pastor model is like that in that there's always more than one way. There's always at least two ways: my way and your way." More than one *way*, however, does not mean more than one *direction*. Because each of us trusts in the other and because of our basic commitments to our relationship and to the work of redevelopment, the potential threat of an *other* way to *my way* is reduced.

> [Because of] our level of trust, which we've built up within our professional work and our marriage, whatever decision I make, even if you might say, "That's probably not the way I would have gone, I'll stand by it and I'll defend it." And the same thing goes for you: "I probably wouldn't have done it that way, Todd, but I will stand by it." That's another way of saying, "You can always have your own way as long as there's more than one way."

Above, Henry noted the difference of Nicole's "admin touch" and my "pastoral touch." The difference built into a shared leadership model does have simple, direct benefits, such as increasing the range of competencies and styles in leadership, but I would argue that it's more than that. Once again, the co-pastor model *embodies* a theological-relational dynamic that was key to the redevelopment at Beneficent Church—namely, what it means to live in the tension of difference and welcome an *other* perspective. We will continue to develop these themes in the following chapters.

One interview respondent, Tim—a longtime member of Beneficent who has held many leadership positions in the church—described the redevelopment process as an oscillation between the familiar and the unfamiliar, the comfortable and uncomfortable. This oscillating movement can be observed in the differentiated aspect of co-pastoring—the "more than one way" of the pastoral office. Nicole observed this oscillating movement in the co-pastors' response to the conflict centered on the EBT (endowment building team) process—which was a proposal to turn all of the church's assets over to two separately incorporated trusts. We will explore the conflict in more detail in the next chapter. Nicole called the EBT the "biggest challenge" to our leadership:

> It was really scary, because it was like, "Hell, no, we cannot allow that to go through," but we also cannot say, "Hell no, I will not allow that." So how do you do that? How do you lead? Somehow we were able to go back and forth: your leadership, my leadership. [Todd] tried doing some meetings. I tried doing some meetings. We assessed, "Well, Nicole is the one that's going to be effective here." I think they expected you to say, "Hell no, I won't allow it," and then when you didn't, they expected me to be cute and cuddly, and I wasn't. Somehow that put things off balance. I guess everyone has their pattern or strategy for getting things done, and somehow [the enactment of the EBT proposal] didn't work.

One of Friedman's concepts is homeostasis, which is the "tendency of any set of relationships to strive perpetually, in self-corrective ways, to preserve the organizing principles of its existence."[4] As we saw in chapter 1, Beneficent Church was born out of conflict surrounding pastoral leadership, which has plagued the church to greater or lesser degrees throughout the centuries. It's in the DNA. The interview study seemed to indicate that somehow the co-pastor leadership model was different enough that the congregation's default, homeostatic patterns of relating to the pastoral office were not able to function. A sort of genetic engineering took place that disrupted the pastor-is-the-enemy gene and turned on another gene, one that functions as if the pastor could possibly be a partner in ministry. This created the need to find new ways for leaders and congregation to relate to each other, which led to shifts throughout the system—shifts that we will come to identify with a postmodern-plural ministry model.

ADAPTIVE CHALLENGE AND
WELL-DIFFERENTIATED LEADERSHIP

Leadership theorists Ronald Heifetz and Edwin Friedman can help us further develop this first, decisive move of defining ministry as redevelopment and leadership as partnership in shared transformation. Heifetz's notion of "adaptive leadership" and Friedman's notion of "well-differentiated leadership" shaped Nicole's and my approach to our roles in the redevelopment process at Beneficent Church. Friedman's "well-differentiated leader . . . has clarity about his or her own life goals" and, therefore, is "someone who is less likely to become lost in the anxious emotional processes swirling about."[5] A pastoral search is an anxious time on all sides. Dying congregations can be particularly anxious and will say many things that candidates will have to sort through carefully. A candidate's clarity of identity and purpose serves as a guide and a tool for assessing redevelopment potential in congregations. Beneficent Church shared with Nicole and me two pieces of information that sounded promising: its history as a New Light church, which we could draw upon to energize and legitimize our redevelopment work, and that it had adequate financial resources to fund redevelopment over a number of years. This would allow us to "pace the change" at a rate tolerable for the congregation.[6]

In chapter 1, we referred to Ronald Heifetz's adaptive leadership in connection to Quinn's deep change and Becker's within-frame and between-frame conflict. Here, we turn to adaptive leadership as "influencing a community to face its problems."[7] Recall that adaptive leadership is based on a distinction between two types of institutional challenges: technical and adaptive. A *technical challenge* is one in which the problem definition is clear and the solution is clear. The role of the leader is to identify the problem and provide the solution. An *adaptive challenge* is one in which the problem definition is unclear and requires learning on the part of leaders and congregation. The solution is also unclear and requires learning for all involved.[8] In an adaptive situation, the role of the leader shifts from providing answers to creating a process-context in which learning can happen. This study describes this context for learning as a safe space in which deconstructive and reconstructive processes operate in an oscillating movement of continuity and change. As we began our leadership at Beneficent Church, defining the work of the congregation-leadership partnership as redevelopment was an important strategy for identifying the adaptive challenge.[9] First, I will describe a negative example of how we defined the adaptive challenge, and then a positive one.

One way Nicole and I began identifying the adaptive challenge during the call process at Beneficent Church was by addressing the issue of the pastor-congregation relationship. One issue that came to light in the interview process was that the church had experienced a series of messy endings with previous pastors. These had left a residue of grief, distrust, and bad feeling in the church that was impeding the congregation's progress and contributing to its decline. As a response to this, we proposed a three-year transitional covenant with the church during which we would engage in redevelopment work. During this three-year period, we would promise not to leave the church, and they would promise not to fire us. After the three years, we would do a full ministry evaluation to see if the relationship was working. This would allow all sides the time and space to do the hard work of setting the pastor-congregation relationship on a new, healthier, and more stable footing. The church's leaders did not agree to this arrangement. Instead, they proposed that we revisit the proposal once we had finished the call process and begun our ministry at Beneficent. That move did two things: it identified the pastor-congregation relationship as a key adaptive issue in the redevelopment process, and it told us (not surprisingly) that developing healthy trust relationships between pastors and congregation would take time and impede (to a certain extent) our initial redevelopment efforts. This was a *negative* strategy of defining our work insofar as it involved church leaders saying no to a piece of the proposed redevelopment process.

A second move to identify the adaptive challenge occurred during an in-person interview with the search committee. Nicole and I met with the sixteen-member committee at the church. They proceeded to take turns asking us questions, and we listened carefully for clues in their questioning about how ready they really were for redevelopment while taking the opportunity to explain our vision for how redevelopment work might proceed in this context. By this time we had learned enough of the church's recent history with conflict, its long history of engagement with mission movements, and its demographic makeup to have a sense of its potential. We had also toured the facilities, including its lovely, historic, recently renovated meetinghouse. At one point someone on the committee asked directly, "What do you envision for this church?" I replied, "You have this beautiful meetinghouse. I want to see it filled." I could tell from the energy in the room that they were interested in this vision. They asked follow-up questions about how we would go about realizing this vision, and we spoke about networking, inviting people, and creating events through which unchurched people could connect with the church in a nonthreatening way. Nicole and I laid out a general direction, and then I said, "If you hire us, we will bring them in. The question is how you will respond once they get here." As wonderful as "filling the meetinghouse" sounded, it would be an adaptive challenge in which the congregation would experience change. This testing strategy in the interview process gave us a sense of what we were up against: we would have to simultaneously bring new people in and deal with longstanding pastor-parish issues. In this way, we were able to begin shaping our strategy even before our official first day on the job.

There is no question that promising to bring new people into the church during an interview process was a bit of a risk. Of course, we could not know with absolute certainty that we would be able to bring new people into this particular church. It was a gut decision based on what we already knew about the church from the interview process—for instance, the amount of attractive space in the church and its high-traffic downtown location—and what we knew about our own previous successes in bringing new people into church. The promise was also a bit of a warning to them based on our previous redevelopment experiences, in which we brought new people into the church only to have the old leaders make life so unpleasant for them that many newcomers left for the sake of their own spiritual health. We wanted to inoculate Beneficent against that kind of behavior out of a sense of moral obligation both to the church and to potential new members. This was a moment of self-definition for us as co-pastors. Self-definition is key for Friedman's well-differentiated leadership. Self-definition is not primarily done through words. Actions speak louder than words, and nothing speaks redevelopment more loudly than actively bringing in new people.

The distinction between adaptive challenge and technical challenge was a key piece of theory that we taught Beneficent's lay leaders. The teaching was mostly done informally. Nicole and I used our monthly meetings with the church co-moderators to introduce the concepts by reading Gil Rendle's *Leading Change in the Congregation*, which applies the concepts of adaptive and technical challenge to church life. Then, when the opportunity would arise in council meetings or other leadership settings, we would apply the concepts to the discussion before the group members and remind them of what the terms mean. In general, church leaders grasped fairly quickly the difference between adaptive and technical challenge and were open to the idea that the problem of decline at Beneficent Church was not amenable to a technical quick fix. They had spent hundreds of thousands of dollars on a staff person they hired to grow the church, which had failed. They had spent tens of thousands of dollars on consultants to tell them what was wrong and how to fix it. They spent hundreds of hours rewriting bylaws to fix the structure and working on trust proposals to fix the finances, and none of this seemed to be giving them the results that they were hoping for, which was a revitalized church. So they were open to the idea that redevelopment would require a radically new approach. This allowed us to talk about redevelopment as an adaptive challenge and then draw implications for how the congregation's leaders—clergy and lay—would need to change in order to create a context in which new life at Beneficent Church could emerge.

In our interview, Steve, a member of the pastoral search committee that brought Nicole and me to Beneficent Church, identified willingness of leaders to lead and congregation to follow as key to successful and faithful church redevelopment. Friedman and Heifetz help us to see more precisely that this willingness is characterized by the commitment and capacity to engage in a process of adaptive change in a way that is open, nonanxious, and oriented toward a mission of redevelopment. Steve clarified that by willing to follow he meant "a congregation willing to accept change and embrace change and be excited about it. A congregation willing to do experimentation and see what works." Leadership is a key to successful and faithful church redevelopment, but, as Steve so eloquently stated, competent, dedicated leaders are not enough. There needs to be a willingness among both leaders and followers—an openness to the redevelopment process and a level of basic trust that makes it possible not only to lead but also to follow. As I regularly and publicly say to Beneficent Church, "We cannot lead you anywhere you don't want to go." Success in redevelopment often depends on the simple factors of how badly people want it and what they are willing to sacrifice to make God's vision real.

WILLINGNESS

In the quotation that leads this chapter, Steve connected willingness to leadership as the key quality needed for redevelopment. Willingness emerged regularly among a number of respondents throughout the interview study in response to a question that asked what it takes to do successful and faithful redevelopment. In the interviews, willingness is often connected to openness—that is, an intellectual, spiritual, and emotional ability to be influenced by perspectives different from one's own. It is not surprising in the shared leadership model being developed at Beneficent Church that the quality of willingness is important for both leaders and those who at a given time in the church's life find themselves in a following role. As Steve said, it takes "leadership that is willing to lead and a congregation that is willing to follow."

The leadership as partnership model takes the form of self-definition and creating the space for others to self-define as well: what Beneficent Church calls "creating safe space for *other* voices." Leaders as partners do not define others for them. Friedman calls that "conversion" or "emotional coercion," trying to change people against their will. [10] It can take the form of cloning— that is, trying to make followers into exact likenesses of the leader or leaders. [11] Clearly, this notion has implications for traditional models of discipleship. Does following Jesus require that we become *exactly like* him? Does good followership of pastoral leaders require congregants to become *exactly like* them? I will leave the first question open. As to the second, my answer is "Heaven forbid!" A postmodern-plural ministry model imagines leadership and discipleship-followership less a matter of convincing others to believe and think alike and more a matter of living in connection with God and community and witnessing to those relationships.

Instead of conversion, leadership, in Friedman's terms, is about making disciples. [12] It is a mutually influencing process of leaders and followers defining their beliefs, values, and perspectives in ways that resonate with the creative genius of the community. Discipleship in this context is marked by respect above all. The openness that characterizes willing leaders and followers is, in the words of Tim, a longtime Beneficent member and deacon, "A questioning mindset that says, 'Well, this is what I believe, but maybe I'm wrong.'" Willingness requires leaders to be open, but distinguishes itself by being rooted in action. Willingness *does* something.

A PARABLE OF WILLINGNESS

Jesus's parable of the two sons found in Matthew 21 could be read as a play of wills and resistances:

> "What do you think? A man had two sons; he went to the first and said, 'Son, go and work in the vineyard today.' He answered, 'I will not'; but later he

changed his mind and went. The father went to the second and said the same; and he answered, 'I go, sir'; but he did not go. Which of the two did the will of his father?" They said, "The first." (vv. 28–31)

Introducing a parable into this story of redevelopment leadership is welcoming an *other* perspective. Reading and preaching parables in the context of Beneficent Church has taught me that parables function as carefully crafted disruption devices specifically designed to dislodge conventional understandings. They lead us directly into the practices of difference and deconstruction. How will this parable disrupt and decenter our story of shared leadership?

Jesus begins by inviting the reader into a questioning mindset: "What do you think?" Matthew places this parable in a series of confrontations between Jesus and the religious authorities of Jerusalem following Jesus's temple action, during which he drove the moneychangers from their places in the temple courtyard. The religious authorities understood this as an attack on established temple practices and responded by questioning Jesus's authority to do "these things" (Matt. 21:27). Jesus responds to their question with a question: "What do you think?" Matthew uses this parable as a setup for Jesus's counterattack on the religious leaders' authority, but for us, in this context, we might read it as a simple invitation to reflect and as an indication that leadership as partnership could also be understood as willingness to engage in conversation.

The situation Jesus invites us to engage begins with a call from a father. A traditional way of reading this parable identifies the father with God, but let's note that the text doesn't require that we read it that way. It could be read otherwise. It could be a call based on a need in the community, a call from a search committee, or—as we will explore later in this book—a call from the other. Nevertheless, in our context of redevelopment work, the pressure to read this as God's call is high. As I mentioned in the introduction, one key to successful and faithful church redevelopment is a sense of calling to the work. Though the work has rewards, it also involves at times incredible pain, suffering, and personal sacrifice. In the famous call story of Moses and the burning bush, the play of God's call and Moses's resistance, on the one hand, gives Moses's leadership a sense of credibility: he's not taking the job of leader for selfish reasons. On the other hand, his resistance says something about the nature of calling: though the decision to accept the call is Moses's choice, there is a sense of destiny about it. Moses cannot *not* lead God's people. My advice would be for leaders to engage in redevelopment work only if you cannot *not* do it. In our case, Nicole was much more certain of the call to Beneficent. She saw the possibilities and promise more strongly. I was much more wary and resistant to the call to Beneficent. I saw the risks and sacrifice. As it turned out, we were both right.

The call is to "go and work in the vineyard today." This phrase tells us several important things about the call. First, the call is to *go*—that is, the call involves movement and direction. Where we presently find ourselves is not where God is calling us to be. One interview study respondent defines redevelopment as "continual evolution." In some cases, redevelopment may involve changing the physical location of the congregation. This has not been the case at Beneficent, though the high cost of maintaining historic buildings has prompted some lay leaders to raise relocation to less costly facilities as a possibility. Successful and faithful redevelopment may or may not involve physical relocation, but at Beneficent Church it most certainly has involved a new movement of the Holy Spirit and willingness of the congregation and leaders to be transformed by the movement. The call is to *go*, to move, but not just anywhere. The call is to go into the "vineyard."

The rich and resonant metaphor of the vineyard has a Hebrew Bible history upon which Matthew is drawing. The vineyard is an image of the people of Israel and the work of the prophets to call God's people into right relationship with God. This vineyard is a missionary image, and the call to work in the vineyard is a call to the mission field. A key to successful and faithful redevelopment is helping the congregation connect to its community. Beneficent has done part of that work in a formal process involving research into the demographics of our neighboring communities. But much of the work, and the most effective pieces of it, has involved informal networking by the pastors, which we will examine in more detail in chapter 5. The fact is, the future of your church is in the people who are *not yet* members of your congregation. The number-one qualifier for leadership in redeveloping congregations is that you love people. It is a contact sport. If you do not have a heart for the community, if you cannot imagine introducing yourself to strangers, making friends, and inviting people to church, you may not have the gifts and graces to lead redevelopment work.

The call to the prophet to go and work in the vineyard is a call to cultivate a community that produces a harvest of *righteousness*—that is, people living in right relationship with God and each other. The product of this right relationship is *shalom*—peace, harmony, creativity, abundant life. The time to work in the vineyard is "today." Not tomorrow, not once we have gotten comfortable with the idea, not once we have had the opportunity to decide what sort of harvest we would prefer, not once we have our ducks in a row, our long-range plan approved, or our bylaws revised. The call is to go into the mission field, to build relationships that help people connect to God in vital ways, and to do it today. In the case of Beneficent Church, this meant that from the first day on the job, Nicole and I began networking in the community and inviting people to church. The call of the father in Jesus's parable is immediately followed by resistance to that same call. The implication of the parable is that we should especially be wary of the type represented by the second son: the one who says yes but does no.

Jesus seems to be indicating that resistance is part and parcel of the call process. One son answers, "I will not," but later he changes his mind and goes. Resistance in redevelopment comes from two places: from leaders and from followers.

Pastors themselves can be sources of resistance to redevelopment. This resistance contains a certain logic. Redevelopment pastors should be prepared to always be leading on the *edge of our competence*. This is because redevelopment involves growing the congregation. As the congregation grows and changes, so will the demands on pastoral leadership. We will have to learn new skills and change our style, to risk failing, looking foolish, and having to admit we don't have all the answers and aren't in control of everything. Since congregations evaluate their pastors based on their competence, leading on the edge of competence is a frightening and risky place to be. There is even the possibility that the congregation will grow and change beyond the point where our leadership can be effective.

In our interview, Nicole talked about how a series of employment and financial crises culminating in the failure of our church-start project prepared us for redevelopment leadership. It taught her to hold her leadership position lightly and to be open to God's leading no matter where that would take the congregation. In other words, it helped us avoid making an idol out of an end result. Perhaps the "continual evolution" of the church would result in its becoming a Haitian congregation or a student ministry for which a different pastor with different gifts would be more appropriate. For Nicole, that would be okay. This willingness as openness counteracts a form of resistance in pastoral leadership that consciously or unconsciously tries to shape the congregation to meet our own leadership expectations and skills. We pastors often tend to keep our congregations at what we envision to be a manageable shape and size. The call to *go* is a call to us as pastors and congregations to risk ourselves for the sake of the kingdom of God.

Resistance also arises among followers in the congregation. This is the resistance that leaders most often find difficult and troublesome. Moses famously complained to God that his people were "stiff-necked" and willful. Heifetz identifies resistance as "work avoidance," which arises from unwillingness among followers to question and examine their values, beliefs, and identities. What people resist, argues Heifetz, is not change per se, but loss— loss of valued traditions, loss of prestige, loss of power, loss of a lifestyle to which they have grown accustomed.[13] Friedman calls resistance "sabotage" and argues that it increases as a leader takes more well-defined stands while staying connected to the emotional-organizational system.[14] Those in the system (congregation) who are least emotionally mature will have an instinctive negative reaction to leaders who call to awareness difference in perspective and sensibility, or the difference that is the gap between the congregation's professed values and its actual behavior. (This is the same gap that Heifetz identifies as the site of adaptive challenge.) Friedman calls this unthinking, sabotaging action a "twitch."[15] The challenge of leadership is to recognize resistance or work avoidance or sabotage for what it is and respond in a nonanxious, well-differentiated way.

For the moment, let us simply notice that Jesus's parable connects both willingness and resistance to the call. There are cases in which resistance indicates an intractable situation that is not conducive to redevelopment. Some churches would rather die than change. In those cases, wise leaders focus their mission energy elsewhere—either in finding another call to a congregation that is interested in going and working in the vineyard or in starting small mission efforts, such as home Bible studies, community mission initiatives, and other entrepreneurial projects, outside the scope of the congregation. The point of the parable seems to be that willingness should not be gauged by words but by action. Redevelopment depends on leaders and followers who don't just say yes but, more important, *do* yes. One son says, "I will not," but then he changes his mind. The second son says to the father, "I go, sir," but he does not go. This brings us back to an issue raised earlier in this chapter about evaluating potential redevelopment opportunities. Many churches will say they want to grow or turn around or something similar. A wise leader will always probe behind the words to look for evidence of actions that indicate willingness to work in the vineyard. Though we serve a God of miracles and second chances, in most cases the best predictor of future behavior is past behavior. A church can kill redevelopment with empty words. Redevelopment lives in mission-focused action.

In Jesus's parable, resistance that leads to willingness passes through a change of mind. The first son in Jesus's parable "later . . . changed his mind." What happened in this mysterious moment? The apostle Paul points to the importance of a change of mind for congregational life when he writes in Romans 12:2, "Do not be conformed to this world, but be transformed by the renewing of your minds, so that you may discern what is the will of God— what is good and acceptable and perfect." The respondents to the interview study spoke of a "change in mindset," a "change of atmosphere," which I interpret to be a change in institutional emotion, a change in culture, a change in institutional perspective, or a change of heart. One church leader identified his leadership role as producing a "change in culture" at the church. This entire book is a meditation on the oscillating dynamic of continuity and change that produces successful and faithful redevelopment. In the process of willingness, resistance and change can lead to action. The interview study identified two primary areas in which leaders need to demonstrate willingness in order for church redevelopment to be successful.

WILLINGNESS TO BE VULNERABLE

Redevelopment leaders risk vulnerability and exposure. Nicole calls this "willingness to go close to the fire." The example she gave in our interview was of a Fourth of July worship service at Beneficent Church in 2011. This worship service was a part of our "Faith and Film" sermon series. In this series, each worship service focused on a film clip and the faith issues it raised. For our Independence Day worship, we chose a clip from the film *Amistad*, which takes its title from a nineteenth-century slave ship that became famous for a mutiny among its captives. Beneficent Church has a historic connection to the *Amistad* because, back in 1841, it, along with other New England Congregational churches, took up a collection to support the enslaved Africans and their bid for freedom. The worship service deconstructed the American ideal of freedom by exposing it to the African American experience of slavery. Insofar as Beneficent had for many years identified with the American religious establishment, it defined its ministry in terms that celebrated American values. What Nicole risked was, on the most sacred of patriotic American holidays, simultaneously exposing the gap, difference, and site of adaptive challenge between American ideals and reality and Beneficent's ideals and reality. She said that although an honoring of the commitment to freedom was part of the experience,

> it was important for me to acknowledge that even though this church has been a cutting-edge social justice church, if we use our lens today to look at what we did in the past with regard to racial justice, we would not be proud of what we did, and [we would see] that we've continued to try to do better. We still had the African Americans sit in the balcony, and there was a black entrance. It was a separate but equal situation, but that . . . it's a progression. We're trying harder, and we know better. We do better. With the leadership of the church changing, our idea of freedom can also change. We should acknowledge that the glory days are still, hopefully, to come. Not that you can rest on "Oh, we've already done all the good that we're going to do."

As if that wasn't enough, among our African American members the worship also risked reopening the shame and wounds of racism and discrimination.

> The other thing that was a little scary was our staff meeting. It might have been one of Elizabeth's [our Minister for Christian Education, who is African American] first staff meetings, and I showed the movie clip that I was using [from the movie *Amistad*] in which Cinque was in chains, and they're referring to the Middle Passage where some Africans were thrown overboard to lighten the load of the ship. It was just so emotional. Elizabeth said, "I just have a hard time with seeing that and going there emotionally." It was a risk, I think, to actually go there, and it still feels scary when I think about it—that I went there. I think it's that *willingness* to go close to the fire that keeps things authentic and real—*not always playing it safe*. It takes a lot, preaching-wise. It's not just putting the words together. It's going to that place heart-wise.

In the multicultural context of Beneficent Church, one way to risk vulnerability is being willing to lead an open and honest conversation on race. That conversation is "close to the fire"—one that is often avoided because it is so easy to get burned. Creating a safe space–holding environment in which hot topics can be addressed is one way in which redevelopment leaders demonstrate willingness. In this case, we created safe space by consulting with Elizabeth on how best we could use the worship service to prepare people for this difficult material and how it could be presented in a way that was sensitive to the feelings of people of color.

Friedman identifies "the willingness to be exposed and to be vulnerable" as a major principle of leadership among the Renaissance explorers and uses them as illustrations of well-differentiated leadership. For Friedman, the willingness to be vulnerable has less to do with a fear of criticism. It is a "fear of being alone, of being in a position that puts one's own resources to the test, a position where one will have to take total responsibility for one's own response to the environment."[16] The explorers of the Age of Discovery, from whom Friedman draws inspiration, risked vulnerability, because they literally moved off the map into uncharted territory.[17] This feeling of stepping off into the unknown—into uncharted territory—was mentioned frequently in the interview study. Tim called it "head scratching":

> You have to be, maybe, a little brave to agree to do things that we haven't tried or to say, "Okay, I want to know how we're going to get there. I want to know what it's going to look like." It's a little more difficult to say, "Hey, you know what? We don't know what it's going to look like. Let's just let it go and see what it turns into."

When we engage fundamental questions of identity and purpose, like those of race and freedom in the example above, when we open ourselves to a fresh encounter with the Divine, when we demonstrate willingness to act on God's call in our lives, we risk the vulnerability that is characteristic of well-differentiated leadership.[18]

WILLINGNESS TO SAY NO

Along with Nicole, several respondents identified the key to saying no while staying connected—namely, define the church's mission and then relate everything we do to that mission. Friedman's well-differentiated leader is "someone who can be separate while still staying connected, and therefore maintain a modifying, nonanxious and sometimes challenging presence" and "someone who can manage his or her own reactivity to the automatic reactivity of others, and therefore be able to take stands at the risk of displeasing."[19] Stated simply, a well-differentiated leader is willing to say no. As Nicole once commented in a conversation about redevelopment, "With every yes, there is a no."

When redevelopment leaders say yes to God's future, they are also saying no to many cherished patterns of behavior that have defined for the congregation "the way we do things here." Nicole was very clear about this in our interview. When I asked her what it takes to do successful and faithful church redevelopment, she replied, "What it takes is just courage and commitment and willingness to not be everything to everyone—to say no, come what may. It's not people pleasing. It's not maintenance. It's not making people feel better or caving in because someone makes a big fuss."

In itself, saying no is not difficult or risky. If one has little or no investment in the relationships, if one does not depend on the relationships in question for support, saying no is easy. When I am in the checkout line at the drugstore and the cashier asks if I would like to buy a candy bar with my purchase, I say no. It is not personal. It is not a big deal. The cashier still takes my money and completes the transaction I *do* want to make.

In redeveloping congregations saying no can sometimes threaten relationships. The difficult work of redevelopment often means saying no while staying connected. Even with a leader's mightiest efforts, redevelopment will likely mean that at some point, one will have to decide between maintaining a relationship and following God's dream for the congregation. Leaders should prepare themselves and the congregation for the eventuality that people will leave the church during the redevelopment process. Because, as Friedman argues, these will most likely be the least emotionally mature; they will rarely, if ever, take responsibility for their decision to leave. They likely will not say, "The church is changing, and I think I might feel more comfortable somewhere else." They likely will say, "The pastors (or other leaders) ruined the church," or "The pastors wouldn't listen to me." Often *listen* is a code word for "They wouldn't do what I want them to do and make the church the way I would like it to be." This can be one of the most painful and frightening aspects of redevelopment. It can be especially painful when redevelopment ruptures a relationship with someone with whom the leaders are particularly close. It can be frightening when someone is trying to hold the church hostage with threats of leaving if something or other is not done to his or her liking. Either way, taking a principled stand on behalf of the church and its future by saying no to certain behavior and individuals, thereby risking displeasure, is a true test of leadership in the redevelopment context.

When I asked Nicole for an example of when she said no, she listed several, including reducing the number of staff positions by two, closing a building—Palmer House—that the church had been renting to not-for-profits at below-market rates, ending the practice of offering free parking to any and every group who wanted it, and discontinuing a hanging-of-the-greens Christmas event to which some longtimers were particularly attached. In a couple of these decisions, we risked not only our relationships with our members but also our reputations and relationships in the wider community.

Saying no to the use of Palmer House for community not-for-profit space was one of the more significant initial moves of our redevelopment work. Beneficent Church moved Palmer House, which is on the National Register of Historic Places, to its property when the building was threatened with demolition back in the 1960s. Forty years of deferred maintenance meant that the building was unsafe. Nevertheless, the church's longstanding relationships with a number of not-for-profit groups (the American Friends Service Committee; the Providence Branch of the NAACP, which Beneficent Church helped found back in 1914; and a homelessness advocacy group that had turned its office space into an unsupervised shelter space without the church's knowledge) were strained when the groups had to move.

When I asked Nicole about the Palmer House transition and how she said no while staying connected, she brought it back to vision: "It's holding out this vision. . . . 'Look, you guys said you needed help. You said you know things aren't working. Well, this is a specific thing that is not working that we've got to let go of.'" There was a period of gathering evidence, which included an insurance assessment of the building. The staff and property team did surprise walk-throughs and discovered evidence of people drinking and doing drugs in Palmer House, including one walk-through during which the team discovered a passed-out man sitting in a chair with a lit cigarette in his hand. Nicole responded:

> We say that the purpose of that space is to help people become not homeless anymore—self-sufficient—and yet we have been housing somebody there for two years, and they're still homeless. Is this really doing what we say said we wanted to do? Are we truly being accountable to our mission?

The irony is that holding out the vision, which exposed the gap between practice and mission, risked accusations that leaders were being un-Christian. While Nicole sensed this fear, in my interview with Henry, he confided that he was, in fact, accused of being un-Christian by church members who didn't agree with some of the changes taking place. Nicole located the risk of this accusation in the tension between individual demands and the leaders' responsibility to the overall mission of the church.

> The accountability is not necessarily to the individual people who are in need; it's to a mission. It's to a broader sense: we want all kinds of people to be served. If serving one person actually puts everyone else being served by this church at risk—for example, the Palmer House burns down or somebody dies

of a drug overdose in the church or something like that—then the church is not going to be able to serve anybody. Are we truly being helpful to somebody by allowing them to be drug addicts in our church and living in our church? I would say, "No, that is not our mission, and we are not equipped and capable of doing that." I guess nobody had said that before.

Willingness to be vulnerable, willingness to say no, willingness to "walk naked into the land of uncertainty"[20] where the ability to listen, learn, and adapt takes precedence over the ability to demonstrate technical expertise and control—all these are qualities of successful and faithful redevelopment leaders at Beneficent Church, but the key leadership lesson from our redevelopment process is that redevelopment leadership is shared leadership. The shared leadership model was put to the test as together we engaged conflict in the congregation.

KEYS FOR REDEVELOPMENT

Leaders—clergy and lay—who are willing to lead and a congregation that is willing to follow.

Pastor(s) and a critical mass of lay leaders who from the beginning define the congregation's mission as redevelopment.

Assessing the congregation's readiness for redevelopment.

Disrupting the congregation's unhealthy patterns of relating to their pastors.

Distinguishing between technical and adaptive challenges, and framing redevelopment as an adaptive challenge.

Helping the congregation connect to its community.

Defining the church's mission and then relating everything you do to that mission.

Chapter Three

Conflict and Conversation

We all needed to calm down.
> —Lucy H., longtime member of Beneficent and church leader

The conflict that Nicole and I encountered when we arrived at Beneficent in 2009 involved two—really three—"camps," as one interview respondent put it. There were the opposing camps identified as *money people* and *mission people*.[1] The unallied group was larger than the first two and comprised the remaining folks. Conflicts over money and mission had something of a history at Beneficent Church. Precisely how far back they went, I don't know. The following are just a few examples of the money and mission conflicts at Beneficent Church of which I am aware.

In 2003 Beneficent Church and the Beneficent Society agreed to work together to make long-overdue capital improvements to the meetinghouse, which the society owns for the purpose of supporting Beneficent Church's "public worship."[2] The money to pay for these capital improvements was to come in part from the society's endowment and in part from a capital campaign led by the church. When the project went over budget and the capital campaign came up short, the society and the church were divided over what to do. The issue was supposedly resolved at a contentious society meeting when a vote was taken to make up the difference in cost out of the society's endowments. As a result, however, the society adopted a new fiscal policy that dramatically reduced their annual contribution to the church for the support of public worship, forcing the church to draw down *its* endowments, thereby weakening its financial position.

Other conflicts over money and mission included the use of Palmer House as low (or no) rent, not-for-profit space and the size and use of the overall mission budget, a conflict that continues at a low level. When Nicole and I arrived in 2009, Beneficent Church was actually giving away more mission money—including contributions to both local service agencies and denominational missions—than it was receiving in pledges to the general fund! The word on the street was that Beneficent Church was a bank. "If I need money, I go to Beneficent Church," one person told me. Conflict over the endowment-funded scholarship program also continues. The program grants scholarships to Beneficent members and qualified nonmember high school applicants for their college education.

The story of this chapter is the interwoven narrative of the dark days and the EBT. This was a money and mission conflict that finally brought the congregation to the point that a critical mass of members said, "If we don't do something different, we're going to die." EBT is an initialism for the endowment building team, a group that formed shortly after the 2006 departure of the senior pastor and that was authorized by the church council to come up with a plan to grow the church's endowments. Somehow, during the three-year interim, the purpose of the EBT morphed from a straightforward fundraising taskforce into a group with the self-designated purpose of saving the church by turning all its assets over to two separately incorporated trusts. The congregation would then receive an annual grant from these trusts to fund its ministries. While intended to save the congregation from its own poor financial practices, the EBT proposal in fact threatened to destroy the redevelopment process before it could even begin; the proposal would cut the congregation off from both its legacy and the funding it would need to do redevelopment work. The idea was to save the church by turning it into a museum, like other historic New England churches and synagogues.

The combination of external and internal threats generated significant conflict, anxiety, and shame. One external threat took the form of broader American cultural shifts that had contributed to Beneficent's institutional decline. The internal threat was the EBT, which one church member described as the "nuclear option." The key to successful and faithful church redevelopment was engaging conflict while protecting the congregational conversation about its future. We were walking a creative edge that, on the one hand, necessitated creating a sense of urgency ("If we do not resolve this conflict, the church will die") and, on the other hand, meant preventing the congregation from falling into despair by casting a hopeful vision ("If we turn to God and get some help, new life is possible"). Through this process, the congregation was able to imagine redevelopment as a third way that avoided the threat of simply continuing on the path of decline and the threat of the self-inflicted dismemberment proposed by the EBT.

THE DARK DAYS

Institutional factors combined with relational distress to produce a chaotic, swirling cloud of anxiety, shame, and despair that characterized the dark days. A key to successful and faithful church redevelopment is a change in atmosphere. Some in the congregation describe the redevelopment at Beneficent as "opening up the windows" and letting in "fresh air" and "sunshine." Anxiety, shame, and conflict had given the church a dark and closed-in feeling that the existing leaders couldn't seem to shake. The anxiety and shame over the congregation's decline produced conflict, which produced more anxiety and shame, which in turn led to more conflict and decline. The story of this chapter is the disruption of this cycle.

Two basic institutional resources are money and people. Both of these were under threat at Beneficent Church. During the dark days the decline in people was frighteningly visible. Though Beneficent had been undergoing a slow membership decline for many years, respondents reported that during the dark days they noticed the decline in worship attendance week to week, to the point that this congregation, which was once the largest in Rhode Island, had only twenty-five to thirty-five people in worship. Members who remembered when the church was full found it extremely difficult to watch this week-to-week decline. One respondent, Steve, reported a certain sense of hesitation and embarrassment when he told his friends about the church he went to. After one of his work colleagues and his family accepted Steve's invitation and attended worship at Beneficent, they never returned and instead joined another Congregational church in Providence. One worship guest who ended up joining the other Congregational church told me shortly after my arrival at Beneficent that he chose the other church because Beneficent seemed like mostly "old people" and it felt "kind of dead." The loss of people and the resulting embarrassment and deadness created an atmosphere that resulted in newcomers looking elsewhere.

At the same time, some leaders in the congregation had become very anxious about the rate at which the church's endowments were diminishing. A number of factors contributed to this diminishment, including declines in the stock market, capital improvements that went over budget, weak congregational stewardship over many years, and a weak budgeting process that permitted spending with little accountability. The endowments—a legacy of both faithful members with limited means and community leaders with substantial resources—had long been a source of pride and community reputation for Beneficent. The thought that, if things did not change, this legacy might be squandered was almost too much to bear. There was no question that the institution, as defined by its human and financial resources, was under threat of extinction. In addition to institutional factors, relational stress also generated significant anxiety and shame.

As chapter 1 showed, Beneficent Church has had a history of bad break-ups with their pastors from the beginning. The dark days were fueled by a series of bad breakups, or "shocks," as the respondents called them, that seemingly were never adequately addressed and lingered as sources of bad feeling, shame, anxiety, and distrust. The previous settled minister had served the church for seven years, during which the church experienced a number of significant accomplishments, including an award-winning $2 million capital project to make the building more accessible. (This was the same project, mentioned in the previous paragraph, that generated resentment and anxiety because it went over budget.) When a church member who was also an ordained minister began publicly challenging the senior minister's leadership, things began to deteriorate, and the senior minister left with bitter feelings on all sides.[3] This produced a profound shock to the congregation. After a brief time of pulpit supply, an interim minister was hired, but her style was so different from what the church had been accustomed to that her ministry was experienced as a series of further shocks. Sensing the urgency of the moment, she tried to lead the congregation through a series of rapid changes that they simply were not prepared for. After eighteen months the church fired her—another traumatic shock. Following this was another interim pastor who managed to provide some stability and enough hope to allow some leaders to believe that all was not yet lost; however, the underlying relational and institutional dis-ease remained.

Interview study respondents remember the dark days as a time when the church felt fragmented, unmoored, shifting, and dangerous. Steve said, "There was always some kind of disagreement about something." Leadership seemed both dangerous and impotent. Andrew reported that the first interim pastor knew what was ailing the church and had a sense that deep change was needed; nevertheless, the relationship between her and the church was "kill-ing the church," and causing the interim pastor grief as well. Meanwhile, lay leaders seemed unable to deal with the situation effectively. There was a sense of "stuckness." Discussions at meetings became maddeningly repetitive. Andrew would say to himself, "Here we go, we're going to have our December meeting again." Another respondent reported that meetings were also at times characterized by "accusations, yelling, hurt feelings, [and] wanting to walk away from the table and not come back." These bad meetings themselves became a source of anxiety. People felt "stunned." Now they were "shocking" each other. They were in "survivor mode."

While the dark days were scary and painful, a small group of leaders also experienced a certain emotional closeness and connectedness in this struggle to survive. One respondent, Phoebe, said,

> It felt like we were all on this lifeboat together. We were just bobbing along. We couldn't see the shore, and we didn't really know where we were going. We were in it together. We lost track of everything. It was like out in the middle of the ocean looking around 360 degrees not seeing anyone else, not seeing land, not seeing the ship, losing track of it.

Phoebe described "the interim lifeboat time" as a "very intense time." Congregational leaders felt like they shared "close quarters." Despite the shocks and conflicts, at other times it felt like "everyone was pulling together" just to "make it through the next several days or months" to do "whatever little thing that we needed to do just to survive." While some in the church seemed to appreciate this extreme closeness, others found it unhelpful. Andrew, for instance, called it "addictive" and found that he felt much healthier emotionally and spiritually once he had some distance from the church.

Several respondents who had lived through the dark days reported a feeling that the church was unchained, disconnected, unmoored, adrift—a sense that things at the church had somehow gotten "unreal." Susan said that the church "wasn't really cohesive" and "that the community was just very much like little groups here and there": "I used to joke with someone else who was in the choir that it felt to me like someday everyone was just going to go up in the dome, and it was going to take off." This paradoxical situation in which some leaders at the church felt extremely close, like survivors at sea in a lifeboat, while others experienced the church as fragmented and ungrounded characterized an environment in which the church lurched from one crisis to the next, allowing lay leaders to avoid dealing with the emotional dynamics and adaptive issues raised by the previous crisis. In response to each crisis, leaders avoided adaptive work by creating scapegoats.

THE ENDOWMENT BUILDING TEAM: A CONFLICT TRANSFORMATION OPPORTUNITY

My first day on the job at Beneficent, I started receiving e-mails and phone calls about the endowment building team. The first e-mail I received was from a member of the search committee, and it listed a series of questions and arguments challenging the EBT proposals. Then I started receiving phone calls from a member of the EBT about how the person who e-mailed me was a troublemaker whom I shouldn't pay attention to. Apparently this conflict had been brewing for some time. It culminated just five weeks later in a three-hour congregational meeting that included shouting, finger-pointing, parliamentary maneuvers, and behind-the-scenes machinations. A vote was taken, but to this day there is disagreement among those who were present about whether the vote indicated congregational approval of putting all the church's assets into trusts or whether it simply indicated approval of continued study of different options for managing the church's assets. As one respondent put it, "There was a sense that something was being taken away from us, but we weren't sure what it was."

In our interview, Nicole called the EBT the "biggest challenge to our ministry." During the call process we had been made aware that the congregation was having a conversation about finances. Tellingly, one of the first interview questions we were asked was whether, in our opinion, the pastor should be able to vote in financial matters. We had a sense that something scary was going on and that it had to do with finances, but we were aware neither of the depth of the crisis nor of the potential threat to redevelopment this conflict posed before our arrival at the church. We addressed the conflict by moving forward on a number of fronts simultaneously. First and foremost, we did not, in Nicole's words, "freak out." Her thought process was as follows: "What's the worst-case scenario? I can still work with that. If the church becomes a museum, and we're working for a foundation or whatever, I'll just go. I'll find some other church." Friedman calls this not freaking out "maintaining a nonanxious presence." In reality, it is not necessary—nor is it possible, I would guess—to be completely without anxiety. A *less anxious* presence will do—that is, less anxious than the system within which you find yourself.

In the case of a highly anxious system like Beneficent Church, being less anxious is not as difficult as one might imagine. The behind-the-scenes political games, laypeople denigrating each other to the pastor, the chaotic congregational meeting—which was an important introduction to and demonstration of the congregation's dis-ease—all indicated very high congregational anxiety. With congregation members focused on organizing to defeat each other, Nicole's and my anxieties—though relatively high—went largely, though not completely, unnoticed. One interview respondent noticed Nicole's and my reactions at that meeting:

> I sat through a congregational meeting, which I thought lasted three hours longer than it needed to. You folks were just here, and you looked like you'd been torpedoed. You really looked scared. I remember looking at your faces, and I could see you saying, "What have we got ourselves into?"

We may not have been able to hide the anxiety we felt from everyone in that room, but our response to the leadership was simply to say, "It looks like you are dealing with some conflict. We will have to resolve that before we can move forward on any redevelopment work." We ended up hiring a consultant to lead us in a conflict transformation process that not only calmed people down but also shifted the norms for relating in the church toward more healthy communication practices.

Our second move for addressing conflict was engaging our support system. Having a support system for both the pastors and the congregation is absolutely critical for successful and faithful redevelopment. As we have said from the beginning, no one can do this on his or her own. *Nonanxious* means "less anxious," and it primarily refers to leaders' interactions with the congregation and its members. Leaders can be as anxious as they want at home, with their families and friends, folks they can trust. A key piece of the support system is a redevelopment coach. The coach we hired for our work at Beneficent Church works with the clergy as well as the congregation in educating, planning, and strategizing for redevelopment. This was so important to us that Nicole and I had it written into our call agreement that the church would agree to work with a coach. A coach will do a number of things to support redevelopment work, including taking some responsibility for communicating difficult realities of change and conflict associated with the process. If the coach is effective, he or she will lend credibility to what leaders are doing and saying. Not freaking out was the start of our success in dealing with the conflict surrounding the EBT, and one thing that helped us stay calm was the support system we began putting in place before we even arrived for our first day on the job.

Third, we put a lot of energy into building relationships within and outside the congregation. This was part of an entrance strategy that Nicole and I had used in other settings. It included Meet the Ministers meetings—a series of ten small-group meetings that laypeople hosted either in their homes or at the church. A total of eighty people participated in these meetings, during which they responded to two sets of questions: (1) What brought you to Beneficent Church? What do you like about Beneficent Church? (2) What visions do you have for the future of Beneficent Church? What would you like to see change? At each meeting, either Nicole or I would record the responses. Once all the data was compiled, I coded it and reported the findings to the congregation. We used the findings to indicate the congregation's priorities for our first year of ministry. Our first annual review was based on the Meet the Ministers data. (See appendix A.)

Building relationships within the congregation was particularly challenging in the early days at Beneficent, because we were trying to build these relationships in the middle of a major congregational conflict, which necessarily means that relationships are fragmented and fraught. People representing different sides in the conflict were continually communicating to us in subtle and not-so-subtle ways that they were wondering whose "side" we were on. I would get calls from people in the congregation warning me about other people in the congregation that I should "watch out for." My response was simply to say that I was called to be pastor to everyone.

During our interviews with the search committee, Nicole and I indicated that a key piece of our redevelopment work would be spending 20 percent of our time networking with people who were *not yet* members of the church. In those early months, our networking included other churches, not-for-profit organizations, the business community, and local politicians. One key networking success was with Johnson and Wales University, whose campus surrounds the church. This partnership has developed into a growing student ministry that continues to bring life to the congregation today. One key networking failure was with our denominational judicatory. Unfortunately, our conference minister at the time had contributed to the conflict at Beneficent during the dark days and was therefore unwelcome at the church. The other Rhode Island Conference churches were focused on dealing with a conference minister whom they didn't like, so there wasn't much of a welcome there either. Instead, to gain support for our redevelopment efforts, we were able to draw on some relationships at the national level that we had built during our church planting days.

Networking outside the church was important for healing the conflict at Beneficent for several reasons:

Networking resulted in increased worship attendance, which helped ease anxiety about the church closing.

Networking brought in ministry partners, which increased our program offerings and ministry capacity so that we were better able to meet congregational needs.

Networking brought in outside voices and consultants to help us with strategies for working through conflict.

Networking helped Nicole and me build allies among legal and financial professionals who consulted with us about forming legal trusts and the implications for the congregation so that we could speak credibly to the situation from another perspective.

ORCHESTRATING CONFLICT AND
PROTECTING CONVERSATION

To do successful and faithful church redevelopment in a postmodern context, congregations need to productively engage conflict. As Alice Mann argues, redevelopment cannot happen without change, and change cannot happen without conflict. Absolutely critical to leading a congregation through conflict is resisting the pressure to take sides. Instead of taking sides, Nicole and I worked to build a partnership of mission people and money people. Heifetz describes adaptive work as a "clash of views." The task of leadership is to "orchestrate these conflicting voices into some sort of harmony." To do that, leaders need to refrain from taking sides and instead bring the factions together so that they can learn from each other's perspective. In this study, we call this work protecting the conversation. To do that, leaders have to build relationships "across boundaries."[4] In the case of the conflict over the EBT, we were dealing with money people and mission people. Henry put it this way:

> I think there's no other church like Beneficent. I think this church has a very big heart. It just doesn't know what to do with it. And the answer's always been spending. It's a sign that our mission has always been writing checks. I think for the longest time we were the largest contributor to the Rhode Island

Conference; yet, population-wise, we were ridiculously small. I think there were two camps. There was a small camp that understood the numbers and wanted to understand the numbers and everyone else. Now the "everyone else"—I don't think it was because they couldn't understand the numbers, it's just that they weren't interested.

The money people—symbolized by the EBT—were afraid that the mission people—symbolized by the congregation and the office of pastor—were spending the church's money irresponsibly. Nicole and I built relationships across boundaries by affirming the need for both money and mission. As I put it at one council meeting, "We need money, because without money there would be no church on the corner of Weybosset and Chestnut Streets. We need mission, because without mission, there would be no reason for a church on the corner of Weybosset and Chestnut Streets." We talked about a partnership of mission and money.

By the time we arrived at Beneficent, the money people had spent years building the EBT plan. The EBT was like a train traveling at top speed. If Nicole and I had tried to step directly in front of it, we would have been flattened. Henry, who works in the trust industry, reported that when he heard the debate about taking the assets out of the church and putting them into a trust, he understood conceptually what the EBT was trying to do, and it made "perfect sense." When he looked at the church budget, his thought was "You [the congregation] are spendthrifts!" Nevertheless, his conclusion from the conflict over the EBT was "This is not going to work, because the people who want it to work are doing it because they feel they have no choice but to save these people from themselves, and what they probably need is a lesson in budgeting." Nicole and I worked with the leaders to make this "lesson in budgeting" an integral part of the redevelopment process, along with growing stewardship, cutting staff, and slowly shifting the congregational culture of mission away from primarily check writing and toward funding hands-on mission initiatives that would engage the wider congregation, which in turn would help to grow the congregation and build energy for redevelopment.

Developing a stewardship program was key to redevelopment at Beneficent Church. When Nicole and I arrived in 2009, Beneficent had recently hired a consultant to help them with a restructuring process to downsize their organization so that it was more manageable for their small number of leaders. In this new structure, the stewardship team was responsible for maintaining the church properties. No formal stewardship education was going on and they had a perfunctory annual pledge campaign. Congregational giving was very low. One of the first organizational issues Nicole and I addressed was forming a property team to deal with the physical plant and refocus the stewardship team on raising money to fund the ministries of the church. It has been slow going, but over a period of four years congregational giving has more than quadrupled.[5]

The result was what Henry called a "culture shift" for the "core group"— that is, the established leadership, who were money people and supported the EBT. He said, "I think that was a cultural change for them, because that process [the EBT] really stopped pretty much after we had a sound footing with our first budget. They backed off completely, and the issue went away entirely." For Henry, the culture shift was marked when the congregation applauded after the first budget following our arrival was approved. The previous church treasurer, who had held that position for forty years, reported that never in the recorded memory of the church had a budget received a round of applause. Henry experienced that as a "good affirmation that something was moving in the right direction" and as a "sense of relief," because the congregation had a sense that the EBT was threatening to "take something away from them," though many still weren't sure what, exactly, that "something" was.

In addition to not freaking out, engaging our support system, networking, and building relationships across factions, Nicole and I also worked to build safe space. Instead of protecting the money, which the money people wanted us to do, or protecting the mission, which the mission people wanted us to do, we exercised adaptive leadership by protecting the conversation. We worked to disrupt unhealthy communication patterns by constructing an environment in which a more effective conversation about the church's future could take place.

One interesting aspect of the EBT process was that some of the leaders who supported the EBT argued that everyone in the congregation was in agreement with the EBT proposals. Lucy, for example, shared in our interview her continuing confusion about the process. She reported that as a team the EBT was "very cohesive." She said that the concept of having two trusts was "well understood by the EBT committee" and that they were "comfortable in the EBT." When over the course of the three-year process the team presented their ideas to the congregation in "dialogue groups" and congregational meetings, "people seemed to be comfortable with the idea and willing to say, 'All right, go to the next step. Go to the next step.'"

Lucy reported that, in her view, "we"—that is, the EBT committee—had given "them"— the congregation—"plenty of chances to come to meetings" to ask questions. She even offered to speak with people individually, but "nobody came to us." The committee "felt that we had spent plenty of time explaining," but after the congregational meeting in which conflict erupted over the proposal, she "didn't feel comfortable going forward."

All of this raises the important question: How was it that conflict suddenly erupted over this proposal when the EBT had been working on it for years and, from Lucy's perspective, there seemed to be overwhelming agreement on it? One phenomenon that Heifetz describes in his discussion of leading without authority is that those in positions of relatively less authority often have access to "frontline information" that those in authority do not, because authority always comes with the constraints of expectations—for example, defending the position of your faction against potentially threatening questions.[6] Those without or with relatively less authority have the flexibility to build relationships across boundaries and factions, and they therefore potentially have credibility, relationships, and thus access to what people are truly thinking and feeling.[7] This seems to be the case with the EBT. The co-pastors had access to frontline information that others in leadership, for whatever reason, could not access. Reflecting on the EBT, Nicole said, "When they [the EBT committee] said, 'Everybody is for this,' we said, 'Oh really?' because we had talked to all these people who were saying to us privately that they were against it."

When we arrived, money and mission were not considered partners; rather, one was continually trying to gain dominance over the other. In 2009 money was making a bid to win a decisive victory. A significant part of the fight was over the pastor's role in church finances. The money people tended to be of the opinion that the pastor should be excluded from financial decisions. This made the pastor automatically a mission person. Our "side" in the conflict had already been chosen for us! This put the authority of the pastoral office itself in question.

Authority, according to Heifetz, is "conferred power to perform a service."[8] Formal authority derives from institutional structures such as office, position, and accreditation.[9] So, for example, a pastor's formal authority is defined by the church's bylaws, by his or her accreditation from the denomination, and by seminary degrees. A lay leader's formal authority is defined by his or her position in the church as chair of a certain committee or a member of a particular board. Informal authority is derived from building relationships of trust with individuals. It comes from having a track record with a particular group of people. According to Heifetz, informal authority is particularly important for adaptive change.

As new co-pastors encountering congregational conflict literally on our first day on the job, we had little authority—either formal (because of Beneficent's extremely fragmented organizational structure) or informal (because we had just arrived and had relatively little opportunity to build relationships and no history with congregation members). Chapter 1 suggests that part of Beneficent's history is to call pastoral authority into question. As Henry put it, "Some people expected you [as pastors] to do you as were told." We also had little informal authority relative to the EBT leadership, most of whom had been church members for many years. Further limiting our authority to directly address the issues raised by the EBT was the ambivalence within the congregation about the relationship of the pastoral office and money. During the interim period, the congregation had formally adopted the policy of the pastor's legitimate leadership role with regard to finances, which had been first proposed by the search committee in 2008. Nevertheless, Lucy seems to be representing a perspective shared by some in the congregation when she said,

> People set up trusts, organizations set up trusts for the long term. Ministers usually come for a much shorter term. And we had had some not-too-good experiences with ministers in the past several years. And we didn't know. You don't know what your ministers are going to be like until they get here and spend several years working with you; [then you] see what they're like and how they think and what they feel and if they're on the same page as you. So some of us felt that a trust would survive any kind of turmoil if there were to be turmoil again. And it would ensure the viability of the congregation and the church.

If Nicole and I were to side, as was expected, with the mission faction, we would simply be fulfilling the role expected of the spendthrift pastors. The mission faction was assumed to be an alliance of the congregation and pastoral office.

Instead of fulfilling the cultural expectations for spendthrift pastors, Nicole and I did something that was surprising for Beneficent Church. Lucy explained how, in her view, the previous pastors simply wanted to spend down the church's endowments until they were gone. When I asked her how she felt about the current pastors, she said that Nicole and I had been trying to rein in spending since our arrival. She said, "It's the first [time] I think I've ever heard at Beneficent that we've got to control our spending and live within our means." Friedman writes that the perspective of well-differentiated leadership sometimes results in surprising and paradoxical responses to anxious situations. Because the well-differentiated leader has a perspective that is less affected by the reactivity of the emotional field and nevertheless connected to it, there is the potential to disrupt the cycle of reactivity by doing something unexpected—like calling for growing the church while shrinking the budget. Again, this is not to suggest that Nicole and I were well-differentiated—only that we were, as it turns out, differentiated enough.

Because of all the factors limiting our authority—whether we were leading without authority (which is really with less authority) or beyond our authority—we had little choice but to approach the conflict over the EBT as an adaptive challenge in which our role was to orchestrate a more effective conversation among the differing perspectives. But this still does not answer the question of how these two very different perspectives on the *decision-making process* about the proposal emerged. For example, Steve articulated the mission people's understanding of the process when he said, "We voted for the committee to keep studying the EBT proposal, not that we approved of it." The money people did not see any significant disagreement over the trust proposals. If there was difference of opinion, it was from a few outliers who simply "didn't understand." The leaders of the EBT were surprised when conflict suddenly erupted at the congregational meeting. Becker gives us a clue to how the leadership was surprised by conflict in her observation that "a lack of conflict can indicate consensus or it can signal that there is no legitimate opportunity to voice dissent."[10]

In our interview, Lucy indicated that from her perspective the EBT provided plenty of opportunity to "ask questions," but could it be that somehow these conversations were framed in such a way as to discourage differing perspectives? Looking back, it seems that the EBT leaders were approaching church decline as a technical challenge to which the trust proposals were a technical solution. The congregational process, then, was simply trying to convince members to accept the solution that the leaders had already decided was the correct one. The pressure would be to suppress differences of perspective as a threat to consensus rather than invite them as resources for a possible adaptive solution. Taking an adaptive approach, Nicole and I gained frontline information that there was dissent and difference of perspective.

The open conflict over the EBT proposals created an opening to try to establish some new communication norms that would allow for the legitimate expression of difference without generating undo anxiety about conflict. The anxiety over difference and conflict may have been generating some of the unhealthy patterns mentioned by respondents in the interview study, including pre-meetings, in which a small group of insiders would try to determine the outcomes of meetings beforehand by withholding vital information, excluding alternate perspectives, and coordinating their votes. In other contexts, some of these behaviors might have been innocuous—a simple matter of being prepared for the meeting—but in the context of conflict where suspicions are high and the impulse to control strong, another process needed to be created in which people could trust that information was being shared openly. One of our primary tool for disrupting these behavior patterns and rebuilding healthy communication was a conflict transformation process called Walking in the Way, which was led by a consultant from the Brookfield Institute.

As is common with declining congregations, members initially resisted and felt anxious about letting an "outsider" lead the congregation through a process for resolving its differences, but the leaders were able to come together enough to engage the Walking in the Way process. The Brookfield Institute's process was selected by the church council and approved by the congregation at a congregational meeting after soliciting proposals from several consultants varying in price, approach, and depth of engagement. A congregation might resist engaging an outside resource for any number of reasons including price. My response is that a wide range of services in a wide range of prices are available, and judicatories will often offer services free of charge. When open, major conflict is present, successful and faithful church redevelopment simply cannot and should not be done without a process in place to effectively deal with the conflict. If a church says, "We cannot afford to engage a conflict transformation process," they are likely saying, "Redevelopment is not a priority for us."

The Walking in the Way process ended up being nine months long. The congregation formed a steering committee that worked with the pastors, consultant, and congregation to guide the process. The consultant coached both the pastors and key lay leaders in person, by phone, and by e-mail throughout the process. (During this time, the congregation and co-pastors *also* continued to work with the redevelopment coach.) We contracted with the consultant for five congregational training sessions in which we learned practices for conflict transformation that we then applied to the conversation about the EBT proposals. Attendance at the training sessions ranged from twenty to forty church members, which constituted about one-third to one-half of the active membership at that time. Two Walking in the Way practices we are continuing to embed in the church's culture are the *talking circle*, in which a talking piece is used to ensure that everyone in a gathering has an opportunity to listen and to speak in turn, and a *relational covenant* that identifies more precisely congregationally defined norms for communication. (See appendix C.) The Walking in the Way process created a safe enough space for the differences in perspective to be expressed about both the EBT *process* and the EBT *proposals* and to influence the direction of the congregation moving forward.

The conflict over the EBT found resolution at a June 2010 congregational meeting in which the congregation voted to receive and affirm the work of the EBT and incorporate its work into the redevelopment process where appropriate. What this meant practically is that the congregation accepted the EBT analysis that drawing down the endowments until they are gone is not an acceptable course; however, the congregation decided not to pursue the option of transferring congregational assets to a separately incorporated trust. Instead, we have been following the course of reducing congregational spending and increasing congregational income. The goal of the EBT was to reduce the congregation's drawdown to 5 percent of endowment income. As of 2012, we are well on our way to meeting that goal through better budgeting and stronger stewardship.

The irony of the EBT conflict is that it created the motivation needed for redevelopment work. In his research on church redevelopment, sociologist Steve McMullin of Acadia Divinity School found that possessing a substantial endowment was one of the most significant barriers to redevelopment among congregations. He found that the sense of security created by an endowment demotivated congregational change.[11] Indeed, that was my top concern in considering the call to Beneficent: Where would the motivation come from when the church was reporting $13 million in the bank? The willingness of the money people to take a hard line on finances, to the point of nearly implementing a "nuclear option," simultaneously threatened to kill redevelopment by locking all the possible financial resources away and motivated the congregation to accept redevelopment by taking the option of status quo off the table.

SHAME AND HOPE

For Phoebe—a woman described by another interview respondent as "the soul of the church"—the dark days at Beneficent felt like living in a lifeboat in the middle of the ocean. The survivors on this lifeboat had no sense of direction, had rapidly diminishing resources, and were vulnerable to sudden, violent storms. She described the beginning of the redevelopment process as the ship coming into view. When I asked her why she thought the congregation got on board with the redevelopment process, she mentioned the personal investment church members had in the church's future despite disagreements as to how best to move into that future. Though these disagreements produced some bouncing around on the ship, on the whole people managed to stay together. For Phoebe, what it came down to was "just the hope that was there": "Even if the vision was dim a little bit or even if there were lots of little visions, people still knew—even if they couldn't articulate what it was—that there was a reason to be here." This heart connection to the church felt by a critical mass of members, while making it difficult for people to do the dispassionate self-evaluation necessary for redevelopment work, is nevertheless critical for the possibility of making any investment in and sacrifices for the future of the church. Simply put, a key to successful and faithful church redevelopment is "a reason to be here."

The interview study revealed that underlying and energizing the strong emotions surrounding the conflicts at Beneficent during the dark days was a sense of shame. Shame is often confused with guilt. Guilt as an emotion is connected to the notion that I have done something bad. The process for overcoming guilt is making amends. By contrast, shame as an emotion is connected to the notion that I am bad. The process for overcoming shame is much less straightforward than that for overcoming guilt. Practical theologian Stephen Pattison calls the process for overcoming shame "integration." It begins with acknowledging shame, working through feelings of victimhood, taking responsibility for one's situation, and living into hope. [12]

Beneficent is not alone in feeling shame over its decline. Nor are we alone in acting out our shame through conflict. Every church I've served has shown symptoms of shame related to its decline and resulting conflict. Theologian Douglas John Hall argues that mainline Protestant Christianity in North America as a whole is suffering shame—with perhaps a touch of depression—over its decline. Hall observes, "Thus, having little spiritual courage for undergoing humiliation at any level, we manifest in our common life today what I can only consider a kind of repressed melancholy—the melancholy of those who wish above all not to appear melancholy."[13] It takes the form of the (often unspoken) sentiment, "What is wrong with us that people don't come to our church anymore? That they don't like the worship we like? That they don't appreciate the programs we hold dear?" Of course, the congregation isn't *bad*—it may be dysfunctional, conflicted, blind to injustices within the institution, but not bad in an irredeemable way. Chronic shame is a hidden and corrosive emotional factor that has to be engaged if church redevelopment is to be successful.

Anxiety and shame feed each other. The impetus for redevelopment at Beneficent Church came from a realization among some leaders that unless they started doing things differently, the church would die. This generated anxiety, which, while it provided energy for action, also created its own problems as leaders went in all different directions at once and ended up simply digging themselves into a deeper hole, which created more anxiety, which led to more fruitless action, which led to even more anxiety and a feeling of being stuck and finally despair that their situation was hopeless: that there was no way the church would be able to reconnect to its legacy. The sense of shame grew as one after another, all the tools in the congregation's toolbox failed to fix the situation. What they didn't realize was the adaptive nature of the situation, which inevitably meant that technical solutions would be inadequate. There were no answers *out there*. Redevelopment is an inside job.

Though there is little consensus among scholars as to what, precisely, emotions are, much less what shame is, Pattison argues, "Shame may well be the most socially significant of all the phenomena that are commonly conceived as emotions."[14] Shame is socially significant because it functions as a barometer of relationships. Pattison draws on microsociologists Suzanne Retzinger and Thomas Scheff, who identify a continuum of unacknowledged shame and genuine pride as informing all relationships. Shame, an indicator that the relationship is somehow out of sync, is the result of evaluation and interpretation: "Shame is the result of a global evaluation of the whole self as inadequate, unworthy, and a failure. It is not triggered by any act of another person or situation but only by our evaluation or interpretation of the situation."[15] It's the shift from "I made a mistake" to "I am a mistake." Human beings are continually and mostly unconsciously evaluating their relationships, so shame, while it can have deleterious effects, also has a positive social function of helping us know where we stand in relationship to others.

Genuine pride is not arrogance, but rather "grows out of self-respect as a result of knowing ourselves to be competent, worthy, compassionate, and honest."[16] Shame as an emotional phenomenon is neither good nor bad. Like power, it is simply a fact of human relationships. Shame becomes a problem, however, when it is chronic and unacknowledged.

Heifetz and Friedman have helped us identify anxiety and fear of loss as emotional barriers to redevelopment. This study suggests that shame is another emotional barrier that needs to be engaged if successful and faithful redevelopment is to take place. In his survey of the literature, Pattison observes the paucity of writing on shame. He attributes this to the nature of shame—that we want to keep it hidden from view. Nevertheless, Pattison argues, "Our dignity as human beings, paradoxically, depends upon the acceptance of our shame."[17] In fact, shame can be revelatory: it helps us to get ourselves in proportion—that is, as a barometer of social relationships, shame helps us find where we fit in community.[18] As Andrew put it, "Beneficent Church is suffering from the institutional memory of when it was the largest church in Rhode Island." On some level, the congregation—and perhaps the core leaders most acutely—were aware of the gap in power, prestige, and pride between their past situation and their current one. In a way, the twisting and turning this way and that for answers is a means of asking, "What's wrong with us that people don't want to come to our church anymore?" One respondent described the congregation's shame as a "lack of confidence" in the church's identity as a church.

Pattison draws on a variety of thinkers and his own experience to write about how churches contribute to chronic shame in individuals and what churches might do to bring healing to people experiencing chronic shame. He identifies himself as a shame-bound person whose religious experiences contributed to his sense of shame. He relates a story of a chance encounter with a friend he had not seen in many years. He recognized the friend as he walked through the train station, but instead of going up to greet him, Pattison continued to read his book and pretended not to see him. Reflecting on this experience, Pattison says that as a shame-bound person his behavior came from a "fear of not being recognized and then not being welcomed or valued."[19] In reading Pattison, it occurred to me that many of the behaviors I was observing at Beneficent seemed to fit the patterns Pattison was describing—for example, the failure of the search committee to disclose the dire nature of the church's situation to Nicole and me during the search and call process, reports from some in the congregation of "secret meetings" in which important decisions affecting the life of the congregation were being made, and the reluctance among some in leadership to embrace the congregation's identity as a silver plate (as opposed to sterling silver) church.[20] Pattison was concerned about the church as an institution shaming others, but what if the church itself was somehow acting out of unacknowledged shame related to the disruption of its internal and external relationships? What if that unacknowledged shame was also contributing to its difficulty in welcoming and valuing people—particularly people whose values and perspectives differed from those to which the congregation had grown accustomed? Douglas John Hall argues precisely this point: The disestablishment and decline of mainline churches has led to *dis-ease*—a pervading sense of shame that needs to be acknowledged.

How does one successfully and faithfully engage shame and disrupt the sense of fear it creates that people will not be, in Pattison's words, "recognized, welcomed, and valued"? One tool we used for creating safe space for acknowledging shame was the pulpit. Instead of trying to cover up our own personal disappointments, failures, and imperfections, Nicole and I used them as illustrations of God's grace at work in our lives—particularly our experience of losing our jobs and our house in the Great Recession of 2007–2009. The congregation noticed this as a difference in leadership from what they had been experiencing. In the interview study, several respondents noted how Nicole and I were approachable. Lydia said, "I like it especially when you guys do the service and we can relate to you with some of your circumstances, and you tell us about it, because sometimes we think that you guys are above us. We're not on the same level. But then, when we see what you went through, I can relate to you."

Publicly acknowledging our own personal limits did four things. First, connecting our own story of loss to God's good news of redemption allowed the congregation to imagine their collective experience of decline as the gospel story. Second, modeling how to appropriately share out of one's brokenness and demonstrating a comfort with that allowed the congregation to get comfortable with and to acknowledge that it was not the church it once was, and that was okay. Third, acknowledging our limits let the church know that we were not there to save them, that this was an adaptive situation in which all of us would be engaging in learning together. Fourth, it created a public space in which hurting and hopeful members of the congregation could give personal testimony to God's work in their lives. We later formalized the practice into a variety of worship features, including stewardship testimonies; a liturgical moment that we call "God Is Still Moving," during which a church member testifies to how God is still moving in her or his life; and "sacred conversations," a preaching practice described in chapter 6. Dealing with shame required leadership on our part as pastors to model how to appropriately talk about limits, disappointments, and hurts that simply are a part of human existence. Pattison writes about "de-idealisation" as a healthy approach to addressing chronic shame. The pastors are not perfect, and that is okay. Beneficent Church is not perfect, and that is okay.

On the other side of the coin, we also worked to build a sense of genuine pride. One early, big success we had was a two hundredth anniversary celebration of the church's meetinghouse. This was a celebration that both Beneficent Church and Beneficent Society, newcomers and longtimers together, could gather around as an expression of pride. During our first month or two at Beneficent Church, one of the staff let me know that the two hundredth anniversary of the meetinghouse's dedication was coming up the next year. I immediately seized the opportunity to create an anniversary committee that would plan a series of events for the anniversary year, culminating in an anniversary-homecoming weekend in the fall. We eventually broke the committee into two subcommittees: The first focused on telling the story of the church's past and inviting "alumni" to come to a special homecoming dinner following worship on anniversary weekend. The second subcommittee, made up of newer members, focused on Beneficent's future and creating a gala community awards evening on the anniversary weekend. At this event, Beneficent Church invited community leaders to celebrate with us as we gave awards to our community ministry partners, including the Rhode Island Coalition for the Homeless, NAACP Providence Branch, RPM Voices of Rhode Island, and others. The mayor and the lieutenant governor attended. The event was talked about in the community and in the church for many months afterward. It created a sense of genuine pride in the history, partnerships, and ministry with our community.

The way we navigated this process of engaging anxiety and shame was to oscillate between encouragement and challenge. Privately—that is, in committee and administrative meetings—we worked to fix weak areas: Palmer House, the budgeting process, the nominating process, and staffing. Publicly, we kept preaching hope. We also began to address issues of power and control.

KEYS FOR REDEVELOPMENT

Engaging conflict while protecting the congregational conversation about its future.

Not freaking out.

Building a support system for the pastor(s) and congregation.

Hiring a redevelopment coach.

Building relationships both within and outside the congregation.

For pastors, spending 20 percent of their time networking with people who are not yet part of the congregation.

Having a plan in place for dealing with conflict before engaging in redevelopment.

For folks in the church, feeling that they have a reason to be here.

Integrating shame and disrupting the anxiety cycle.

Taking steps to increase the fiscal health of the congregation, including examining spending and focusing on stewardship education.

Chapter Four

Shifting Power

We're trying to be a multicultural church. You need to have a multicultural voice—not a monocultural voice—trying to lead a multicultural church.
—Grace, multicultural educator and member of Beneficent Church

A key to successful and faithful church redevelopment at Beneficent Church was moving new staff and laypeople into positions of leadership. This chapter tells the stories of leadership transitions on two key church committees—the scholarship committee and the health and wellness committee—and the power shifts that resulted. Addressing issues of power in the congregation were difficult for two reasons: First, like other churches I've served, Beneficent did not have a language or a process for openly addressing the exercise of power in the congregation. Second, the changes involved in shifting and sharing power are changes that involve an experience of loss for some. In other words, they are adaptive challenges that involve deep change.

Adaptive work teaches us that congregational change in and of itself is not a problem. Even a change as significant as changing a pastor is not so difficult if the basic power structure of the congregation remains intact; however, when pastors exercise their power on behalf of marginalized people in the congregation, there is potential both for loss and for new life. The interview study showed that, for Beneficent, social justice means an equitable exercise of power. It turns out that at Beneficent Church, redevelopment work is justice work. Making this power shift is the heart of redevelopment.

A key to successful and faithful church redevelopment practice is redefining power relationships away from patronizing dominance and control and toward mutual influence. This shift in how power is exercised is decisive for the model of church redevelopment being constructed here. Strategies for church growth that do not address the exercise of power in the congregation are not likely to bring about the depth of transformation necessary to bring new life to a dying congregation. And power as patronizing dominance and control is precisely what feeds the death spiral of anxiety, "stuckness," and conflict. In this and the following chapters, we will explore the deconstructive movements of shifting power and the reconstructive practices of building systems of equity.

SCHOLARSHIP COMMITTEE

Grace and her family had been members of Beneficent for more than ten years when I interviewed her about her experience of redevelopment at the church. She, her husband, and their two young children had joined at the invitation of another young family who were members of Beneficent. Grace and her husband had been baptized but were not practicing Christians at the time they joined Beneficent. Grace became involved with the Sunday school because of her children. Her husband was involved in church leadership during the dark days, but he withdrew after being discouraged by behavior he described as "sneaky, Machiavellian, and inappropriate." Both Grace and her husband are professional educators who specialize in issues of diversity and multicultural education. For Grace, a key aspect of redevelopment was a power shift that she participated in at a meeting of the scholarship committee.

The scholarship committee at Beneficent Church manages a historic endowment that allows it to award $80,000–$90,000 a year in scholarships for secondary education. When I asked Grace to give an example of one thing she was excited about that illustrates what redevelopment at Beneficent Church has been for her, she began by talking about arriving at church for a scholarship committee meeting. She spoke about all the energy, activity, and people around the church on a weekday evening: "[It] just felt like the church was alive." For Grace, there was a connection between the change in atmosphere at the church and the shift in power on the scholarship committee.

This experience of arriving at a church full of energy and people was emblematic of many positive changes at Beneficent. As a young parent, Grace felt personally responsible for years for keeping the Christian education program afloat. Taking her children to church was a chore, because she had to drag them. They did not want to be there, because the Christian education program was so small and unstable. Now they have friends at church whom they want to see. Several other respondents also mentioned how their children want to go to church now and how it not only pleased them that the church was supporting them in passing on their faith to their children but also made churchgoing much easier on their families. A combination of people new to the church and folks who had been around for a while but, for a variety of reasons, had been on the margins of church life were beginning to influence decision making at the church. Grace was one of those people whose voice was beginning to be heard in a new and powerful way.

Grace describes the "voices thing" on the scholarship committee as "so important." In her view, "there's more willingness to be open to alternative perspectives." The example she gave was a meeting at which scholarships for several church members were up for renewal. One student had "done well" despite being "on her own" without family support. Several on the committee thought that increasing her scholarship was both deserved and needed, but one committee member said no. According to Grace, this was a member "who's very strong in the community and has *lots of voice*" (italics mine). But instead of deferring to her no, which had been the practice in both the committee and the wider congregation, "people felt much more able to say, 'Well, this is what I believe, and I think we should do this.'"

It so happened that Grace was facilitating the meeting in place of the chair, who couldn't be there. This shift in leadership—even though temporary—had a profound effect on the conversation. Grace reported:

> I felt that I had the voice to say, "So tell me about why you're saying no. Tell me about your reasons. Tell us how you're feeling about that." The person didn't have any reasons—ended up just saying, "I don't think we should." I think that was an example of how things were at Beneficent in the past. It was like, "I don't think we should. I don't have a reason we just shouldn't. I have the power, and that's it." People wouldn't speak into "Well here's how I'm feeling about that" or "Let's have a conversation about that."

This was a "huge change," according to Grace. Grace recalls being anxious—even though she was facilitating the meeting and even though her perspective was shared by a number of members of the committee—that the veto of the longtime member would end the conversation. Grace was relieved to discover that "on her part she was open to hearing the reasons why we thought it would be helpful for the student to get more aid through the committee." The proposed increase passed. While this might seem to be an insignificant incident, Grace identified it as "an example where someone who's been here forever, who has that power, that the power seems to be shifting a bit."

HEALTH AND WELLNESS COMMITTEE

A second example of shifting power, which had a much more visible (and audible!) impact on the congregation, was the Zumba exercise class that resulted from a change in leadership on the health and wellness committee. It so happens that the same person who had "lots of voice"—let's call her Eunice—from the above example had also served as chair of the health and wellness committee for many years. At this point I will point out that the example illustrates a common dynamic of entrenched power in dying churches: Power becomes concentrated in the hands of a decreasing number of people, so that you have, in Grace's words, people wearing "multiple hats." This dynamic was replicated in many areas of Beneficent Church and—while improving—continues to be an issue as new members go through the slow process of getting involved in church life, training for leadership, and getting nominated for leadership roles.

In the case of the health and wellness committee, transformation happened when a new member, Karen, who was both young and an experienced church leader from another congregation, agreed to cochair the committee with another, longer-tenured member. Ever since my arrival at Beneficent, Eunice, who was in her late eighties, had spoken to me about stepping back from chairing the health and wellness committee. Over the course of the next two years I approached different church members to take over for Eunice, but none would agree because all were worried that Eunice would sabotage their leadership unless they did things as Eunice would have them done. After years of searching, I finally found a pair of leaders whom Eunice approved of and who were willing to risk Eunice's disapproval.

Once again, the new leadership was able to shift power and transform the program by creating a space in which new and diverse voices could be heard and have influence. Karen accomplished this with the simple suggestion of doing a congregational survey and building the program around what the congregation indicated as their needs and interests. Tim, a respondent in the interview study who had observed the changes in the health and wellness committee, characterized the planning process that transformed the program as "the bottom-up model," as opposed to the "old model." With some irony, he said, "I think of the startlingly new idea of actually asking people what they would like to do or see the Health and Wellness come up with, and they said, 'Zumba.' Okay. Wow. What a shock. It turns out to be a success."

The committee had been dominated by longtimers, who ran the same programs year after year. The committee and programs were losing steam. They would ask questions like "How can we get more people involved?" I would respond, "Why don't you ask them what sort of programs they would be interested in?" They couldn't or wouldn't hear that suggestion from me, but with Karen's leadership and credibility with the committee, it finally happened.

The survey showed exercise as the number-one need and interest among the congregation. Karen had a personal connection with a Zumba teacher, who agreed to run a program for six weeks. Every week the class grew as people invited their friends. Folks from the neighborhood heard about it and started attending. At the end of the six weeks, we decided to make it an ongoing redevelopment program. Today, it is an ongoing health and wellness program that has expanded to two nights a week.

Nicole, who works out with the Zumba class every week and uses it as an evangelism opportunity, describes it as one of the most exciting pieces of redevelopment so far:

> I meet colleagues, and I'll say, "Oh, we have this great Zumba class," and they kind of chuckle or laugh, and I say, "No, really, this is a ministry tool—a Zumba class." For some it's hard to imagine how an exercise class could be part of the mission of the church. [This is] the way that it fits: We've had a health and wellness committee at the church for years and parish nurses and all of that, and they'll have programs in which they talk about *how to be healthy.* They talk about the healthy things that *one could do* to be more healthy. The Zumba class is actually doing something that is making you healthy.

The old model of doing health and wellness ministry was connected to an academic model that consists of imparting information from the party that has it to another that does not. In this age awash in information, this approach is making less sense. For example, when it comes to the overall ministry of the church for mission and witness to the good news of Jesus, people do not necessarily need information about Jesus. If they want information about Jesus, they can Google "Jesus" and get a lot of information. People are not looking to the church for information about Jesus; they are looking for an experience of Jesus. In this way, a postmodern practical theology of redevelopment could be said to be *incarnational*—that is, redevelopment focuses on finding creative ways to embody the gospel message. In the same way, the folks at Beneficent were looking for less information about health and wellness and more opportunities to experience health and wellness in their lives.

ENTRENCHED POWER AND BUNKER MODE

A number of respondents connected redevelopment with a shift in power in the congregation. Almost all of them recognized both the gains and the losses associated with the change in leadership. Grace, for example, while celebrating that other new voices along with hers are being heard, also said, "I think it was hard for the member who's been here a long time to see things changing and to see the power shift." Henry was also sensitive to the feelings of those who now find themselves sharing power with new voices: "There seems to be a group of leaders who've been leaders for so long. I think they may have single-handedly kept the lights on for a long period—'bunker mode,' as it were." According to Henry, as power shifted, the "we-kept-the-lights-on group" had "a feeling that either they're being marginalized or their vision of the future isn't what is happening." In his view, "they are hurt but they don't realize it." Henry connects this feeling of marginalization and inability to realize vision with the old model of exercising power, which was no longer working. It's a model that, in Henry's words, takes "the reins [and says,] 'I'm just going to do it.'" He observes that some people weren't ready for this power shift, and some "did it gracefully."

At the center of every declining church I have served is a small, tightly organized core group of leaders who are surrounded by a larger, more diffuse group of marginal voices. As anxiety about decline increases, the core group increasingly exercises its power in "bunker mode," or survival mode. Another term for this power pattern is *circling the wagons*, which refers to the practice of nineteenth-century covered wagons or prairie schooners on their journeys through the American West. When the caravan came under attack, the wagon drivers would circle the wagons for protection. In congregations, this power pattern creates a wall that defends against threat, including new ideas, new leaders with differing perspectives, new initiatives, new life, and creativity. The practice of circling the wagons comes out of the legitimate leadership function of protection. What congregations are protecting is their establishment. The protection, however, creates a system that is rigid, anxious, and controlling. As church redeveloper and consultant Bill Easum puts it, "Established churches worship at the feet of the sacred cow of CON-TROL."[1] Unfortunately, the more leaders try to control the situation, the more things tend to spiral out of control. Like Phoebe's lifeboat bobbing in the open ocean out of sight of land or ship, the congregation loses sight of its purpose and identity. The overarching purpose of Beneficent Church during the dark days became survival, and its identity became wrapped up in preserving the past. Eventually, the spiral of anxiety and control served only to dig the church deeper into the hole it found itself in.

Beneficent Church called and welcomed Nicole and me to do redevelopment, but that welcome was not shared equally by everyone. From the beginning, members articulated a fear that people "not like us" would "take over." Grace sensed this fear, and in our interview she articulated it in terms of creating an equitable system of sharing power—of "opening" the congregation to new voices and expanding the circle of "who has access to participation in public arenas of discourse."[2] Grace commented, "I think some of the fear about opening the church up is that people are going to come in and take over, take away, take or want the things we have." Though these fears primarily circle around money, they also touch on worship, particularly music style, and programming, including engaging the community as partners rather than patrons. One way Nicole and I dealt with that fear was by working on some things the core leaders were concerned about and thereby building relationships and gaining a level of trust.

Ronald Heifetz writes about the key role trust plays in leadership—particularly in constructing a "holding environment," one way power is exercised to facilitate adaptive work. According to Heifetz, "a holding environment consists of any relationship in which one party has the power to hold the attention of another party and facilitate adaptive work."[3] Remember, adaptive work requires learning on the part of leaders and followers alike—everyone confronted by an adaptive challenge. The learning process demands that people be open to new ideas and differing perspectives. Bunker mode is not a mindset oriented toward learning. The holding environment is a relational space in which anxiety can be contained and regulated at manageable levels—enough to motivate learning but not so much that the anxiety cycle kicks in. Leaders create this holding environment by building "relationships of informal authority derived primarily from trust." The last chapter outlined some of the strategies we employed for building relationships, including the Meet the Ministers meetings and the Walking in the Way process. We also built the holding environment by being competent enough and consistent enough.

Heifetz writes, "Trust in authority relationships is a matter of *predictability* along two dimensions: values and skill."[4] In chapter 2 we discussed the importance of being consistent in values related to redevelopment beginning with the call process. This consistency is a contrast, for example, to the dark days of the interim during which the pastor initiated a series of changes that were experienced by the church as destabilizing "shocks." The point of redevelopment is not to shake things up, but rather to deconstruct entrenched power in a consistent, methodical way that serves to make the congregation more just and compassionate. According to Nicole, it's the confidence that "everything that you do fits within an integrity that is going to hold water."

While acting consistently out of your values and vision for ministry—in Friedman's words, being "well-differentiated"—creates a certain amount of anxiety and pushback, it also begins to build the trust needed for adaptive work. Remember that Friedman's well-differentiated leaders should expect resistance and sabotage proportional to their principled stand. In fact, a leader's ability to recognize sabotage as a "systemic phenomenon connected to shifting balances in the emotional system" is the "key to the kingdom."[5] For redevelopment pastors, it is better to be trusted than to be "loved."

Paired with consistent values is the skill to show concretely the fruit of those values—in the case of redevelopment, that fruit is signs of new life. At the beginning of redevelopment we painted a picture in folks' imaginations of a full meetinghouse, and as new people began to show up, the leadership began to trust that we were competent enough to lead redevelopment work. New people in the pews are absolutely key to redevelopment for several reasons:

New faces give hope for the church's future.

They demonstrate your competence to make good on your promises.

They are the source of new leadership that disrupts entrenched power patterns.

They represent an opportunity for the practice of Christian hospitality— what I call *impossible hospitality*—which produces spiritual growth in the congregation.

For these reasons, while increasing worship attendance and membership numbers are not everything, they are definitely something and a key piece to successful and faithful church redevelopment.

Heifetz argues that predictability alone is not enough to build trust. People also need to feel that you have their best interests at heart and will not take advantage of them.[6] Beginning in chapter 1, we saw that Beneficent Church has an anxiety that some renegade pastor is going to spend all of its money. Some of the ways in which Nicole and I showed the leaders of Beneficent Church that we shared their concern about the organizational health of the church were (1) publicly saying that the status quo of the church finances and administration were not okay; (2) investing significant time in administrative tasks like creating job descriptions, managing staff, cutting spending, and improving communication; (3) closing Palmer House, a difficult administrative issue that cost us some members who were invested in the ministries housed there but reduced overall anxiety about the budget; and (4) staffing for redevelopment (an ongoing issue!), which involved some staff cuts, was messy and difficult, and again cost us some members, but it helped decrease the level of anxiety even further. These measures helped us build up enough trust to make possible the power shifting necessary for adaptive work. Slowly the church began to climb out of bunker mode.

Creating a holding environment for adaptive work is necessary for church redevelopment, but a holding environment by itself is not going to provoke the learning needed for adaptive change. The hybrid, postmodern model I am developing in these chapters needs a critical mass of new and formerly marginalized voices to begin speaking to the situation from their perspectives. In our interview, Grace raised the necessity of including *multiple* new voices in church leadership. She said she was looking forward to her new leadership roles in the church—particularly that of moderator. She saw this as another example of shifting power. Then she remembered an example of another new leader, Peter, who was moderator during the dark days. For Grace, Peter's was the story of a new leader who had a bad experience trying lead the old system:

> It was just so challenging for him because I think he was in there on his own. Here's this newer member, and he's on his own as the moderator of the council, but he was still being the moderator for the old guard. So he didn't have any other voice beyond his own voice to try to shift things or make change, so it's like he got run out of there. He couldn't wait for it to be over.

Being a lone "voice in the wilderness" may be a place to start, but it is probably not going to affect a shift in power. For that, you need a critical mass of new voices. New voices and what Heifetz calls "creative deviants" are much more easily neutralized if they have no support. That is why redevelopment pastors need to pay close attention to the nominating process to ensure that new voices are not excluded from the outset. Our redevelopment coach, Paul Nickerson, calls it "getting a hold on the nominating process."

By contrast, now Beneficent has enough new voices that the bunker-mode power patterns are less effective. For example, Grace identified pre-meetings as one strategy used by the core group to maintain their entrenched power. These were patterns of communication whereby core leaders would work out together how to ensure that their agenda would be enacted. Grace described this pattern as "pre-meeting meetings with the plan, and then the plan comes in, and it's already decided, and then there's really not a meeting because all the pre-stuff happened." The key to disrupting this pattern is the new, empowered voices in committees that are willing to question what in the past seemed like a fait accompli. In Grace's words, "So those pre-meetings may be happening, but there are not as many key players once you come back into the meeting. There are still a lot of alternative voices, so you really have to work through things. It's not going to just be the pre-meeting people getting what they wanted."

From the perspective of entrenched power, these alternative voices are "creative deviants," but I would like to find a new name for them.[7] *Deviant* has a pejorative connotation based on the assumption that there is a commonly accepted norm. In redevelopment, where prevailing norms are questioned, those who think otherwise aren't so much deviant as they are simply different. A key to successful and faithful redevelopment is cultivating and protecting these *different* and *differing* voices.

This raises a further issue of the different expectations new and marginalized people bring to their connections to the life and ministry of the church. It is perhaps a stereotype of new church members and younger generations that they are not interested in serving on church boards, committees, or ministry teams and that they do not contribute financially to the church in any significant way. At Beneficent Church, we have found reality to be a bit more complex than that generalized claim. The following are several things we have found to be true of how newer, younger, and formerly marginalized people understand church leadership and ministry in the church:

1. People who have been overlooked for positions of responsibility in the church—because of race, age, length of membership in the church, sexual orientation, socioeconomic status, or gender—generally regard

being invited to serve in positions of responsibility in the church as an honor, though they feel some of the hesitancy that comes with lingering fear that their voices or perspectives will be disregarded.

2. Younger people and newer members tend to want to spend more time *doing* ministry and less time *talking* about ministry. Therefore, the task of leadership is to design short-term, hands-on, accessible ministry projects and to ensure that healthy communication patterns are practiced in meetings.

3. Younger people and newer members are faced with considerable time pressures and therefore are looking for meetings that are focused and productive and not a "waste" of time, meaning they don't want to devote time to socializing at church business meetings, because (thank God!) they have social lives outside the church.

4. Younger people and newer members are generally not interested in hierarchical decision-making processes in which one group of people decides what the ministry priorities of another group of people should be. People want to be empowered to do the mission God is calling them to do.

5. Some of our newest members—particularly those with previous church experience—are our biggest financial contributors.

The role of the pastors in this process is simply to leverage their power on behalf of the marginalized in the congregation—to keep the space open, to practice direct, covenantal communication, and to graciously, nonanxiously hold to the redevelopment process leaders and congregation have agreed upon together, even in the face of sabotage and threats. What happens then is that these new voices—those that had been marginalized—begin to deconstruct the established power structure simply by "speaking the truth in love" (Eph. 4:15) from their perspectives as excluded others. They deconstruct entrenched power as they expose underlying constructed assumptions, like "We don't have any leaders" or "Things will never change" or "We'll never make it" or "People don't give" or "Nobody will volunteer" or "People are too busy" or "We've tried everything" or "We have no choice" or "They can't be trusted."

Often people find themselves excluded from power precisely because they ask questions like "What if we try this?" or "I wonder what those people think?" or "What's the worst that could happen?" or "Why do we do it this way?" or "What if we asked them?" or "What does the Bible say?" or "What do you think God is up to?" or "Why not?" The trick is making space for these questions that make controllers uncomfortable while at the same time being a compassionate pastor to everyone—insiders and outsiders alike. This means absorbing some of the anxiety and reactivity of longtimers who are being challenged and disoriented by the inevitable changes that redevelopment brings, while helping newcomers find ways to use their unique perspectives, gifts, and energy in coordinated ways for building up the church. Theologian Catherine Keller argues that through decisive actions of leaders to open space for new voices, an organic "self-organizing complexity" begins to emerge. In my experience, "self-organizing" is a bit of stretch. In reality, redevelopment pastors should expect to carry a heavy load organizationally. Nevertheless, on our best days, the redevelopment process at Beneficent is neither the order of imposed will nor the chaos of dissolution, but rather a third way of mutually influencing, transformative cocreativity.[8]

Not all of those in the "we-kept-the-lights-on group" resented the shifting power. Some welcomed it gracefully. Gene—a longtime leader—saw new people taking leadership as something the church "desperately needs." While the changes going on at the church have meant that he has had to give up some things that have been meaningful to him personally—the primary one being a shift from the classical music–focused worship service to a multicultural worship service—he was willing to give up singing only the old hymns if new music means new people. People like Gene—I call them spiritual giants—who find purpose and meaning in helping newcomers find purpose and meaning are key to successful and faithful church redevelopment in a postmodern context.

Successful and faithful church redevelopment in a postmodern context takes shifting and sharing power and enough existing members who are willing not simply to welcome newcomers to sit in *their* worship and participate in *their* programs but also to truly make space, to move over and welcome the hopes, dreams, identities, values, and ways of doing things that newcomers bring to the church. It also takes pastors who, when necessary, have the stomach to stand up to powerful lay leaders in order to protect the voices and perspectives of newcomers.

CHRISTENDOM AND GOSPEL REDUCTIONISM

In chapter 1, we turned to Penny Edgell Becker's research on conflict and congregational models for a hermeneutic key—that is, a tool for interpreting the culture and history of Beneficent Church—to unlock the redevelopment potential of the congregation. In analyzing Beneficent's spiritual DNA through the lens (this is a magic key that can transform into a lens!) of Becker's congregational models, we noticed certain resonances. First, we noticed that in the beginning there was a big bang of between-frame conflict that erupted at First Congregational Church of Providence when Great Awakening evangelists came to town. When some members of First Congregational heard the evangelists' preaching, they began to question their pastor's piety and theology. We noticed that two groups, both responding to the movement of the Spirit, began to construct distinct identities that emanated from different understandings of truth, knowledge, and covenant. When Deacon Snow's group left to form their own congregation, First Congregational Church continued—in a diminished capacity—as an establishment congregation operating out of a leader model, whose primary function is protecting and passing down denominational tradition in order to change the world.

The process of separation that produced Beneficent Church gave the congregation a mixed inheritance of spiritual DNA. Though Deacon Snow maintained to his dying day that his was the "true and original" Congregational church in Providence, Beneficent was by no means an establishment church. The Spirit that formed and informed Beneficent *disrupted* the established Congregational order, and local Congregational leaders were none too happy about it! This ambiguous and ambivalent relationship with its denominational heritage produced in Beneficent a tension between leader model aspirations in which the congregation conforms to denominational identity and community model demands, which focus on congregational process and locally defined identities. Trying to sort out this confusing leader-community model mix at Beneficent, which was reflected in the data generated by my 2011 interview study, led me to wonder about other ways of reading Beneficent Church.

Brian McLaren's analysis of contemporary American Christianity using modern and postmodern approaches to faith seemed to open a way forward. Could a conversation among modern and postmodern thinkers point toward a new theological language that could connect Beneficent's particular mixed heritage of evangelical enthusiasm and establishment rationalism to the diverse, largely unchurched mission field in which it now found itself? This new reading led me to postulate a shift at Beneficent Church from a predominantly modern-patronage ministry model to a mixed postmodern-plural ministry model. This particular postmodern-plural ministry model looks like a disrupted modern model that embraces a not-quite-establishment or disestablished posture toward its community and tradition.

This analysis is based on a broader theological reading of the shifting relationships among mainline Protestant Christianities and mainstream American culture and how they come into conversation with the local processes of redevelopment at Beneficent Church. In this chapter, I have outlined how a postmodern-plural ministry model deconstructs entrenched power at a local level. The postmodern-plural model also calls into question the close historical connection between Protestant Christianity and Western cultural forms.

Modern-patronage ministry models are connected with a much broader modern Christian mission model—a model that theologian Darrell Guder calls the Christendom mission model, which he describes in *The Continuing Conversion of the Church*. He traces its history in detail, beginning with the establishment of Christianity as an accepted religion of the Roman Empire under Constantine—known as "Constantinianization."[9] At this point the Roman Empire began drawing on Christian thought and practice to legitimize its imperial agendas, and Christianity began taking advantage of the empire's resources to strengthen its institutions and extend its reach. The resulting mix of empire and church gave birth to Christendom, which, Guder argues, has fallen into the "sin" of reducing the gospel to Western cultural forms. Evangelism then becomes making *them*, non-Western people, like *us*, the ambassadors not only of Christ but also of empire.

Christendom has been guilty of reducing salvation to adopting Western ways. In the American context, the Christendom model morphed into civil religion, which conflates being a "good Christian" with being a good American citizen.[10] Recall, for example, Rev. Hall and his *Discourses Comprising a History of the First Congregational Church in Providence*. In his first discourse, he writes,

> Our civil polity has been our religious polity. Or rather, the religious preceded and controlled the civil. Religion led the way. It laid the foundation. It reared the superstructure. It built not the church only but the school, it founded the college, it guarded the laws, it wielded the power, it threw its strong voice and stronger energy into all the forms and fashions, the institutions and interests, of the new State, and the new world.[11]

This sentiment was echoed by Rev. Vose in his 1894 *Sketches on Congregationalism in Rhode Island* on the 150th anniversary of Beneficent Church.

Both First Congregational and Beneficent Church claimed an establishment heritage. Beneficent disrupted the establishment not to call Christendom into question, but rather to reestablish it on the basis of a "different sentiment." This study argues much along the lines of Guder that successful and faithful church redevelopment in a postmodern context takes an awareness of the ways in which Western cultural assumptions and Christianity have been welded together. [12] Redevelopment at Beneficent has been a process of directing the congregation's tendency to disrupt toward efforts that call Christendom into question, as it had called established Congregationalism into question more than two centuries earlier. This raising of awareness is a deconstructive process that opens a space for new readings of Christian texts and traditions.

For Guder, the modern Christendom mission model is exemplified by Christian missionaries who traveled to foreign countries and cultures not only to bring the gospel message to those places but also to "civilize" the people there. This gave a moral cast to a whole host of cultural forms—from liturgies to music, to organizational structures, to architecture, to norms of leadership, communication, and relationships—that a postmodern-plural model calls into question. For example, in chapter 5, we will examine the transformations in Beneficent Church's music program to include, in a much more intentional and integrated way, non-Western music forms—in this case, gospel music. While Beneficent has made this transition for the most part successfully and gracefully, initially some longtimers expressed a worry that gospel music is "entertainment"—that is, somehow spiritually more shallow or deficient compared to the organ music to which they were accustomed. For a few, gospel music is not simply *different*—it is *deficient*. Tracing the history of this subtle form of patronizing racism helps to surface it, deconstruct it, and reduce its impact. For Guder, conversion happens and the "cultural captivity of the Church" to the sin of gospel reductionism is broken when churches stop reducing the gospel to Western cultural forms and instead engage in God's mission of spiritual and relational transformation. [13]

The church's captivity has been a theme at least since the time of Martin Luther and his "Babylonian Captivity" of the church—with a capital *C* denoting what was at the time a battle over Christendom. What began as a war of words, with ninety-five theses on the door of the castle church at Wittenberg, eventually led to a bloody conflict in Europe that came to be known as the Thirty Years' War. That religious language was used to justify military violence discredited the whole religious project for many in Europe—or at least brought the role of religion in public, political life into question. European thinkers began calling for an enlightened politics based on scientific reason instead of religious superstition. Christians responded to this cultural shift in a variety of ways, including, but not limited to, (1) rejecting Enlightenment modernity as antithetical to Christianity, (2) accommodating Enlightenment demands by demonstrating the reasonableness of Christianity, and (3) focusing on Christianity as a private, individual choice for moral edification and existential comfort, especially appropriate for childrearing and the home. The first response above represents the choice made by fundamentalist and more conservative groups. The second and third were the preferred responses of mainline Protestant churches in the United States. In short (and an admittedly rough reading of history this is!), Luther's liberation of the church from the ecclesiastical empire of the Roman Catholic Church did not liberate churches from a deeper cultural Christendom forged in the fires of the cultural shift to Enlightenment modernity.

The colonial violence of the seventeenth through the nineteenth centuries, including the American slavery system, sowed the seeds of the Enlightenment project's disintegration. The unprecedented violence of the twentieth century—of which World War I is only one example and the only one to which Guder refers—has contributed greatly to the further disintegration of the Enlightenment project. The demise has led to a radical critique of the very categories of Western thought, which are based on binary pairs, one dominating *the other*: intelligible over sensible, reason over unreason, God over humanity, good over evil, white over black, man over woman, rich over poor, America over the world, and so forth. *The other* is often defined by lack—evil is the absence of good. Once again, this is an extremely rough outline of one trajectory of postmodern critique.

Guder is headed in the right direction with his "'cultural captivity' of the gospel and churches' compromises with their surrounding contexts," but I am not sure at this point whether he understands or is willing to acknowledge the depth of the critique of Western culture and Western Christendom going on right now.[14] The only piece that I would like to examine a little more closely here is how he understands God's relationship to humans in mission. In short, his understanding that God is "the author, the subject, the initiator," that "no witness articulates an original word," and that God's intention in revelation is "to be recognized and submitted to and served" are claims that folks in the multicultural ministry context of Beneficent Church, where people are very sensitive to language of dominance (and the implicit threat of violence), might want to call into question.[15] Until we can deal directly with issues of power in churches and the extent to which we replicate these power relationships in our theologies, I am not sure we will be able to free ourselves from the cultural captivity that Guder identifies.

Nevertheless, in my reading of Guder, his shift from the "Salvation of Man" to "Mission of God" opens a space for the plural identities of congregations to experience life-giving, life-changing encounters with the others of our world.[16] Evangelism is no longer turning *them* into us, but rather a mutually transformative encounter in which all turn toward God. Guder invites a rereading of "the beginning of the good news of Jesus Christ, the Son of God" (Mark 1:1). Jesus's word in Mark 1:15—"The time is fulfilled, and the kingdom of God has come near; repent, and believe in the good news"— is no longer simply a modern call to people to humbly accept salvation from the omnipotent God, but more a postmodern call to the mission of mutually transforming encounter with *others*. Successful and faithful redevelopment at Beneficent Church has meant engaging in a theological conversation at this level of depth. Redevelopment is not simply a new website or a praise band but also a theological transformation with profound implications. Congregational transformation is a call to this mission of continual mutual transformation—what Guder calls "the continuing conversion of the Church," which I would characterize as a process in which patronizing binaries of helper and helped, civilized and uncivilized, churched and unchurched, longtimer and newcomer, are continually opened up to surprising reversals and mutually empowering partnerships.

Nicole sees the modern-patronage ministry model and its hierarchical binaries as perhaps being appropriate at a certain point in Beneficent Church's history. It may have had its place, but it is no longer appropriate for it to hold the primary position. For her, this line of thinking emerged during our Meet the Ministers meetings and other initial conversations with church members. Though the congregation had a strong consensus that Beneficent Church had "always," to some degree, been a multicultural church, among the established leaders there was a recurring theme that the role of people of color in the church was to be receivers of services. Nicole understood this viewpoint as emerging historically seventy-five years ago when the church started to do a lot of outreach to immigrant groups. Many of the immigrants were "really marginalized people and disadvantaged and ha[d] a lot needs, and maybe that is how they related to the people of color, because they were persons of color and they were immigrants and marginalized in that way, but that is not the community that we have now." According to Nicole, what disrupted this hierarchical binary was the operation of "difference"—that is, "the way the congregation related to itself vis-a-vis its various cultures." Nicole and I didn't approach our ministry at Beneficent intending to create a multicultural congregation. Rather, "we just started doing our thing"—that is, engaging established leadership and entrenched power—"and the church started becoming more multicultural." The result was that ministry-as-patronage became a "big issue."

The communication tools we had learned during the Walking in the Way process made it possible to identify and talk about issues of race, class, and power. According to Nicole, "What we started hearing was the reason the things have been this way has something to do with race and racism and maybe some classism." We also heard that people of color did not "want to be the ones who are just receiving services. They want to be full partners and participants." This frank and open conversation produced a shift in the operation of power at the church so that today, when we welcome immigrants, we recognize that

> even the immigrants can have a contribution to make. So there is something about being able to articulate in a loving and authentic and real way what is really going on at the church. It could be about money. It could be about power dynamics. It can be about culture and race. But whatever those difficult things are, we have more tools now to talk about those. And that has made a big difference.

Our faith tells us that churches are the body of Christ broken for the healing of the world. We now recognize at Beneficent Church both the brokenness of the modern-patronage model and the healing that God accomplished through it. That model allowed us to host political refugees from a number of countries and support them in building a new life. It motivated the church to provide hospitality to a variety of immigrant groups—Swedish, Armenian, Chinese, Laotian, and others. But the model was based on unexamined assumptions about culture and power that no longer fit our multicultural, pluralist, postmodern context. The emerging postmodern-plural model is perhaps no less broken than the modern-patronage model, but it takes a different approach to mission. Instead of trying to assimilate marginalized peoples into a Western cultural *center* that the church imagines itself to occupy and master, we recognize that the church itself is now marginal to mainstream culture, and from that margin we are relearning together how to be and do church as a Christian culture marked by difference.

Grace calls her vision of an alternative to the patronage model "systems of equity." It is a shift toward a pluralist process in which a wider range of people are given "access to participation in public arenas of discourse."[17] At Beneficent, this shift toward systems of equity produced a self-reinforcing feedback loop that reversed the anxiety-control spiral characteristic of decline. As controlling behaviors like "pre-meetings or having one voice or just a couple of voices dominate the conversation" were disrupted, more voices were able to join the conversation, which in turn made the controlling behaviors less effective, which reinforced the welcoming and safe atmosphere, which allowed still more new voices to be heard and have an influence. The growing number of new and diverse voices has created the necessity to revise, expand, and formalize systems of equity.

According to Grace, the patronage-dominance system, while intending to help people, sets up inequities that "end up helping fewer people than you could if you had a system for it."

> When you create systems—if they're created well—they can eliminate bias and balance the power; whereas, if you just go with your feelings and the people with which you're connected, then that leaves out so many other people who you may not have the feelings for or you may not have the connection with, and if it's only the people who are one type of person—who is in a certain group—then it really keeps out a lot of different people.

In the case of the scholarship committee, creating a system of equity was mostly a matter of leaders simply applying the already existing rules for awarding and maintaining scholarships fairly and consistently. In the preceding years, the committee had moved away from holding certain scholarship recipients accountable for grades, getting required information to the committee in a timely manner, and the like. They were given preferential treatment because they had personal relationships with people on the committee. At the same time, qualified applicants who didn't have a personal connection to someone on the committee could find it difficult to get an application. Systems of equity are also systems of accountability.

Grace's leadership called the scholarship committee to be accountable to its stated vision, values, and rules while raising awareness for the need for diverse voices in the decision-making process. Anticipating her role as church moderator, Grace envisioned activating the power shifts taking place at the committee level in church leadership as a whole. To articulate this vision, she borrowed an example from her work as an educator:

> We're trying to be a multicultural church. You need to have a multicultural voice, not a monocultural voice, trying to lead a multicultural church. That would just never happen. It's like if you set kids out, and you let the girls be in charge, but they are making decisions for the boys *and* the girls. There would be some boys who would be fine with it, but there would be a lot who would be like "Wait a minute. I don't want to do that game, or I don't want to be a part of this thing. I want to say what we should do or have."

Beneficent has been a multicultural church for many years and over the years has developed different models multicultural ministry. The modern-patronage ministry model at Beneficent was successful in helping vulnerable and marginalized immigrant groups establish themselves in Providence. The redevelopment process at Beneficent, which included the work of deconstructing entrenched power, exposed the limitations of the modern-patronage model and opened space for a new, pluralist model. This new model envisions a church organized around systems of equity that expand access to participation in public arenas of discourse by paying attention to not only those who have "lots of voice" but also those who have not yet even been invited to the table.

STAFFING FOR MULTICULTURAL MINISTRY

Beneficent Church's ministry turn toward the postmodern-plural model produced surprising and significant growth in the Christian education program. Christian education really took off when, through Nicole's networking, we found a talented new leader for the program. Nicole described her as "a trained pastor who has a lot of roots in the community and really understands ministry."

> She comes from a more evangelistic background—not UCC, not Congregationalist—but I think that's a really positive thing because that fits the redevelopment part—the evangelism part—and the fact that we've also been working on this idea of diversifying ethnically our staff. As an ethnically diverse congregation, it's really important to have some diversity in the staff. She is African American. She comes from an AME [African Methodist Episcopal] tradition. She grew up in the city. She has a lot of gifts that we don't have in

terms of being from here—being able to relate better . . . culturally to the people of color in our community.

The thing that struck me about Nicole's response is that she relates the effectiveness of the new CE director to *difference*—religious, cultural, social, and racial. While it was easy for me to see the benefit of those differences in terms of new skills and different perspectives, what was striking to me was that difference had been such a source of anxiety and conflict at Beneficent Church up until recently.

What was it that made difference key to redevelopment in this case? Once again, Nicole came back to the Walking in the Way process, the safe space or holding environment, and the communication tools we had developed as a congregation in the first year or so of our ministry together. According to Nicole, "It [the Walking in the Way process] did slow things down and give us some tools and a perspective on difference: difference is not bad, it's just different. There are all kinds of perspectives." Though we did not set out to *make* the church multicultural, the leadership style we adopted for redevelopment work opened the space for this new model of multicultural ministry.

It appears that Heifetz's adaptive leadership as a learning modality and Quinn's idea that leadership requires a "willingness to be vulnerable" served us well when it came to multicultural ministry. According to Nicole, it's a "humility," or what "comes across as humility" (note a touch of irony here!), that says, "Look, we don't have all the answers." In theological terms, it's respecting the mystery of the other: "We're doing our best. We're not persons of color. We don't understand all of that, but we're willing to engage that question with humility and with an openness." The key is "just to love the people that come through the door and try to understand who they are and what they're about and give ourselves fully to that." Nicole links adaptive leadership to postmodern ideas about difference. The result is movement toward a nondominating notion of leadership.

> Maybe what you're getting at is this idea of embracing the difference as a gift instead of something [that's] a problem to overcome. Maybe that has been a key shift in perspective. Difference does not have to be scary. I guess that is more of a postmodern idea, that we're not trying to make everyone the same or initiate them into a culture that is monolithic. It [congregational culture] is something that is growing and changing as the congregation grows and changes and we need to be open to that.

The dream of a "monolithic," or at least a united or universal, Christendom is a notion in tension with postmodern difference and diversity—a tension this study does not seek to resolve (which would only lead to another "dominology," or, to use Mobley's term, an "idol," that of the postmodern); rather, it is a dynamic to be lived, explored, and negotiated.

The key to successful and faithful church redevelopment is redefining power relationships away from patronizing dominance or control and toward mutual influence. This shift in the exercise of power is decisive for the model of church redevelopment being constructed here. Strategies for church growth that do not address the exercise of power in the congregation are not likely to bring about the depth of transformation necessary to bring new life to a dying congregation. And it is precisely the exercise of power as patronizing dominance and control that feeds the death spiral of anxiety, "stuckness," and conflict. By contrast, the exercise of power to create systems of equity produces a self-reinforcing feedback loop. While that loop doesn't eliminate tension, and in fact generates new tensions as new differences express themselves, it does generate new life and vitality. In the next chapter, we will explore in more detail how Beneficent Church has begun constructing a community that more closely resembles what Grace refers to as a "system of equity."

KEYS FOR REDEVELOPMENT

Moving new staff and laypeople into positions of leadership.

Redefining power relationships, moving away from patronizing dominance and toward mutual influence.

Bringing new people into worship services.

Exerting influence on the nominating process.

Protecting those whose perspectives differ from the established norms.

Involving the spiritual giants who find purpose and meaning in helping newcomers find purpose and meaning.

Longtimers who are willing to move over and make space in leadership for newcomers.

For pastors, having the stomach to stand up to entrenched power.

Building an awareness of the ways in which Western cultural assumptions and Christianity have been welded together.

Loving the people who come through the door, trying to understand who they are and what they're about, and giving yourself fully to that.

Chapter Five

Extending Welcome

I've prayed a lot this year and probably more than I have previous years. I think it's because I'm looking. I'm seeking God's way and trying to put myself and my own biases and my own preferences aside and *listen.*
—Cindy, longtime Beneficent Church member

Lydia began attending Beneficent Church when she was twelve years old at the invitation of her boyfriend, who sang in the choir with his sister. He wanted Lydia not only to hear him sing but also to see the large, nineteenth-century crystal chandelier that hangs in the center of the meetinghouse. In 1964 they were married under that chandelier. Before leaving to serve in the US Army, where he would be the first African American from Rhode Island to sacrifice his life in the Vietnam War, Gary made Lydia promise that she would continue going to Beneficent Church. Lydia kept her promise. Over the years, Lydia and her extended family would attend worship and occasionally host church suppers.

For Lydia, church and family are closely connected. The primary theme of our interview was the ways in which faith and family were woven together in Lydia's life. For Lydia, the faith values of Beneficent Church reinforce the family values she seeks to instill in her children, grandchildren, and great-grandchildren. Lydia's family is large, and her leadership responsibilities are significant. She is an elder of the Northern Narragansett Indian Tribe, which numbers more than three hundred members. Since hers is the largest family of the tribe, she wields significant influence in the group. Lydia traces her leadership legacy back to an ancestor who was tribal translator and scribe when English colonists began settling Narragansett land in the seventeenth century. Despite her deep devotion to her faith and family, Lydia's worship attendance had fallen off during Beneficent's dark days. She said the church had become "boring," which was her assessment of the depressed atmosphere of the church at the time.

Lydia and I met at her house, where she has lived with her extended family for many years. When I asked her what excited her most about redevelopment at Beneficent Church, she told the story of how word got to her that the church had new pastors and she should "try it." She said she would "give it a few weeks." She has missed very few weekly worship services since then. What she likes about redevelopment is the "openness" that it has brought to the church. She experiences this in how she is greeted at the church. This gesture of welcome is significant to her as a mark of genuine respect. When I asked for an example, Lydia spoke of a time when Nicole paid a visit to the church kitchen. Lydia and her family were cleaning up after hosting a church meal. Hosting church meals is a significant part of her family's ministry at the church. It reflects her Native American cultural heritage, which uses social suppers to build relationships, teach culture to younger generations, and advance the interests of the group. Lydia said:

> [Pastor Nicole] came up to me, she introduced herself, and she said, "Lydia, I've heard a lot about you, but I've never met you." She was just talking to me and asking me about what changes and things that we would like to see, and she was just very welcoming. And you know what? We were cleaning up, and she says, "Well, what can I do in here to help you?" It was nice.

What was new for Lydia and remarkable was church leadership—in her words, "extending a hand" in a "genuine way." The "outgoing" way that the pastors welcomed her and her family communicated that "Now, it isn't just 'You're welcome if you come.'"

These small, seemingly insignificant gestures of welcome have had huge effects on Beneficent Church. The attitude of "You're welcome if you come" was not experienced as particularly welcoming by Lydia and other people of color at Beneficent Church. Successful and faithful redevelopment at Beneficent Church has hinged on moving beyond simple tolerance of *other* people and their *other* cultures to actively extending a hand to people of diverse cultures within the congregation and in our neighboring communities. It has demanded that we open ourselves to *other* traditions, histories, and values so that together we can relearn how to follow Jesus, worship God, and practice community. We have had to develop the ability to extend hospitality to people in a way that respects cultural difference and opens space for expression of that difference. Expressing difference in this way deconstructs the dominating power in the congregation. Cultural difference at Beneficent Church is marked by racial and ethnic differences; generational differences; social, economic, and political differences; sexual orientation and gender differences; and differences in ability, needs, beliefs, religious experience, and values.

Nicole's initial extension of welcome eventually led to Lydia's election to deacon at Beneficent Church. Lydia had been a member of Beneficent for more than fifty years and, as previously mentioned, was an elder of the Northern Narragansett Indian Tribe—a community larger and older than Beneficent Church, and one that has faced (and continues to face) hardships far greater than any Beneficent Church has—yet she had never been invited to serve in any official leadership capacity at the church. Like leaders of every dying church that I've encountered, Beneficent's established leaders had complained about being burned out. They complained that no one would volunteer for leadership, so the same people played a game of musical chairs, rotating through different committees. Many served as leaders on most of the committees, which sometimes created conflicts of interest—Grace called this "wearing different hats" a barrier to "systems of equity." Yet here was a gifted, spiritually mature leader who had been overlooked for fifty years. I met with Lydia and her family in her home. I attended social suppers and built relationships among the Northern Narragansett people. Nicole and I worked with Beneficent's nominating committee, and within a matter of months Lydia was elected deacon at a congregational meeting.

What Nicole and I discovered when we extended ourselves to those who did not identify with the predominant cultural assumptions of the church— and who identified with cultures different from our own—was that the experience of being overlooked was painful. When the nominating committee approached Lydia about serving as deacon—which, in Beneficent Church, is a role that has responsibility for the spiritual well-being of the congregation—Lydia's first reaction was "Why? Most of the people in the church don't even really know me. Nobody knew much about me, because, like I said, as long as I've been going to that church, nobody extended a hand to me."

Successful and faithful church redevelopment in postmodern contexts begins with looking at a congregation with "fresh eyes," as pastor and redeveloper Mary Louise Gifford puts it. Nicole identified Beneficent's difficulties as stemming from a "lack of imagination." In the early days, it seemed to me that the story of the established leadership was one of missed opportunities. In the Gospels, stories of Jesus's healing of blindness serve as a metaphor for spiritual transformation. Redevelopment involves healing and justice that turns to God for the gift of sight so that leaders might see clearly the gifts, resources, and opportunities right before us.

The modern-patronage ministry model has contributed in significant ways to the multicultural diversity of Beneficent Church. Various mission societies birthed out of the vision, energy, and resources of Beneficent Church members have been building cross-cultural relationships for centuries, the most significant and enduring ones being European American ties to African Americans, Native Americans, and Chinese immigrants. The Great Awakening evangelical impulse that gave birth to Beneficent Church provides the congregation with a strong social justice and mission orientation. However, Western cultural assumptions, which for many years served to connect Beneficent to its mission fields, began over the last several decades to function as an invisible cultural force field against the cultural diversity that now characterizes Beneficent's mission fields. Undeconstructed cultural assumptions, coupled with the anxiety of decline, narrowed the leadership's view of the congregation's situation. This chapter documents how Beneficent Church came to have an awareness of its cultural assumptions, how this awareness has supported the redevelopment process, and how the congregation overcame its anxiety toward welcoming others of different cultures.

GOSPEL MUSIC AND PRACTICING FREEDOM

When I asked Nicole what she found most exciting about the redevelopment at Beneficent Church, she said the introduction of gospel music to the church. In her opinion, gospel music has made "the biggest difference" to the life of the church. A number of other respondents agreed. Henry, for example, called the changes in the music program "massive," from the perspective of internal administrative processes, internal church culture, and public program changes—which include not only worship but also new, popular music-education programs.

Nicole began her story with the networking she had been doing with the church's neighbor, Johnson and Wales University. One of the folks she met was the director of service learning at the university. This person also happened to be a member of a community gospel chorus called RPM (Reaching

People through Music) Voices of Rhode Island. RPM happened to have just lost its home at Brown University. They had been planning a Christmas concert and suddenly were in need of a venue. The director, Clarice LaVerne Thompson, called Nicole.

> It was very short notice. It was maybe less than a month away. We talked, and I said, "There are two kinds of ways you could use this building: one is you rent it, and one is you become a ministry partner." I made a calculation in my head like "Oooh, this sounds like not a rental but a possible partnership."

The ministry partnership model we have developed at Beneficent Church has been key to our successful and faithful redevelopment. It takes us beyond the attitude of "you can come if you want to." It is an active extension of our hospitality. It says to a particular group or organization, "We have things that we can learn and do together in ways that build up both of our communities." Our ministry partnerships are based on a shared sense of mission and sealed by a sacred covenant. (For Beneficent Church's covenant with RPM, see appendix D.)

Together Nicole and RPM's director agreed to begin building a ministry partnership. They started by defining both the resources and the needs that each group brought to the table:

> [RPM] didn't have any money. They were in the process of becoming their own 501(c)(3). So they said, "The most we could afford would be $75." I said, "The cost is really $350 to rent space, but would you be willing to trade use of the space for coming to sing at worship as our special musical guests?" They said yes they would, and we set the date for Martin Luther King Sunday. Now it is on our regular calendar.

Beneficent could offer RPM performance and rehearsal space, but the extension of welcome in the form of ministry partnership offered more than bare space. We were saying, "Make Beneficent your home." What RPM offered was the people and the know-how for building a successful, multicultural music program. For example, because of our partnership with RPM, Martin Luther King Sunday is one of our most well-attended worship services of the year. Today, almost all Beneficent Church intergenerational choir members also sing with RPM. Beneficent Church has also gained choir members, musicians, and church members through our partnership with RPM. Both organizations have grown.

The partnership with RPM began when through her networking Nicole was made aware of a community need—a not-for-profit community group needed space. Beneficent Church has rented space and continues to rent space to any number of community groups. This was different. Nicole sensed an opportunity to enter into a different kind of relationship—to offer a different kind of hospitality: one in which the other, the guest, the stranger, is invited not simply to share physical space but also to share a spiritual and emotional space that has the potential to transform relationships, shift perspectives, and prepare hearts for spiritual and congregational growth. The "ownership" of the ministry is held lightly. It is not Beneficent's ministry. It is not RPM's ministry. It is ours together. Our missions are not exactly the same, but they are close enough to both establish a real connection and preserve significant difference. The partnership itself is an example of the postmodern-plural approach of building identity through difference.

Beneficent offered RPM a home. RPM offered Beneficent an education in how to do multicultural ministry through music. Nicole described it as follows: "We had talked with our music director about doing gospel music or non-European music. She had tried herself to do these gospel Sundays, and it just really did not work out. It didn't feel very different. It was the same director trying to do gospel music, but it wasn't really gospel style." Then it just so happened that Beneficent's music director took maternity leave, and we invited Dr. Clarice, RPM's artistic director, to be Beneficent's guest director during that time. We framed it to the congregation that together we would be doing an experimental gospel workshop during worship for the next six weeks.

Nicole described our gospel workshop experiment:

> We did the traditional hymns, but it is different when you play it gospel style than when you play it European style. It's not like we said to Clarice, "Now Clarice, you play it gospel style." She just played it how she plays, and it made a big difference, and honestly the best choir participation we've ever had has been when Clarice comes, so I think that is the proof [that it was working].

The congregational learning that produced actual transformation was that gospel music is more than notes played or the rhythms performed. It is a comprehensive approach to worship, community, and expression that is defined by freedom. We learned by experiencing the *way* Dr. Clarice led the choir and the process by which the music was produced. The hospitality we extended, which went beyond "You're welcome if you come," opened a space for deconstruction in which we questioned our assumptions about "the way we do things here" and what is "good" music. Dr. Clarice is music director at another church in town, but the experiment at Beneficent went so well that we hired Dr. Clarice to be our gospel choir director, and once a month she leads Sunday morning gospel worship at Beneficent.

What we discovered was that a domination-defined version of the modern-patronage ministry model was operating in our music program. When Nicole and I began our ministry at Beneficent, the choir had four paid section leaders—who were not church members—in addition to our music director. The section leaders were, in Nicole's words, "dominating the choir." The typical makeup of the choir at that time was the four section leaders and two to three volunteer singers from the congregation. That meant the section leaders didn't have sections to lead. Instead, the volunteers "were almost accompanying the section leaders." All four section leaders were classically trained musicians who either worked professionally as teachers and performers or were in training to do so. They were very talented and sang wonderfully. Unfortunately, the dynamics of this situation sent the message to the congregation that unless they had a similar level of musicianship, their voices were not welcome. Nicole contrasted this approach to making music with Dr. Clarice's approach:

> The way Clarice directed there were no section leaders. Everybody was equal. Lots of people had solos—not just one person. She started working with different people—not the paid people—and it really signaled something different to the congregation. We had to overcome this idea that "Oh, I couldn't possibly sing in the choir, because I can't read music. I don't like that kind of [classical, European] music. That doesn't move me," or "I can't imagine myself doing that." The gospel music communicated to people in a different way, and people thought, "I could do that. I like that music."

I am not ready to attach particular power assumptions or patterns to particular music styles in any inherent way. It just so happened that at Beneficent Church the modern-patronage model, which tends to divide people in hierarchical ways, seemed to have attached itself to the traditional—that is, European, classical—music program at the church. The result was that untrained volunteers didn't feel like they could participate in the choir next to the trained voices of the paid section leaders. When I suggested that the section leaders take on a training and supporting role with the volunteers, they resisted. Because RPM approached music with a community model, their music carried the message of freedom and equality not only in the lyrics but also in the way they approached making the music. This multicultural approach was more in line with the emerging postmodern-plural approach to redevelopment at the church.

Beneficent's partnership with RPM has also affected the racial makeup of our intergenerational choir, which has, in turn, reflected an increasing diversity in our congregation. Before our partnership with RPM, we had only one person of color who was a regular member of the choir. Since working with Dr. Clarice, both the choir and our congregation are about 50 percent people of color. Dr. Clarice is African American. The powerful symbolism of a person of color leading worship cannot be underestimated. The significance of this shift was confirmed by the anxiety it initially generated in the congregation. In an interview study with more than 170 multiracial congregations in the United States, sociologist Gerardo Marti documents the significance of multiracial worship leadership in building multiracial congregations. He calls this practice "multiracial ritual inclusion." What he found is that, contrary to popular opinion, music style does not contribute to increasing racial diversity in congregations. Instead, he found that worship music can contribute to increasing racial diversity in two ways: when people of diverse races and ethnicities are given publicly visible music leadership roles in worship, and when music rehearsals give choir members and other musicians opportunities to build cross-racial friendships. [1]

We would not have had the same success transitioning to a multicultural gospel music style program had our current music director, Laura, not had the ability and willingness to build a collaborative partnership with Dr. Clarice and RPM. Nicole calls it Laura's "greatest gift." Laura is conservatory trained in the classical music tradition, but she willingly took on an immersion experience in the gospel workshop model, and RPM hired her to be their accompanist. Successful and faithful church redevelopment at Beneficent Church depended less on the technical skill of its current music director and more on her social skills and leadership abilities.

In our interview, Laura described what this evolution from traditional European American, Protestant, classical style to multicultural gospel style has been like: "It's been positive. There've been growing pains here and there, just because it's such a different [style]. I've felt challenged to expand in different directions that I hadn't done in previous jobs and situations." Before the redevelopment process began, Laura and the music program had been "left on [their] own to do the music [they] liked." She said, "It was very easy to stay there and just to do the music that we all had grown to love." By contrast, "The more diverse your program is, then you're looking in all these different places. I guess it gets more exciting, but there's just so much out there that you have to look. It's not like there's a clear path. We've had a lot of trial and error of certain things." In Laura's assessment, we can hear the theme of disorientation that Heifetz describes as characteristic of adaptive change and both the excitement and the challenge of uncharted territory that characterizes Friedman's spirit of adventure.

Laura described the music style prior to redevelopment as *contemporary choral*, which included gospel pieces, but the arrangements were "pretty involved." She reported that her experience with RPM and Dr. Clarice gave her a "different perspective [on] all the different varieties of spiritual arrangements and gospel arrangements." She learned that gospel music is not "one thing" and that much of what she was familiar with was "concertized" gospel music. The difference between concertized gospel music and the music the choir learned in partnership with RPM lay in "people's approach to it." What she had learned previously was an approach to gospel music that tried to fit it into an established European-classical choral ideal. By contrast, the approach of RPM emphasized freedom: "It's not requiring people to learn within the parameters of the standard choral literature. [Classical European style and gospel style are] both really exciting for singers, but there is such a huge difference. There's a lot to learn there."

What Laura discovered is that what she had thought was diversity in her music actually "fit very well into [her] comfort zone," so that the music was not having the same impact as what she was learning with RPM, which she experienced as more organic. In Laura's assessment, what made RPM multicultural was not so much the particular pieces, notes, instrumentation, and other technical aspects of the music, but rather that they were trying to give people an experience of both approaches. The question, then, does not become one of "either-or," but instead "where is the right place for this, and where is the right place for that?" The key, according to Laura, was that Dr. Clarice has this "other experience" that for Laura and the Beneficent music program "opened the door" to "learning a new approach."

"It's not an easy path to make it all cohesively work together," according to Laura. Nicole agreed that multicultural practice at Beneficent Church was still a bit like multiple personality disorder. Though the worship leaders might feel a lack of cohesion, others in the congregation experience the multicultural approach at Beneficent as "natural" and "authentic." In an interview, Martha, a relatively new church member, said,

> I think the thing that really is very energizing for me is how naturally multicultural Beneficent Church is. I think that it started out this way, or has a history of that certainly, but I think over the past couple of years that has intensified so that there really is a breadth of participation of many ages, many colors, many different social and economic groups, young, old. There's really a nice mix, and I think that's something that naturally is happening and it feels natural and that's very, very exciting for me.

When I asked Martha to describe what a Sunday morning was like for her, she mentioned "a lot of good energy." She observed people "enjoying themselves." They are not "constricted to pews." Instead, "there's just a lot of movement" and a "sense of excitement." "People are talking amongst themselves—the young and old and various different ethnic groups—without any seeming strain." People are "integrating," as seen by where they sit for worship. "There isn't a sense of anger or constraint. It feels very open."

The increasingly multicultural character of Beneficent Church was not a part of any master plan. The transformations in the music program happened in a haphazard, piecemeal way through natural connections and a genuine interest in the community. It was an instance of going into "the vineyard *today*" (Matt. 21:28, italics mine). In working with the music director and choir, my mission for them was simple—grow the choir and help create a warm and welcoming worship experience. "If you can do that with Bach and Brahms, go for it." It turns out that, in this context, because the modern-patronage ministry model was welded to classical European church music, Bach and Brahms were not effective either in growing the choir or in creating a warm and welcoming worship environment. It took *other* non-European musical styles and traditions to do that.

Though the transition from a classical worship experience to a multicultural one has been largely successful, it was by no means a smooth and painless process. Two interview respondents shared the pain they themselves experienced and that the congregation felt when three of the four section leaders were let go. One mentioned the tears she shed. In her opinion, transforming the choir could have been done more "gently." Henry admitted that the process was a mess and that, looking back, the church's lay leaders could have done more to prepare the staff for the changes that redevelopment would bring. Though the congregation had approved a budget that eliminated two section leaders, Phoebe experienced the change process in the music program as "one way." She would have liked more opportunities for congregational input. I experienced mixed messages from the congregation about what their visions for the music program were, which made it difficult to know how I should lead the staff through this process. All this is simply to say that extending welcome can be messy and difficult. Even successful and faithful redevelopment involves, unfortunately, missteps, confusion, and (at times) pain.

WHO OR WHAT IS (THE) OTHER?

In a *New York Times* obituary for Jacques Derrida, theologian Mark C. Taylor argues that deconstruction is widely misunderstood as a process of dismantling or taking things apart. Correcting that view, he writes, "The guiding insight of deconstruction is that every structure—be it literary, psychological, social, economic, political, or religious—that organizes our experience is constituted and maintained through acts of exclusion. In the process of creating something, something else inevitably gets left out."[2] The other is simply that "something else"—the remainder that remains and disturbs the repose of the self-identical same.

In constructing his discourse on the other, Derrida built on and borrowed from the thought of philosopher Emmanuel Levinas. Levinas and Derrida agreed that the remainder—the leftover—is the mark of the other—that is, the mark of difference. Simultaneously exterior to organizing structure and erupting from within, the other cannot be completely assimilated, understood, or controlled. It is to be respected. It's the outside within. It's that within that is always beyond. To describe this paradoxical operation of the other, Derrida coined the tautology *Tout autre est tout autre*: "The (every) other is the (wholly) other."[3] They disagreed as to whether God was wholly other in a way that could be distinguished from the otherness of humans: Levinas wanted to preserve that distinction; Derrida wanted to leave it open for questioning.[4] Jesus certainly creates some space for questioning the distinction of divine and human otherness when he says, "Just as you did it to one of the least of these who are members of my family, you did it to me" (Matt. 25:40). Along those same lines, the epistle to the Hebrews states, "Do not neglect to show hospitality to strangers, for by doing that some have entertained angels without knowing it" (13:2). According to Derrida, Levinas, and the Bible, the other confronts us with a moral imperative.

Derrida understands the work of deconstruction as a vocation—a response to a call that comes from the other. In the words of philosopher John D. Caputo, "Everything turns on the turn toward the other." This response—our response-ability—takes the form of hospitality. For this reason, Caputo can write, "Deconstruction *is* hospitality."[5] Deconstruction creates space at the table for the other, the one marked by difference (whether racial, ethnic, economic, or otherwise), and deconstruction maintains that space, allowing that difference to disrupt "the way we do things here."

This space is an awkward and difficult place to live as a community—a place of unease. It means that mastery and control, qualities highly valued in our North American cultural context, will be by design decentered and called into question. Successful and faithful leaders operating out of this ministry model will find it necessary to develop strategies for practicing nonanxious presence while leading at the edge of their competence. "Speaking the truth in love," confession, forgiveness, reconciliation, and perseverance are all necessary spiritual disciplines. Ministry with and on the porous margin where diverse others interact requires above all a congregation bathed in grace—a living, breathing community that regularly gathers and disperses, a congregation that maintains open space where individuals, with their idiosyncratic perspectives, shape identity and practice and in turn are spiritually informed by the histories, traditions, missions, visions, and values of the congregation.

Postmodern thinkers have noticed how modern organizing structures in the West often produce hierarchically constructed binaries. These binaries in themselves are not necessarily bad. They just represent how thinking works. Knowledge works such that we identify something by constructing its other. We know about man by constructing woman. I know about me by constructing you. We know about church redevelopment by constructing a discourse of congregational decline. Injustice happens when we confuse these constructed binaries with reality. We then attempt to reify, institutionalize, and build a foundation for certainty upon this knowledge. Postmodern thinkers have shown how these binaries—which include, for example, man or woman, black or white, up or down, rich or poor, and so forth—create totalizing systems, sometimes called "dominologies," that erase differences.[6] These systems erase differences in two ways: first, by marginalizing and potentially annihilating the excluded other (for example, male-dominated institutions silencing or disenfranchising women), or, second, by appropriating the other as a deficient or an idealized expression of the same (women are an "irrational" version of man or man's "better half"). Postmodern thought tries to open up either-or logic in order to imagine and construct new ways of writing, thinking, relating in the world, and, in the case of Beneficent, becoming a congregation. Let's look at an admittedly brief example of how Derrida's discourse of the other connects to theology.

The connection between deconstruction, exclusion, and the other—the stranger at the gate—resonates with liberation theology. Liberation theology was born in twentieth-century Latin America "when faith confronted the injustice done to the poor."[7] Liberation theology claims God's preferential option for the poor and calls on Christians to work on behalf of justice for oppressed and marginalized peoples. Some are cautious about connecting liberation theology and deconstruction, because liberation theology claims that the goal of history (teleology) is justice, while deconstruction wants to step outside of origins and ends entirely.[8] Liberation theologian Enrique Dussel, however, draws on Levinas's notion of the other in his *Philosophy of Liberation*, which calls for justice on behalf of the marginalized other.[9] All this is to say that the redevelopment model developing at Beneficent Church connects justice to an impossible hospitality that welcomes the wholly other in all his or her difference—that is, the church gives itself over to the influence of the others, puts itself in the others' power—while simultaneously maintaining its identity and difference. This means that leadership is continually called into question and has to answer for itself. It is a place of unease that gracefully engages spiritual, social, and emotional dis-ease in order to bring healing.[10] This is hospitality as more than just "You're welcome if you come," as Lydia put it. It genuinely recognizes and respects difference and allows difference to disrupt and destabilize community boundaries to keep them open and porous yet recognizable.

IMPOSSIBLE HOSPITALITY

In the paragraph above I used the word *community* as a synonym for congregation. In chapter 1, I described Becker's Community Model congregation and suggested that the dynamics of Beneficent Church reflect that model to a significant degree. It is common for churches to describe themselves as faith communities. My point is that we like to think of our congregations as a special kind of community. With that word *community* comes a vision for everyone being together, sharing good feelings, being like-minded and peaceful, perhaps holding hands and singing "Kum Ba Yah." In Derrida's words, we humans have an "irrepressible desire" for community because of this need to be connected on some deep emotional and spiritual level.[11] Unfortunately, this Kum Ba Yah community has been a rare experience in my years of pastoral ministry. Why is that?

Our friend Derrida might shed a little light on this conundrum of community. He was actually quite uncomfortable with the whole idea of community. The reason is that community has connotations of "fusion" and a homogenizing kind of "identification."[12] Derrida's worries about community resonate with Friedman's observations on fusion, emotional coersion, and cloning in anxious congregations. The danger is that our desire for connection, for comfort, for like-mindedness, for an absence of tension, for a Kum Ba Yah community, might become so insistent that it will not tolerate difference— that it will welcome others only when they become just like us, in which case, they cease to be others in Derrida's sense of the word. When this happens we really aren't welcoming anyone. We're simply consuming, assimilating, and potentially obliterating them.

Instead of *community*, Derrida prefers the word *hospitality*. Referring to an unpublished lecture given by Derrida at Johns Hopkins University in March 1996, Caputo interprets Derrida's understanding of hospitality. This understanding comes from a deconstructive etymological reading of the word *hospitality*. This etymology notices that the word "carries its opposite within itself." Hospitality derives from the combination of two Latin words. The first is "*hospes*, which is formed from *hostis*, which originally meant 'stranger' and came to take on the meaning of the enemy or 'hostile.'"[13] The second is *pets*, which has the cognates *potis*, *potes*, and *potentia*, with the meaning "to have power." Caputo brings out the hostility in hospitality by coining a new term: "hostil/pitality."

The tricky thing about this interpretation of hospitality is that it points in two opposite directions at the same time. It points to *both* the host standing at the door *and* the stranger at the gate, from which emerges the fraught relationship that appears in this encounter. This is precisely what Derrida wants to surface—the inherent paradox and self-limiting nature of words we too often take for granted. When we put *hospitality* under the electron microscope, what we discover is that *hospes* refers to the host and *pets* to the power of the host to remain master of her domain. As we say, "My house, my rules." I would not be providing hospitality if I invited you over to *someone else's* house. Hospitality refers to the power of the host to maintain her integrity and her identity in the face of the stranger who demands welcome.

At the same time, *hospes* refers to the stranger or enemy (hostis/hostility) and *pets* to the moral power of the other to demand accommodation. In Derrida's understanding, true hospitality demands a temporary suspension of the rules of the house, a hospitality beyond hospitality; as the saying goes, "*Mi casa es su casa.*" But if I give my house over to the stranger, it's no longer my house, and I've lost my power to host. Derridean hospitality turns on this logical paradox. For this reason, it could be called an impossible hospitality. It is welcome extended past the breaking point. It can't be logically explained; it can only be enacted. It can't be preprogrammed. I can't give you a recipe to follow. It can only be practiced. The result of the practice of impossible hospitality is a "community without community"—a community whose borders are porous, a community that is always to a certain extent under construction, a community that is continually called into question by the call of the other.[14]

Deconstruction is hospitality. Derrida writes:

> Far from being a methodical technique, a possible or necessary procedure, unrolling the law of a program and applying the rules, that is, unfolding possibilities, deconstruction has often been defined as the very experience of the (impossible) possibility of the impossible, of the most impossible, a condition that deconstruction shares with the gift, the "yes," the "come," decision, testimony, the secret, etc. And perhaps death.[15]

For Derrida, deconstruction is an unspeakable transforming or transformative experience that puts one in a new relationship with the other. This experience tends toward a justice that cannot be reduced to a system of laws—what Derrida refers to as "co-responsibility," a covenant of unconditional availability to the other that defines hospitality.[16] The condition of deconstruction—the paradoxical possibility of the impossible (a condition that deconstruction might even share with death)—begins to sound a little like the way of the cross that Jesus describes to his disciples in Mark 8.[17] Surprisingly, perhaps even heretically for some, deconstruction begins to open a space for a postmodern reimagining of justice and discipleship.

Derrida makes it clear that the paradox of hospitality cannot be reduced to a philosophical formula. Hospitality can only be enacted. It cannot be explained. Its practical result at Beneficent Church is a back-and-forth motion, what theologian Catherine Keller calls "oscillation," which she associates with the Spirit of God "vibrating" over the waters of creation in Genesis 1:2.[18] In our interview, Tim put it this way: "I think the back and forth between clinging onto what we like, what we're comfortable with, and trying things that appeal to a group of people who we really don't know or understand keeps you on the track." It means allowing space for the expression of difference—sometimes even in small ways. For example, one respondent confided that even though Beneficent Church uses the language "forgive us our trespasses as we forgive those who trespass against us" in reciting the Lord's Prayer, he honors his different heritage by saying to himself "forgive us our debts as we forgive our debtors."

A more striking example of impossible hospitality was our "Native American Cultures and Christian Worship" workshop and worship service, which we organized and hosted as a part of our 2012–2013 worship renewal grant program, funded by the Calvin Institute for Christian Worship. Nicole, who served as grant administrator, gathered a team of local and national Native American leaders to work with Beneficent Church's grant implementation team to plan and present a day-long workshop on Native American culture and worship to which we invited congregations from all over New England. Our guest leaders included Navajo Christian leader Mark Charles, the Eastern Medicine Singers, Wampanoag leader Anawan Weeden, and Beneficent members Valerie Tutson (an internationally known storyteller) and Northern Narragansett elder Lydia (whose family hosted the feast following Sunday worship). We did our best to give each guest the space to bring his or her unique cultural gifts to the conversation.

Despite the massive amount of planning and preparation, the Spirit moved, creating spontaneous moments of connection and new learning. And it was not without a big bang. Though we did our best to keep the space open for impossible hospitality, we discovered during worship that the Spirit had been working in surprising ways to open a new space. Anawan was responsible for leading the "Litany of the Four Directions," with which we opened the service. We found out afterward that he had experienced a lot of anxiety about participating in our worship service because he did not consider himself a Christian and did not see the connections between his Wampanoag way of believing and being and what he imagined Christianity at Beneficent Church to be. Anawan needed to ensure that the history of Christendom's assimilation and annihilation of Native Americans would not be reenacted. Respecting difference was a matter of vital importance.

He responded to this tension by leading the congregation out of the meetinghouse and into the small park next to the church, where he had us form a circle. He shared from his heart what it has been like for him and the Wampanoag people to be hosts to American guests on their land for the past four hundred years. While issuing a strong call for respect of difference not only between Wampanoag and nonnative Americans but also between Wampanoag and our Navajo guest, he initiated an exchange of gifts among leaders of all the communities represented that morning in a powerful gesture of reconciliation. I understand this as an instance of *hostil/pitality* in which roles of host and guest were for a moment reversed and blurred so that reconciliation and peacemaking could take place.

EDUCATION AND POWER

Successful and faithful church redevelopment as it relates to hospitality begins with education. Education helps the congregation learn "what's going on outside," as Tim says. When I asked Tim to name the most exciting thing about redevelopment at Beneficent, he said, "The evolution of the music." He first mentioned the symbolic, spiritual, cultural, and emotional significance of music in church life. He spoke of a congregational canon of familiar hymns and songs that evoke memories and emotional responses from congregation members. He was speaking from the perspective of a longtimer for whom the canon of mostly European American hymns of the classical Protestant Christendom tradition have a particularly deep resonance. "When you start talking about tinkering with the canon, you hit a lot of nerves" throughout the congregational culture, including the people in the pews and the music staff, who were hired, in this case, to maintain the musical canon.

To begin to make space for *other* musical cultures, the congregation first needed to be educated that other legitimate options were out there. Tim notes that Beneficent is

> fairly insular in that the members of the church just come to that church. They don't go to other churches on a consistent basis to find out what other people do. So, you're sort of set, and that's good, and that's what you expect, but then you don't know what's going on outside. It seems to me that a first part of the redevelopment process is educating people as to what the rest of the world is like.

We engaged this educational process in a number of ways, including working with the music director and choir on building a vision for redevelopment in the music program and making field trips to other churches with leadership teams. But the biggest shift happened through our ministry partnership with RPM Voices of Rhode Island.

Education for impossible hospitality began with the awareness that other legitimate and credible options were out there. It continued with an imaginative exercise in seeing the congregation as an *other* would see it—seeing it *otherwise*. This move is analogous to what Derrida understands as the task of deconstruction. For Derrida, the *task* of deconstruction is discovering the "nonsite" from which "philosophy as such [can] appear to itself as other than itself, so that it can interrogate and reflect upon itself in an original manner."[19] In educating for impossible hospitality, we are looking for an oscillating nonsite—the back-and-forth shifting of perspective—that allows the congregation to see itself as others see it so that through original reflection and interrogation a space might open up to welcome the other. Tim said, "There are people who I don't know. So, how do they view things? If they come in the door, what are they going to see, and is what they're going to see inviting? Is it energizing or not?" Because Beneficent had a significant level of cultural diversity when we arrived, we did not need to go too far to get an *other* perspective.

During our Meet the Ministers meetings, a number of people—particularly people of color—said that the worship music at Beneficent did not speak to their culture in a meaningful way. In Beneficent's redevelopment, it was enough simply to create a safe space where the diversity already present in the congregation could speak the truths of their cultures to begin the conversation of what it would really look and feel like to make people of non–European American cultures feel at home in worship. A leadership that *extended* itself to the other, that had taken the time to build genuine relationships of trust with *others* and then intentionally invited their perspectives, was an important part of this process and a key insight for redevelopment in this multicultural setting.

Another key piece was a commitment to justice that takes the form of an *equitably shared* sacrifice that impossible hospitality invites us to practice. In her 2008 study of an interracial church near Columbus, Ohio, sociologist Korie Edwards discovered that unjust racial dynamics persisted despite the church's transition from majority European American to majority African American membership. Though the church had hired an African American senior minister, it continued to expect that African Americans would express their cultural preferences only to the extent that the white members were comfortable with them. In other words, the sacrifices involved in worshiping, working, and caring for people of *other* cultures were disproportionately put on African American members. Successful and faithful church redevelopment in a postmodern context takes an equitable sharing of the discomfort and sacrifice to which impossible hospitality invites us. For example, several respondents for this interview study expressed how difficult the introduction of gospel music and the transition to multicultural worship was for them. Gene said, "I've lost some of the things that I had appreciated in this church in order to see other things that the church desperately needs." But what Gene and other longtime Beneficent leaders didn't realize was that African American, Latino, Chinese American, and Native American members had been sacrificing their cultural preferences to the dominant white culture for generations.

A key to education for impossible hospitality in a multicultural context is raising an awareness of our own internal cultural assumptions—particularly our assumptions related to power. Theologian and educator Eric H. F. Law helped Beneficent Church move forward at this point in our conversation. In his book *The Wolf Shall Dwell with the Lamb: A Spirituality for Leadership in a Multicultural Community*, Law paints a vision for churches as "peaceable realms" spoken of by the prophet Isaiah (11:6–9) in which "the wolf shall live with the lamb." Multicultural communities have some of the dynamics of a wolf-and-lamb relationship in which there are critical power differences, differences in perception of power, tendencies to attack or flee (or both), a need for safety, feelings of fear, and a need for people to act against their own cultural instincts. The wolf and the lamb can begin to dwell more peaceably with each other when they can begin to identify their own internal cultural differences. These *internal* cultural differences are largely unconscious and have to do with assumptions about power and how people should relate to each other. These are distinct from *external* cultural differences like music, food, dress, holidays, art, and the like.

Over the years Beneficent Church had done quite a bit to welcome cultural differences on an external level—celebrating the Chinese New Year, performing choral arrangements of gospel music, hosting concerts, celebrating World Communion Sunday, and so on. What was needed was the much more difficult work of making conscious, and then critically examining, internal cultural differences—particularly as they relate to power. Law compares internal culture to the water that a fish swims in. When a person steps out of that internal culture, he can feel like a fish out of water—a frightening and threatening situation indeed. Law calls Christians to do this work based on Jesus's courageous and self-sacrificial example and vision of a peaceable realm.

Philosopher Hans-Georg Gadamer argues that all knowledge takes the form of conversation. For Gadamer, conversation means a specific type of process. It "means to be beyond oneself, to think with the other and to come back to oneself as if to another."[20] To be "beyond oneself" means to find oneself outside the bounds of mastery, control, and self-same identity. By *self-same identity*, I mean this Kum Ba Yah community that assumes we're all the same when in actuality we're not. Beyond that, self-same identity instinctively moves to erase differences when they express themselves. Remember, difference is the mark of the other and therefore an invitation to impossible hospitality—that uncomfortable, deconstructive, and potentially transformative space where established power relationships are called into question. Gadamer calls us to "think with the other." How that is possible when we don't know the other, as interview respondent Tim observed—when we can't *know* the other without appropriating or idealizing her, making her *like* (meaning, the same as) us—is a mystery and a gift. It is also the practice of testimony.

According to Derrida, "Deconstruction has often been defined as the very experience of the (impossible) possibility of the impossible," a condition it perhaps shares with testimony.[21] The turn toward the other, the turn that unblocks the flow of ongoing creativity at Beneficent Church, is a turn toward what theologian Rebecca Chopp calls a "poetics of testimony." Chopp understands testimony as an invention of contemporary writers expressing their experience of marginalization from a site "outside the representation of modern, rational discourse." Testimony is a narrative that emerges from the experience of a "group of people." It is a discursive practice that seeks to tell the truth from the perspective of marginalized people as they see and experience it. These witnesses also seek to articulate what this truth "means to their communities." The testimony is a discourse of "survival for hope and hope for survival."[22]

At Beneficent Church, the practice of testimony was key to successful and faithful church redevelopment. It took a number of forms, including the Walking in the Way process, which we will return to below. Gospel music, as we learned to practice and understand it through our partnership with RPM, is a form of testimony as Chopp defines it. Other examples include a worship practice we developed called "What the Lord Has Done in Me," which features congregation members speaking for two to three minutes about how God had a made a difference in their lives. We also developed a "sacred conversations" sermon series, which is described in chapter 6. It included a formerly homeless church member, Jane, whom the congregation had helped transition into housing and employment, and who throughout her ordeal had continued to tithe to the church. When it came time for our annual Season of Stewardship, we invited Jane to speak. With tears in her eyes, she testified, "I give because I believe that God will take care of me. And he has." In a congregation with some relatively wealthy longtime members who gave relatively little financially and yet expected to call the shots, this was testimony as speaking truth to power outside the bounds of rational discourse. The result of thinking with the other through the practice of testimony, however, is "to come back to oneself as if to another"—that is, to be changed, to recognize oneself as unrecognizable. [23] Maybe Law's "fish out of water" grows lungs! At Beneficent Church, there have been some members who, because we have attempted to think with the other, have left the church, complaining that it is no longer "their" church. It became *other* to them.

Law argues that the peaceable realm cannot be separated from justice, which he defines as an equal distribution of and access to power and privilege—power being defined as a person's ability to change his or her environment. [24] Internal culture connects with doing justice where there are internal cultural assumptions about power, about people's ability to change their environment and how they should relate to authority.

Law makes a basic distinction is between "high power distance" cultures and "low power distance" cultures. Low power distance cultures perceive a "low power distance" between leaders and followers. Followers feel like they have an ability to effect change in their environment and tend to speak out directly when they feel an injustice has been done to them. White middle-class American cultures tend to be low power distance cultures. When they do not like something at church or elsewhere, they complain, speak up at congregational meetings, get themselves on committees, and work to change the situation. They feel they have the right and ability to do so. High power distance cultures perceive a "high power distance" between leaders and followers. Leaders tend to be held in high regard and have the responsibility for ensuring that justice is done and voices are heard. People of color and poor people tend to operate with an internal culture of high power distance. [25]

For this reason, Beneficent Church's leadership—particularly pastoral leadership—extending themselves, creating safe space in which all voices could be heard and respected, was important *culturally*. Just saying "Well, you can come to a meeting," in Tim's words, or "You're welcome if you come," in Lydia's words, was not enough. The church needed to practice a genuine and impossible hospitality coupled with an awareness of internal cultural assumptions that would invite people operating out of high power distance assumptions to speak from their perspectives without fear that they would be disregarded. As I noted in chapter 2, just because no one is expressing dissent doesn't mean that there is no disagreement. It could mean that leaders—wittingly or unwittingly—are creating a process that precludes or discourages dissent by doing all the talking in meetings, dominating conversations, and using subtle cues to communicate that differing perspectives are unwelcome. Those operating out of low power distance assumptions need to be quiet and listen in the knowledge that together we are trying to build a multicultural community that more closely resembles our value of diversity and the biblical vision of a peaceable realm.

The apostle Paul writes to the Romans, "Do not be conformed to this world, but be transformed by the renewing of your minds, so that you may discern what is the will of God—what is good and acceptable and perfect" (Rom. 12:2). There are times when each of us needs to speak his or her mind, and times when each of us needs to change his or her mind. Unfortunately, in dying churches those who need to change their minds end up doing all the talking, and those who need to speak their minds end up doing all the changing. Nothing will change until those who are used to speaking listen up, and those who are used to listening speak up. A key to successful and faithful redevelopment is the spiritual transformation that happens when the "right" people are speaking up and the "right" people are listening up.

The Walking in the Way process gave the congregation a number of tools so that we could begin practicing Law's peaceable realm. The first was the practice of deep listening. Several respondents mentioned how learning to listen was important to the process of redevelopment. Grace related deep listening to creating "systems in which the church can run in a more equitable way." For her, deep or "open" listening is "not just hearing and waiting to jump in and say what you have to say," but also taking the time to truly understand another's perspective. This kind of listening and understanding is closely related to Derrida's impossible hospitality and Gadamer's conversation. One respondent connected listening directly to her spiritual growth: "I've prayed a lot this year and probably more than I have previous years. I think it's because I'm looking. I'm seeking God's way and trying to put myself and my own biases and my own preferences aside and *listen*." The group practice we developed to facilitate listening was the talking circle, which empowers an individual to speak when he or she is holding a talking piece; the rest of the group practices deep listening. We mostly used this practice at the beginning and ending of meetings to make sure everyone had a chance to speak. We also used it in discussions that were sensitive and carried potential for conflict.

A second Walking in the Way tool was the relational covenant, developed through a group process and adopted by the congregation, which expressed how the congregation would live out its value of "speaking the truth in love." The document itself was lengthy and detailed, but the primary and most transforming provision was the first: "We will speak directly to each other using the first person and 'I' statements." Nicole and I then connected this provision to an early Christian conflict resolution process found in Matthew 18. I had learned of this process a number of years ago in training at the Lombard Mennonite Peace Center. As I noted in chapter 1, it was also the process at the heart of the conflict that gave birth to Beneficent Church. In a sense, the whole reason for Beneficent's being was an argument for this process. That gave it particular power in this context. We combined this principle of direct communication with some teaching with the leadership about Friedman's concept of triangling. To make things crystal clear, we wrote a script for how the leadership could deal with complaints in a healthy way. You can find the relational covenant, with the script for direct communication, in appendix C.

All this leads to a point at which deconstruction-hospitality as it is unfolding at Beneficent Church perhaps adds a dimension to Derrida's notion of receiving the other. At Beneficent Church, the impossible possibility of maintaining a domicile without dominating the stranger has happened not simply by passively receiving the "stranger at the gate." At Beneficent Church we have actively sought to extend ourselves toward the other in a humble, openhanded gesture. Hospitality at Beneficent is both an invitation to *come in* and an invitation that is *sent out*, a gently transgressive missionary hospitality. By *transgressive*, I mean respectfully crossing that cultural border into the territory of the other. Caputo calls Derrida an "apostle of the impossible." This apostleship aspect of deconstruction seems to be at play in the hospitality model under construction at Beneficent Church.

In our interview, Gene identified people—especially new people—as key to successful and faithful church redevelopment. New people, with their "fresh eyes," "other" cultures, and "different" perspectives, were, according to Gene, "something the church desperately needs," not only for institutional maintenance but also for spiritual growth. In the postmodern-plural redevelopment model under construction at Beneficent, spiritual and numerical growth cannot be separated, because it is precisely in the impossible gift of apostolic hospitality that our blindness to our cultural force fields is healed. We are saved from the "sin" of "gospel reductionism." We learn to listen with respect and to speak the truth in love. In my work with dying churches, I frequently encounter leaders who want to separate growth in church membership from spiritual growth. Not surprising, they always elevate spiritual growth and denigrate numerical growth. This study calls that attitude into question. Spiritual growth without numerical growth is not redevelopment; it is hospice, which is its own legitimate but separate form of ministry. At Beneficent Church, spiritual growth is not an academic exercise. Spiritual growth happens only when theology is put into action as impossible, apostolic hospitality.

KEYS FOR REDEVELOPMENT

Moving beyond simple tolerance of *other* people and their *other* cultures and actively extending a hand to people of diverse cultures within the congregation and in neighboring communities.

Developing ministry partnerships.

Being prepared for missteps, confusion, and sometimes pain.

Educating the congregation about what the rest of the world is like.

Working to ensure an equitable sharing of discomfort and sacrifice.

Raising awareness of internal cultural assumptions related to power.

Learning and engaging the practice of testimony.

Creating a safe space where the "right" people can speak up and the "right" people can listen up.

Chapter Six

Becoming Church

You could feel a change in atmosphere.

—Steve, Beneficent Church member

The story of the Sacred Conversations series begins in spring 2010 with informal conversations among Nicole, Grace, and me about developing a program for Beneficent Church based on our denomination's program "Sacred Conversations on Race." We talked about the diversities at Beneficent, the need for developing language and practices to communicate in and through our differences, and the best ways to begin this conversation, which we agreed was vital to successful and faithful redevelopment at Beneficent Church. We decided to begin by introducing the concept of sacred conversation to the congregation. We did this by featuring a sacred conversation in each of our worship services for the season of Lent. The sacred conversations took a variety of forms, but each conversation took place during the sermon portion of worship and featured at least two voices speaking from their experience about an issue vital to their faith and vital to our community.

At the same time that Nicole and I were developing a vision for sacred conversations, we were also developing a vision for a creative arts team (CATS), whose purpose, as expressed in its 2010 mission statement, was "creating a warm, welcoming worship experience through the arts and creating invitational arts-related events for the purpose of praising God and growing the church." CATS brought together members of Beneficent who were musicians, visual artists, and performing artists. Its first project was building a partnership with Elemental Theater—a local theater group—to offer arts programming at Beneficent Church. In exchange for helping us get CATS off the ground, we made our fellowship hall available as rehearsal space for an upcoming Elemental Theater production. For their first program, CATS and Elemental Theater decided to introduce the Sacred Conversations series.

Our first sacred conversation emerged from several planning sessions among CATS and Elemental Theater members, which itself was understood to be a sacred conversation. It was carefully designed to be a safe space in which differences were respected and hospitality practiced. We would not have even had the opportunity to engage in this conversation with Elemental Theater had Nicole and I not spent a couple of years building relationships with its leaders, including hosting one of their productions in our church and providing rehearsal space for another of their productions. Out of these planning sessions, CATS and Elemental Theater developed a process for designing the first Lenten worship service of the Sacred Conversations series. The vision for this first worship service was to invite the congregation into an experience of talking with God. This invitation began with a simple questionnaire that worship attenders were invited to fill out several weeks before the service was to take place. It asked people to respond anonymously to one of three questions:

What would you whisper in God's ear?
What brought you here?
When have you felt God's presence?

The responses were collected and formed the basis for a reader's theater piece that CATS/Elemental Theater wrote, staged, and performed for the sermon element of our first worship service in Lent. This piece wove together direct quotations from Beneficent folks' responses to the questionnaire to create a chorus collage of diverse voices, their authentic experiences of God's presence and God's absence, their longings for God, their connections and failures to connect. From this introduction, the series continued for the next five weeks and featured sacred conversations on race, mental illness, poverty, sexuality, and youth. Several months later, in the summer of 2011, eleven out of the thirteen interview study respondents mentioned the Sacred Conversations series during Lent as a turning point in the redevelopment process.

Though we weren't fully aware of it at the time, upon reflection it seems that the Sacred Conversations series took the work we as a congregation had been doing behind the scenes in creating safe space for marginalized voices to speak the truth in love and made it public in worship. In fact, the process took years. It began with our Meet the Ministers meetings and our initial efforts as pastors to listen to marginalized voices like Lydia's and Grace's one on one—to hear their stories and learn from them. It continued in our Walking in the Way process, which included congregational forums during which we learned skills like deep listening, circle process, direct communication, and "speaking the truth in love." Worship was the biggest and most public space in which we would attempt as a community to speak and listen with care and respect to congregation members who courageously spoke out of their own experience of the broken places in their lives. Together we walked in places potentially shaming and shameful for both the individuals and the congregation, and we were able to hold that sacred space in such a way that healing could take place. [1]

The experience was empowering because neither Nicole nor I spoke *for* anyone. This disrupted a modern-patronage model as it had been manifested at Beneficent Church, in which the pulpit was reserved for the pastor, whose role was to be the "great orator." In the sacred conversations, Nicole and I deployed our training and expertise differently. Instead of reserving our knowledge of crafting sermons, we used it to coach, apprentice, and support gifted and called lay leaders to participate directly in the sermon-creating and delivering process. It was an instance of sharing leadership in the most highly charged and public aspect of the church's life.

What was that experience like for people in the congregation? Tim was particularly moved by the sacred conversations. When I asked him to give an example of a time when he felt like the congregation was really allowed to speak, he said, "The first creative arts team service," which featured the theater piece described above. With tears in his eyes and emotion in his voice, he said, "You hear these echoes [and] you knew it was coming from the congregation. . . . It was like you were hearing the congregation vibrating. . . . It was drilling down, at least one or two layers below the layer that we normally work on."

> It was an intentional process designed to let the congregation speak in really authentic and deep-rooted ways. From the service, it sounded to me like people heard that and felt, "Oh, good, I've been wanting to say this," or "This is a way that I can speak with a little protection. It's a way I can speak, and I appreciate that people feel that it's important that I have an opportunity to do that." [This] speaks to the culture and, basically, I would say also speaks authentically to our tradition as a Congregational church.

For Tim, what gave the sacred conversations power was that the *other* voices, which disrupted established dominologies and called the congregation into unfamiliar spiritual territories, erupted from within the congregation itself. In fact, in a wonderfully paradoxical way, this journey into the unknown, this moving off the map, this adventure "beyond the wilderness" (Exod. 3:1), was also a return, a speaking "authentically to our tradition as a Congregational church." Our hospitality toward strangers—in this case, Elemental Theater—inviting them to help us rearrange what we hold most sacred—our worship—catalyzed a vibration, a genesis moment that tapped into the "different sentiment" of the Great Awakening, which was the sentiment that produced the big bang out of which Beneficent Church evolved way back in 1743.

Though Tim had been a member of the church for many years, he had never had the opportunity to connect with his fellow church members in a deep and genuine way. Their newfound intimacy was close but not fused. Appropriate boundaries were maintained. It was a controlled explosion. As one respondent put it, the key was that no one had to say anything they did not want to say. People were able to speak out of their brokenness, their need, and their desire without being shamed. It's also interesting to note that the one key worship moment mentioned in the interview study did not include a pastor preaching some inspired word that suddenly made everyone "get it." The pastors' role was receiving and communicating the vision of a worship experience in which the congregation experienced God speaking through *them*. The phrase Nicole and I use to describe this work is "holding the space." Much of the leadership work in this postmodern-plural model is holding the space.

In our interview, Phoebe, who coordinated CATS and was a part of the team that designed the service, described the process and what made it safe. For Phoebe, safety meant the permission to claim her identity as "a seeker who spiritually still feels like [she's] in a lifeboat." She described her relationship with God as "up and down." In Phoebe's experience, God is "there sometimes" and sometimes "isn't there": "A safe place would be a place that would say, 'That's okay'; that would acknowledge frailties but say, 'That's okay'; would acknowledge pain but say, 'That's okay.'" The sacred conversations were "so important" for Phoebe because "that was a time where people could be very vulnerable, and it was safe to do that. For me, a church—particularly a worship service—should be a time when you can bring all those vulnerable, half-formed, broken pieces of yourself, and it's okay, and there's acknowledgment of that." In other words, no fixing—just witnessing. Safety came not only from the permission to be open and vulnerable without shame but also because "we kind of knew what was going to happen and yet there was still open space." Out of a vision for a full meeting-house carefully developed with many hands contributing their unique gifts to preparation and planning, the Spirit swept over, expanded, and broke through our small, bounded space in a play of ritual and spontaneity.

A safe space in this context was a bounded space that was predictable enough ("We kind of knew what was going to happen"), yet still open enough to acknowledge and respect difference, doubts, and weakness: a creative edge between what is too chaotic and what is too limiting. The safe space created in the pastor-congregation relationship, in the Walking in the Way process, in clarifying decision-making processes, and in worship served to create a holding environment in which people could begin to make the connections among their own personal healing, spiritual growth, and the adaptive challenges of redevelopment. These adaptive challenges included church programs, policies, and structures, as well as the *atmosphere* as it manifested in public worship and church meetings.

In postmodern cultures characterized by consumerism and choice, how the church makes people feel (is it a *positive* experience?) is key to successful and faithful redevelopment. The holding environment of the safe space allows leaders to make the critical adaptive move of "giving the work back to the people"[2]—in this case, to critically assess how their attitudes and choices contributed to a church culture that was "harsh, self-absorbed, self-obsessed" and to envision a church culture "that is relaxed and happy."[3] The holding environment of worship is an exceptional opportunity to do this heart work, the essential work of leadership—work that is key to successful and faithful church redevelopment. That holding environment begins in the hearts of leaders who have a heart for their communities.[4]

THEOLOGY OF BECOMING

Tim said of the Sacred Conversations series, "You were hearing the congregation vibrating." Was this an incarnation of Genesis 1:2, where we read that the *ruach elohim*—the spirit or wind or breath of God—hovered, swept, brooded over, or vibrated upon the face of the waters? Was this a small Pentecost in the form of a new genesis for Beneficent Church? In her book *Face of the Deep: A Theology of Becoming*, constructive theologian Catherine Keller uses the framework of process thought—a theology developed in conversation with the work of philosopher Alfred North Whitehead—to re-read Genesis 1:1–2. In addition, Keller draws in postmodern themes of deconstruction and difference and weaves them together with feminist and liberation theologies. In her book Keller argues for a theology of creation *ex profundis*—that is, out of *tehom*, or "the Deep," which she defines as "primal chaos" out of which God created and is creating the universe. Before she constructs a theology of the Deep, however, she deconstructs what for centuries has been the dominant and dominating "orthodox" doctrine of God's creating *ex nihilo*—out of nothing.

Keller's purpose is not to "destroy" the *ex nihilo* doctrine—deconstruction, by her definition, is *not* destroying—but to "expose" its "underlying constructed presumptions."[5] Keller deconstructs creation *ex nihilo* by showing how a variety of theologians over the centuries have read Genesis 1:1–2 through the lens of ancient Greek philosophical categories that privileged certain ideas of harmony, order, purity, goodness, and power.[6] These ideas emerged out of an imagined world of pure, disembodied, immutable, rational being. This philosophy of being came to be known as ontology (from the Greek *ontos* = "being"). Ancient Christians connected the concept of ultimate being to God. Postmodern thinkers call this concept of God as ultimate being ontotheology, a concept that has dominated Western thought until the last half of the twentieth century.

This ancient Greek worldview led some thinkers, including a significant number of ancient Christians, to the "logical" conclusion that if the intelligible world (the world of pure ideas and reason) is good, then the material world (creation) is bad. This logic (operation of the *logos*, or "word")[7] contradicts Genesis 1:31, which proclaims, "God saw everything that he had made, and indeed, it was very good." This fundamental contradiction has led to thousands of years of Christian theological convolutions and conundrums. Once these underlying constructed presumptions are exposed, Keller can question whether it is appropriate to privilege the lens of ancient Greek philosophy over other possible readings of Genesis 1:1–2.

Keller constructs an *other* understanding of creation by reading Genesis 1:1–2 *otherwise*. The conventional reading of creation *ex nihilo* separates Genesis 1:1 ("In the beginning when God created the heavens and the earth") from verse 2 ("The earth was a formless void and darkness covered the face of the deep, while a wind from God swept over the face of the waters"). This interpretive move is made so that we can imagine God as the *pure origin* of creation, unlimited and untainted by any *other*—such as the "formless void," "the deep," or "the waters." Reading otherwise, Keller appeals to other ancient traditions that read verses 1–2 together as a creative process including all these elements: "When in the beginning *Elohim* [God] created heaven and earth, the earth was *tohu va bohu* [formless and void], darkness was on the face of *tehom* [the deep], and the *ruach elohim* [Spirit of God] vibrating on the face of the waters."[8] In this reading, God and the Deep, or the primordial chaos, are neither opposed to each other in a relationship of domination-annihilation nor identical with each other in a relationship of appropriation-assimilation. Instead, Keller reads the Deep as that "site of difference" or "abyss" out of which meaning, creation, justice, and genuine connection emerge. In Keller's words, the Deep is "a primal Other not separate from but within God."[9]

When we read verse 1 separated from verse 2, we tend to imagine the God-creation relationship in one of two ways that diminish the other: (1) we imagine a God separated from creation either as a distant establisher of the laws of the universe or as an intimate but wholly other dominator who directs events through "His" divine will, or (2) we imagine God as identical with creation. Keller's reading otherwise helps us imagine God and creation as mutually influencing—both intimately connected and significantly different. "God in All and All in God."[10]

This theological position, known as *panentheism*, offers a suggestive model for the practical theology of church redevelopment under construction at Beneficent Church. At the very least, it offers an analogy between God's creative process *ex profundis* and the work of redevelopment, since Nicole and I did not begin the re-creative process at Beneficent Church with a blank slate or any other sort of *nothing*. Instead, redevelopment meant a creative engagement with a chaos known as the "dark days." While *ex profundis* provides a rich and resonant theological reading of how we humans engage the creative process in partnership with the power of the Spirit, I'm not sure Keller's panentheism does justice to the biblical insistence on God's absolute freedom, which God willingly and with pathos binds in covenant to the broken shards of God's creation. This absolutely free and wholly other God is, as Phoebe says, "there sometimes and sometimes isn't there." This God who creates *ex nihilo* is the mystery before which we tremble, the one in whose presence worshipers at Beneficent Church can at times "hear the congregation vibrating."

Chapter 6

CHANGE IN ATMOSPHERE

Successful and faithful church redevelopment in a postmodern context is irreducibly theological.[11] Training in best practices for organizational leadership is absolutely necessary for successful and faithful redevelopment, but it is not enough. Theological work and organizational work go together. Theology is important for redevelopment because it is the mother tongue of the church. It is the native language that erupts from within—it deconstructs the congregation's paralyzed relational structure—while simultaneously reconnecting the congregation to its creative spirit. Only theology has the authority to reread and rewrite a congregation's story. Practical theology is observing and meditating upon the gap between the theology that the church declares and the theology that the church does.[12] A slogan for successful and faithful redevelopment might be borrowed from the London Tube: "Mind the Gap" (referring to the space between the subway platform and door into the train). It's simply felicitous British phrasing for the more American expression, "Watch your step."

The abyss that opened up in the dark days was incredibly frightening for Beneficent Church. Monsters emerged from this deep—anxiety, conflict, shame, Other, not-me, change, hypocrisy, the threat of death. Established

leaders tended to resist the notion that their actions might have contributed to the church's decline. They desperately wanted to save face. The safe space needed to be safe for them too. Nevertheless, facing the theology that the church *does* (that is, its practical theology) and brooding over the gap that inevitably opens up—an impossible gap that left us vulnerable to our own hypocrisy—miraculously gave us the chance for a new spirit to sweep over us. This spirit manifested itself in new members, increased worship attendance, new programs, increased effectiveness, new leadership, increased giving, and all those other institutional markers, but pervading all this is a manifestation of spirit as atmosphere. Every respondent in my interview study mentioned a change in "atmosphere" or "energy" as a result of or as key to doing successful and faithful church redevelopment. Whether atmosphere change is a product of or precursor to redevelopment is a chicken-and-egg situation that for this study remains undetermined. Rather, it seems that atmosphere and redevelopment are co-arising.

When Tim talked about the change in atmosphere, he recalled a movie from his childhood. He contrasted the new energy he experienced in worship at Beneficent with an image of mainline Protestant worship from *Mrs. Miniver*, a movie made during World War II that starred Greer Garson, his father's favorite actress. [13] The scene, which he understood as the idealized mainline Protestant worship of his childhood, depicted people gathered in a bombed-out Anglican church in a village outside London. In a climactic scene, the rector is telling his congregation why their fight against fascism is good. According to Tim, "Roosevelt ordered copies of it sent to every movie theater in the country, because, [as the president] said, 'This is why we fight.'" Tim continued, with some irony in his voice, "In all those church things in the movies, the meetinghouse is always packed. They're all singing, and it's just very dignified." Tim saw this idealized image from his childhood as communicating a "very, very different atmosphere from what we were experiencing [at Beneficent Church]. And I'm thinking, this [Beneficent's changed atmosphere] is the future. What used to be the norm and accepted is not the future."

The established Protestant church, the church of Tim's memory, had a particular atmosphere that could be described as "dignified" and somber on occasions when that was appropriate—definitely sober, well-mannered, polite. It fit well with American established society and those who aspired to it. It assumed a close continuity between America's mission and the church's mission, which is presumably why Roosevelt saw this movie as such an effective piece of propaganda. When establishment leaders (the Roosevelts, the Aldriches, and their descendents, for example) left Beneficent Church—when they moved out to the suburbs, when they moved on to other churches or out of church altogether—the atmosphere at the Great Awakening church, the anti-establishment turned establishment and now becoming disestablished church, turned from dignified to anxious tinged with shame and confusion. Redevelopment meant a change in atmosphere.[14]

Steve noticed a change in atmosphere that he connected to the Walking in the Way process:

> It just seemed like meetings got a lot less contentious and people just seemed to be more agreeable, less argumentative at the meetings. Definitely you could feel it. You could feel a change in the atmosphere. Their level of stress seemed to go down. 'Cause people would sit there all tense sometimes, because they were ready to argue about something. It seems like that isn't happening anymore. I don't see it anymore. Well, hardly ever, anyway.

Steve connected this change in atmosphere through the Walking in the Way process to theology, what he calls "the God aspect," and to a change of mind:

> I really feel like some people were totally forgetting about the God aspect of church and thinking about it in a business sense, which was causing a lot of the problem. By bringing religion back into it, it forces them to rethink a little bit, hopefully. When you can say, "Is that really what a church should be doing? Maybe that's what you want to do in business, but is that how a church should be?" So, yeah, that a huge part of a getting people's minds turned around.

The "business sense" that Steve referred to was the technical challenge approach to church decline adopted by the money faction during the dark days. In the case of Beneficent Church, reclaiming a theological-missional identity opened up the space to begin asking adaptive questions (such as "Who are we and how do we do things here?"). Several other respondents connected redevelopment to God and claiming a theological identity. John, a lifelong member of Beneficent, saw the church as "constantly denying or apologizing for" its faith identity. The atmosphere at the church began to change as the congregation acknowledged its shame and confusion, faced its decline and disestablishment, and began to reclaim its identity as a New Light congregation born of the Great Awakening.

In John's view, a distinguishing feature of Christianity is that of a missionary religion that asks its adherents to make a decision—to claim that identity. To claim that identity, one needs to have "a certain clarity as to what that even is." For John, this clarity had been a missing piece at Beneficent Church, and he saw it as a wider problem for mainline Protestant churches. In a paradoxical way, John linked the lack of clear identity both to the "Holy Ghost" going away and to "something [that is] really there and we find every excuse not to identify with it." The result is that in many ways we had turned ourselves into a social service agency that talked about God for an hour a week on Sundays.

What John saw missing was "a real sense that there's a purpose to what [we're] doing and that the purpose is spiritual and that it communicates confidence. That's what people are looking for." John identified a barrier to this sense of confidence and purpose as "feeling guilty," which is elsewhere in this study identified as shame—not simply that we as a church have done bad (guilt) but also that our decline exposes an underlying weakness and vulnerability that we want to hide, much like Adam and Eve's impulse to cover their nakedness after eating the forbidden fruit (Gen. 3:10). According to John, this sense of shame made it difficult for the church to "identify with itself"—that is, its impulse to hide and deny fragments, aspects, and pieces of its history that it judged less desirable, its unwillingness to "mind the gaps" between its proclamation and practice, its marginalization of creative deviants, and its attempts to erase difference and enforce a European American cultural conformity made it difficult to engage the healing process of integration. Instead of accepting itself as a clay vessel (2 Cor. 4:7) full of cracks through which new light might shine, it spent its energy in fruitless attempts to paint them over.

For John, successful and faithful redevelopment depends on the courage to claim all our fragmentary identities and on identity as fragmentation without shame.

> I think once you do that, you become open minded, because you know where you stand. It's not a position of apology, it's a position of assertion, and when you're in that position, you can welcome, you can love, you can appreciate differences, and so forth and not be threatened by them, nor necessarily feel that in some sense your inherently superior. I think it's a position of strength that we have available to us that we're lacking the ability to articulate.

Connecting spiritual growth and numerical growth, John argues that redevelopment needs to flow from a sense of purpose that is "deeper than simply bringing in a lot of people." For John, this is the "spiritual part" from which everything else flows. Currently, Beneficent Church is developing a mission statement that declares we are "Christ centered." As together we call all other homogenizing cultural, doctrinal, and social identifiers into question, we are discovering that in a postmodern context the Christian difference is the sometimes seemingly slight difference that makes all the difference. In the wake of our institutional collapse, we have found it necessary to strip the accretions of the centuries away so that we can start again at the beginning with the simplest of creeds: "Jesus is Lord" (1 Cor. 12:3). Focusing our ministry on saying and doing that simple testimony with every ounce of our being in every aspect of our life together turns out to be incredibly powerful and countercultural in our context. Newcomers regularly tell us that they "never knew there was a church like this."

The "response-ability" that is the justice work of impossible hospitality, the constructing and claiming of purpose and identity, the change of atmosphere, energy, and mind, all are connected to theological work at a deep level that is not primarily theology as a debate over rational propositions, but rather theology as lived Christian practice. This is a powerful theology—not the theology that is said, but the theology that is done.[15] Approaching redevelopment as an adaptive challenge allows us to begin to diminish the gap (without closing it!) between our espoused values and our actual practices of community, testimony, hospitality, respect, and love. Though much remains unclear theologically at Beneficent Church, it is clear that theology at Beneficent is under construction. It is less a theology that shines with the triumphant light of changeless, eternal being—though at times it is shiny and bright and beautiful—and more a theology at home in the mess of human suffering and hope that nevertheless holds the possibility of endless becoming.[16]

UNBLOCKING THE FLOW

Church redevelopment is the practice of imagining and realizing new life in dying churches. As such, it participates in the great Christian narrative of resurrection. In this case, redevelopment looks a bit like resurrection as re-creation. It is not only irreducibly theological but also irreducibly contextual. In the context of Beneficent Church, redevelopment work has a particular trajectory produced by the socio-theological big bang called the Great Awakening. It has a particular spiritual DNA informed by the theological matrix of colonial New England. The local history of the Great Awakening in Rhode

Island revolved around unauthorized itinerant preachers, such as Gilbert Tennent, who served as catalysts for a "different sentiment" of religious expression that included a reformulation of religious authority based not on ecclesiastical endorsement, but rather on personal testimony of conversion and a more rigorous practical piety. Tennent was a Presbyterian minister born in 1703 in County Armagh, Ireland, whose family emigrated to Pennsylvania in 1718. He became friends with Congregationalist minister Jonathan Edwards, who in the early 1740s encouraged him do a preaching tour of New England. Tennent gained fame (or notoriety, depending on one's opinion of the Great Awakening) for his sermon titled "The Danger of an Unconverted Ministry." When in 1741 Beneficent Church founder Joseph Snow Jr., who at the time was a faithful member of First Congregational Church in Providence, heard Tennent's preaching, he "felt that he had never been a Christian before"—such was the power of his awakening. [17]

The language of sin and repentance figured prominently in Great Awakening preaching and practice—perhaps the most famous expression of which is Connecticut clergyman Jonathan Edwards's sermon "Sinners in the Hands of an Angry God." Turning to Beneficent's particular history, we hear resonances with Great Awakening themes in the fireworks of calls to "true faith" and—when that didn't work—mutual recriminations set off by Snow, Cotton, and their respective followers. Great Awakening preachers rooted their faith and practice in Scriptures that connected conversion, resurrection, and re-creation, such as the apostle Paul's famous exhortation to the Corinthians: "So if anyone is in Christ, there is a new creation: everything old has passed away; see, everything has become new!" (2 Cor. 5:17). But what is this new creation? What does it mean "everything old has passed away" and "everything has become new"? Is our history obliterated and all memory erased? Is our DNA—spiritual and otherwise—disassembled, decomposed, and dissolved without a trace so that God can create *ex nihilo*—out of nothing?

The process of becoming church—of brooding over the formational question, "Who are we and how do we do things here?"—was not one of destruction that wiped the slate clean and imposed a new regime; it was a one of deconstruction that creatively engaged the chaos of decline in order to release the Great Awakening energy always already erupting within the congregation but covered over, domesticated, and pressed into service as a kind of "chaplaincy to authority." [18] We heard the voices of our ancestors calling across the generations, "Don't let us fade." Derrida associates this quality of the past erupting within the present, the ancient dislocating the modern, with deconstruction, "so that the new is not so much that which occurs for the first time but that 'very ancient' dimension which recurs in the 'very modern.' . . . No matter how novel or unprecedented a modern meaning may appear, it is never exclusively *modernist* but also and at the same time a phenomenon of *repetition*."[19]

Becoming church, then, isn't simply a modern-patronage style of unfolding a program, making progress, and marching triumphantly into a new "Christian century," though it does at points involve developing and following disciplined processes. Becoming church is instead this odd, paradoxical, nonlogical practice of repentance in which making new is a restoration that is not a return to the past. It is both rupture and repetition. It is healing that always leaves the trace of the wound—a scar.

What is this God-prepared re-creation–restoration that "no eye has seen, nor ear heard, nor the human heart conceived" (1 Cor. 2:9)? Reflecting upon redevelopment at Beneficent Church, Tim recalled that it was "difficult because I didn't have a really good idea of what redevelopment looked like, what it was going to be at the end." He characterized redevelopment as an "organic; let's see how this procedure works." Then he broke off his sentence. Another movie image had disrupted his train of thought. Unable to continue his linear description of this nonlinear procedure, he said,

> All I can think of is one of those World War II movies. Clint Eastwood had to be in it. . . . They're sent into Yugoslavia to blow up a dam because it'll wipe out a bridge and the Germans won't be able to get from here to there. So, they send their bomb expert in, and he sets up his charge and hits the button, and there's nothing. Nothing happens.

The dark days—an advancing poison cloud of anxiety, shame, and spiraling conflict—at Beneficent Church posed an existential threat to the congregation perhaps not unlike the threat of national socialism in twentieth-century Europe—at least it felt that scary to some members of the church. For Tim, redevelopment was that strategic intervention intended to disrupt the advancing threat. The "expert" is duly brought in. (Is Tim referring to Nicole and me—redevelopment pastors as "bomb experts"? Now there's an image I haven't encountered before!) However, "nothing" happens. The threat isn't immediately eradicated with a technical quick fix. There is a pause, a suspension, waiting with bated breath. Tim's thought? "You [the experts] blew it." Things didn't immediately change. In the early weeks, conflict and reactivity in the congregation actually increased. Heifetz writes about "ripening the issue," "turning up the heat" of anxiety, and "giving the work back to the people" as keys to the adaptive process.[20] As redevelopment pastors, Nicole and I had to be willing to get our hands dirty and engage the conflict. We also needed to resist the quick fix and take the heat for doing adaptive work, which might look like *nothing* to some. Anything less would be a failure of nerve.

The ability of leaders to maintain a less anxious presence strengthened Tim's nerve. Looking back on redevelopment, Tim said, "You've just got to wait": "It was a little tiny bomb, but it was put in the right place, and then after maybe ten, fifteen, twenty minutes, all of a sudden things start to happen. Then Mother Nature takes her course, she finds the weak point and, kaboom, and away it goes."[21] How does one disperse a noxious cloud and change the atmosphere? Only a power as great as Mother Nature—as the *ruach elohim*, the Spirit of God with her wings spread, brooding over the face of the Deep—can halt that advance and open up new channels of healing energy. Unblocking the healing flow of the Spirit is a matter of a little, tiny bomb, the smallest disruption of the status quo, a strategic shift in power that is almost nothing—a breath. It seems completely inadequate to the size of the obstacle. If you never find yourself on your knees feeling completely overwhelmed and inadequate to the task, you may not be doing redevelopment work in the mode outlined in this study.[22]

Re-creation *ex profundis*—out of the Deep—means that in the beginning God is always already calling order out of chaos and life out of death, that the story of Genesis 1:1–2, of Christ's resurrection, of St. Paul's conversion, can be stories of a redeveloping congregation, and that successful and faithful redevelopment calls us to continually participate with God in these creative events. Rereading Augustine—and the history of Reformed teaching on sin to which Beneficent Church is heir—through the ancient church father Origen, Keller suggests, "Is *blockage* the problem—rather than a shame-blame model of sin?"[23] Elsewhere: "The 'original sin' would be first of all a *blockage*: a habitual obstruction of the originary flow," a hardening of the heart resulting from phobia.[24] According to Keller, phobia "is not just fear, which warns of danger," but also "the obsessive reiteration of fear, which cripples the ability to face fear"—in other words, chronic anxiety along the lines of Friedman's systems theory.[25] What phobias gripped the Congregationalists of colonial New England that compelled them to (unwittingly) pave over the flow of the Spirit layer upon layer until the Great Awakening erupted and rent in two churches like the First Congregational Church in Providence?

Was it fear of chaos, dissolution, the endless American wilderness that pressed against their farms and villages?

But perhaps this is attributing too much agency to our ancestors. While the practices of repentance and forgiveness are key to successful and faithful church redevelopment, we are still liberating the word *sin* from centuries of shame-blame baggage. Shedding the weight of the past, experiencing a fresh start, reconciling history—all aspects of this event of re-creation—are absolutely necessary. But we don't quite have the language to articulate it yet.

In his book *Church on the Other Side*, author Brian McLaren uses the image of seismic activity to describe the eruptions happening in our world and in our churches as modern and postmodern tectonic plates shift past each other.[26] This image calls to mind the shocks described by Phoebe that generated so much anxiety during the dark days at Beneficent Church. Heifetz describes one aspect of adaptive work as the unleashing of "uncontrollable social forces" that risk "social disaster."[27] Redeveloping churches are "unmanageable organizations."[28] This suggests to me that this work of redevelopment has no guarantees. The same Spirit explodes old wineskins and fills new ones. Why did the "different sentiment" of 1743 lead to a church-splitting eruption while the "change in atmosphere" in 2010 led to church-strengthening growth? Can it really be attributed to *sin* in the sense of moral culpability, or is it simply how the Spirit moves and how congregations respond—the *pathos*, or "passion," of the infinite in the finite and the finite in the infinite? How can there not be natural disasters when we are called to build communities on this creative edge? Perhaps repentance is simply to acknowledge this ever-present possibility of impossible hospitality. Perhaps this is why the apostle Paul admonishes Christian communities to "work out your own salvation with fear and trembling" (Phil. 2:12). Perhaps conversion is this willingness to turn and return to God in the face of disaster, to gather the fragments, heal the wounds, and wait with expectant hope for the call of the other that inevitably comes.

In a moving introduction to the final chapter of *Face of the Deep*, Keller reflects on the contemporary state of theology and Christian institutions. "Theology has been growing uncertain for decades," she writes. Meanwhile, local congregations and the denominational structures that link them—constituencies to whom theologians and theological educators have traditionally been accountable—exhibit an exasperating vacillation between desperate grasping for the latest quick fix and stubborn retrenchment, characterized by willful ignorance of contemporary needs and opportunities. Dependent upon local congregations for financial support and new generations of students, seminaries and divinity schools can't help but be caught up in this perfect storm of cultural shifts and generational transitions, the result of which is the disestablishment and marginalization of the mainline Protestant establishment. Like an appliance with a short circuit or a nervous system with Parkinson's disease, the institutional machine that is the body of Christ shows signs of going haywire. The theological result? "We tumble off the timeline of progress." The gaps that have opened up in the modern-patronage ministry model and its vision of Christendom have left congregations wandering in the desert without a clear path forward. Keller admits, "I did not always recognize this confusion as a gift."[29]

That Christianity has lost its dominating influence among the American cultural elite, which journalist Ross Douthat bemoans as he documents it, means not only a loss of power and prestige but also an opportunity for congregations to reclaim their distinct identities and practices. Liberation theologians tell us that truth is spoken from the margins. What choice do we have but to turn and return to that animating Spirit that gives us life? What is left but to ascend the mountain with Moses and enter the cloud of unknowing?[30] Or "perhaps there is nothing to do but deepen the repetition," writes Keller.[31]

As we repeat our history at Beneficent Church, we notice that the disruptions in our evolution as a congregation have resulted in mutations of our spiritual DNA. We were marked by differences from the beginning. The Great Awakening in Providence brought together Congregationalists (who practiced infant baptism), Baptists (who practiced believer baptism), and Quakers (who practiced baptism of the spirit) into one worshiping community. Our records contain evidence that Beneficent practiced both infant and believer baptism (and, presumably, baptism of the spirit) from its beginnings in 1743. We are not aware of any other congregation that was doing this at the time. While much of Providence's historic wealth was gained through the slave trade, Beneficent actively participated in the abolitionist movement, raising money for the defense of the *Amistad* captives (1839–1841) and serving as a stop on the underground railroad. We have nineteenth-century records of African American worshipers and weddings performed at Beneficent Church.

Though an adequate rereading of our history could characterize the church as multiracial/multicultural, *how* the congregation has embodied that spirit has evolved. For example, at some point it decided to do away with its black entrance to the meetinghouse. As together the congregation presses deeper into the twenty-first century, our practical theology continues to evolve. Successful and faithful redevelopment at Beneficent Church has meant a transgressive repetition of our history that deconstructs its assumptions, unblocks the flow of its animating Spirit, and reframes our identity, not in terms that necessarily align with the values of our wider communities, but rather in terms that can hopefully communicate with them.

MINISTRY ON THE MARGINS

Almost two years after my interviews with Tim, Steve, John, Henry, Gene, Grace, Lydia, and the rest of my Beneficent co-researchers, we are completing our third annual Lenten Sacred Conversations series. Though it no longer has the same level of revelatory surprise that the first series did, it is an anticipated event and well received. This year we featured three sacred conversations: one on the topic of multicultural worship, one on leadership, and one on marriage. The congregation has come to embrace sacred conversations as a valuable spiritual practice. For example, one of our senior groups is having a sacred conversation on elder care. The atmosphere of anxiety and shame that threatened the church during the dark days has receded into congregational memory.

In fact, today the majority of Beneficent's worship attenders and church members have no personal memory of the dark days, because they have joined in the years since that time. For them, the church has always been joyful, diverse, hospitable, and cutting edge. Talk of the dark days or ghosts of past conflicts come as a surprise to them. Some have suggested we stop telling the story, since it is an uncomfortable and scary one. The major conversation for our church today concerns our mission, vision, values, and long-range plan. We have found that we can't stay in an indeterminate state of flux forever. Once the flow is unblocked, channels are needed to direct it; otherwise, it just floods everything and goes nowhere. We're shifting our focus from stopping the bleeding, which involved getting a handle on budget, cash flow, staffing, stewardship, property, nominations, membership loss, and the like, to reconstructing an organization that will serve a redefined mission.[32]

In the dark days, the specter of dissolution loomed before us like an insurmountable obstacle or, perhaps because we couldn't get a handle on it, an inescapable threat. We rejoice that the toxic cloud has dissipated, but it has revealed yet another daunting prospect: Can a disestablished, outside-the-mainstream, multiracial, multicultural, Open and Affirming, socioeconomically diverse congregation in an economically distressed city in an economically distressed state come up with the human and financial resources to support a church infrastructure built by and for established mainline Protestants at a time when Providence, Rhode Island, was at the peak of its prosperity? Though our congregational giving has increased dramatically, will it be able to keep pace with our growing needs? Will we be able to grow and train a new generation of leaders—both staff and lay—quickly enough to support the programs we need to continue to grow? Will we be able to make the transition from pastoral- to program-sized church without the whole project collapsing around us? These are the formidable questions we face, which perhaps have implications for other historic mainline churches hoping to offer their legacy to future generations.

Theologian Douglas John Hall, in a series of 1993 lectures to the Presbyterian Church (USA), responded to the decline crisis in that denomination by proclaiming a message to the churches in North America: "Dis-establish yourselves!" He argues that there is a widespread, though unarticulated, sense of shame and humiliation among churches that, when looking back over the past one hundred years at what was supposed to be the Christian century, read their recent history as one of failure to establish Christianity as the global dominant religion. More shameful still is not only the failure to establish world dominance but also the decline of Christianity in its own "homelands" of Europe and North America.

Hall argues further that the form of establishment in North America as opposed to Europe is of a much more deeply engrained type. In Europe, says Hall, Christianity's establishment was primarily formal and legal and therefore much more easily dissolved. By contrast, Christianity's establishment in North America is much more deeply connected to the American project itself. The establishment is at a cultural level, corresponding perhaps to Law's internal culture—the culture of who we are and how we do things here. The disestablishment of mainline churches in North America, therefore, is much more difficult, intricate, and painful, because it carries with it religious (as well as national and cultural) implications. Reading Douthat, one might get the impression that America itself is having an identity crisis because of mainline (and other established Christianities') decline.

Hall's challenge is for mainline churches to take charge of their disestablishment. Not only does he see the process as inevitable, but he also sees great benefit to churches, who no longer carry the burden of being a "chaplaincy to authority."[33] Hall describes this work of intentional disestablishment as theological work that produces changes in "understanding and will."[34] In particular, what needs to be sorted out are the differences between white middle-class values and Christian values. I wonder what Hall would think of the deconstructive work of this study—the search for the "nonplace" where faith can appear as *other* to itself. The result of this intentional disestablishment is churches embracing what Hall calls their "awkwardness." This awkwardness comes from a refusal to take a position as either cultural insiders or cultural outsiders. He warns against churches that try to resolve their relationships with the wider culture by building their identity on taking radical stands on social issues. While he is sympathetic to social justice issues raised by feminists, environmentalists, economic justice advocates, and the like, those positions should be arrived at as the *consequence* of Christian faith, not the basis of it. A second alternative that Hall wants to avoid is a complete separation that could result in withdrawal from or antagonism toward culture. This leaves us in an awkward place—neither completely congruous with nor completely separate from the culture that mainline churches have so decisively shaped. It is a place of nondominance, not quite establishment strength revealed in weakness, power demonstrated in not quite having it all together. It is a position from which churches—instead of arguing the universal truth of their claims—might testify to the faithfulness of their God.[35]

A disestablished church is a church that takes its place on the margins of power. Redevelopment work along the lines of the postmodern-plural model under construction at Beneficent Church could be thought of as ministry on the margins. It is the testimony of a marginalized community among the marginalized of society. This marginalization expresses itself in many ways—those more obvious to the wider culture include marginalization based on economic class, race, sexual orientation, gender identity, immigrant status, and the like; those less obvious include the spiritual marginalization of those who have an ambivalent relationship with God and religious institutions, the millions who inhabit the margins of faith, who cry out with the father of the boy with the unclean spirit, "I believe; help my unbelief!" (Mark 9:24).[36]

In addition to offering words of truth, testimony is a moral summons to "sanctify life."[37] In sum, what a turn to the poetics of testimony offers is a means of survival for the marginal community. What they testify to is that the demise of the ontotheological project and the disestablishment of churches shaped by the modern-patronage ministry model have not spelled the end of mainline legacies; that despite finding ourselves "dispossessed," we continue to receive blessing; that despite the eruption of the other and of difference in history, the faithful community is able to reconstitute itself and discern a fragmentary continuity.[38] Including these voices of testimony as "coauthors" of a postmodern practical theology of redevelopment will help those of us on the margin that joins belief and unbelief reweave the fabric of our faith communities.[39] It will help us dance through this dis-ease, if you will. As we do so, we will keep turning and returning to the God of Abraham, Isaac, and Jacob. As the Shaker hymn so beautifully puts it, "To turn, turn shall be our delight 'til by turning, turning we come round right."[40]

KEYS TO REDEVELOPMENT

Creating a framework for conversations that are safe, sacred, and public in which there is no fixing, just witnessing.

Minding the gap between the theology the congregation declares and the theology the congregation does.

Practicing repentance (without shaming or wallowing in despair) to unblock the creative flow of the Spirit in the congregation.

Claiming the power of testimony from the margins of power.

Without Conclusion

Every reading that seeks understanding is only a step on a path that never ends.[1]

—Hans-Georg Gadamer, "Reply to Jacques Derrida"

It worked because the spirit of adventure triumphed over the concern for safety and security.[2]

—Edwin Friedman, *A Failure of Nerve*

WHAT DOES IT TAKE?

What does it take to do successful and faithful church redevelopment in postmodern contexts? The answer to our guiding question in this study is multiple. It is never just one thing that leads to successful and faithful redevelopment, and it is never just one thing that leads to a church's decline. There's no magic bullet, no easy answer, no prepackaged program developed by experts that will change your congregation's life. There's only you, your congregation, its context, and your willingness to risk everything for God's mission. The purpose of this book is to spark your own creative thinking and your own courage to act in your particular situation, which will have its own unique opportunities and constraints. As Becker observes about her study, "This is a particular case, and its importance as a case lies in its particularity."[3] That being said, at this point in the study, we can consider a summary of some of the learnings gained through this practical theological work.

The interview study that informs this work identified multiple beginnings for the story of imagining and realizing new life at Beneficent Church. For

157

example, Nicole mentioned our work as church planters, which helped us clarify our mission as church redevelopers. Another example of a possible beginning were the dark days so vividly described by Phoebe as a time of trial that opened the hearts of a critical mass of congregation members to the possibility of redevelopment as a preferable way forward. The clearest, and perhaps most decisive, beginning was the call of Nicole and me to serve as co-pastors to the church. Every interview respondent pointed to the call as the moment when things started to change. Other research cited in this study supports the notion that most often successful and faithful redevelopment begins with the call of new pastoral leadership. This book suggests, however, that simply calling a new pastor is not enough. A number of factors contributed to the successful call process at Beneficent.

Chapter 2 identified some key contributions to the call process. One was an adequate reading of the redevelopment context. Nicole and I were intentional in choosing Beneficent Church for our redevelopment work. Before we settled on Beneficent, we had considered quite a number of dying churches trying to avoid death. Our past experience serving churches taught us that not every congregation has the institutional resources necessary for redevelopment—that is, they've declined past the point of no return. Not every congregation is located in a context that presents redevelopment opportunities—that is, a socially dynamic community that is an adequate cultural match for the congregation. Most important, not every congregation—despite their protestations to the contrary—is willing to do whatever it takes for successful and faithful redevelopment. The principle that Nicole and I followed in making our assessments is that the best predictor of future behavior is past behavior, so we did all we could to assess the congregation's spiritual DNA: Did they show evidence in their history and theology of effective outreach within their communities that contributed to the institutional and spiritual growth of the congregation? Simultaneous to the assessment process was defining our ministry as redevelopment from the beginning.

The initial weeks and months of our call to Beneficent Church were marked by between-frame conflict—that is, factions within the congregation broadly identified as money people and mission people engaged in a power struggle over the identity of the church, while a number of other subgroups who didn't identify strongly with either faction looked on in confusion. Key to successful and faithful church redevelopment was publicly naming this conflict and using our influence as co-pastors to engage the services of a conflict transformation consultant. Meanwhile, Nicole and I focused our ministry on networking both within the congregation and in our wider community. We surprised the money people—who were biased toward viewing the pastoral office as spendthrift—by cutting staff and slashing the budget. At the same time, we supported the claim of the mission people that the identity of Beneficent was not, in fact, a not-for-profit museum to religion, but rather a living spiritual community with a fundamental moral obligation to pass on its legacy to future generations. We offered redevelopment as a third way forward—an alternative to irresponsibly spending endowments until nothing was left or irreversibly cutting off the congregation's access to the assets with which past members had endowed it by turning the church into a museum.

Between-frame conflicts are power struggles over fundamental questions of identity. Nicole and I worked to focus the congregation's attention on the questions of who we are and how we do things here while drawing on resources from Beneficent's history to offer our own vision of what it might mean to be a New Light church in the twenty-first century. Between-frame conflicts are messy, involve factions, and can easily compromise a pastor's ability to lead the redevelopment process. Establishment forces within the congregation will try to destroy the seed of redevelopment before it gets a chance to take root. People can be extremely sensitive to what they perceive as threats to their power and will automatically respond with sabotage. The challenge of adaptive, nonanxious leadership is to respond with clarity and grace. Ultimately, successful and faithful redevelopment asks congregation and pastors to construct fundamentally new answers to the questions of congregational identity and purpose that are nevertheless authentic mutations of the congregation's spiritual DNA.

The adaptive work of orchestrating between-frame conflict demanded that leaders, particularly pastoral leaders, engage in networking both within and outside the congregation. The insider-outsider dynamic generated by anxiety over congregational decline meant that within the congregation there were marginalized voices—creative deviants, if you will—who represented overlooked spiritual, human, and financial resources. Established leaders had responded to congregational anxiety by trying to control the situation. Alternative perspectives were marginalized, which only generated more anxiety as marginalized voices struggled harder to be heard, withdrew from leadership, or left the church altogether. A key to successful and faithful redevelopment was shifting power away from patronizing control and toward systems of equity. As newcomers, Nicole and I were marginal to the power structure ourselves; we leveraged the power of our office and the power of our vision to create safe space in which marginalized voices could begin to deconstruct the operation of power in the congregation. In the language of adaptive leadership, this work corresponded to creating a "holding environment" and "giving the work back to the people."[4] The congregation did this by calling into question who they were and how they did things here. This power shift brought new leadership—both staff and lay—into positions where they could begin shaping a new direction for the congregation.

The new voices that began to have influence in the congregation expressed cultures different from the classic European-American Protestant perspective that had dominated the congregation for generations. In most cases, these voices had been present in the congregation for many years. Why was the congregation having such a difficult time hearing and affirming their perspectives? Based on the interview study, I constructed the hypothesis that a modern-patronage ministry model, which defined Western cultural values and practices as normal, made it difficult for people of other cultures to feel fully valued and respected. It was as if—except for special Sundays—they had to leave those pieces of themselves that made them culturally different at the door. As these new voices found themselves heard and validated, the church began to grow more multicultural, or multicultural in a new way, which I described as a postmodern-plural ministry model.

What made this shift faithful and successful was that the congregation was *not* trying to be something it wasn't. Beneficent Church was simply embracing on a deeper level aspects of its identity that had been on the margins. Though paradoxical, this made the practice of *impossible hospitality*—welcoming the other in a way that disrupts identity—feel authentic for Beneficent Church. Beneficent had to move beyond a modern-patronage model of assimilation, which communicated to people of nonestablishment cultures "You're welcome if you come," in order to move toward a postmodern-plural model of impossible, apostolic hospitality that extends itself to the other in mutual respect and partnership. Connecting the emerging model to the spiritual DNA of the congregation in explicit and public ways was key to successful and faithful redevelopment.

The change in atmosphere at Beneficent Church was difficult to grasp and impossible to ignore. Interview respondents used images like "breath of fresh air," "opening the curtains and letting the sunshine in," "the whole congregation 'vibrating,'" "enthusiasm," and "warmth." The threat of the dark days had been all the more frightening because of its amorphous quality—like a toxic emotional cloud that hung over every interaction. Dispersing this cloud was key to successful and faithful redevelopment. Interview respondents also identified this work as clearly spiritual and theological in nature. As one respondent put it, the church had forgotten "the God aspect." Not that Beneficent had stopped worshiping or praying at meetings or doing Bible study or calling itself a church. It had simply lost sight of the connection between the faith it professed and its practices as a community. In other words, it had forgotten how to do *practical theology*. The result was an organization that was neither a full-fledged secular social-service organization nor a robust Christian church. Without a clear sense of identity, purpose, or direction, Beneficent was doing a pretty poor job at both.[5]

Dispersing the toxic atmosphere at Beneficent Church was clearly the work of the Holy Spirit. As co-pastors, Nicole and I worked with church leaders to create practices, events, worship experiences, and conversations that tapped into the Great Awakening spiritual DNA of the church. At first, all that these little victories did was momentarily part the clouds so that the congregation could regain a sense of hope. One example of this was the two hundredth anniversary celebration. The key to the success of this event was that Nicole and I created *two* committees—one of longtimers who were primarily interested in reliving the past and one of newcomers who had a vision of how aspects of Beneficent's past might meet the needs of the current community. We focused most of our energy on working with this second committee to create an invitational event that would reintroduce Beneficent to our community. Another little victory, the Sacred Conversations series, created safe space for a public articulation of the longings and hopes of a new generation of spiritual seekers. These voices served not only to connect with new people who represented the future of Beneficent but also to awaken the almost-extinguished flame of spiritual vitality in many of the longtimers. As more and more new people joined the church and connected to this vision of new life, the breeze shifted and blew stronger. Today, the dark days are a past reality that, while retained in memory, no longer dominates the church atmosphere.

CAN WE REMAIN OPEN TO POSSIBILITIES?

Can a postmodern-plural ministry model replace a modern-patronage ministry model? In a word, no. *Postmodern* is an unsettled and unsettling term that invites controversy, revels in contradiction, and simply would not be postmodern if it could be pinned down. It points to strategies for disruption of certainties. It resists fixed meanings and final answers. Its purpose is to create new openings for fresh thought. A postmodern-plural ministry model is not a model in the sense of a coherent, step-by-step, money-back-guaranteed program for fixing your church. Rather, it is a series of experiments, improvisations, and gutsy maneuvers. In the introduction to this story-study, Professor Mobley warned against making an idol of postmodern thought. Rather, we should view the various reading and writing strategies, aesthetic movements, cultural critiques, theological adventures, and political engagements that somehow touch upon the term *postmodern* as "weed-eaters" designed to clear away the "overgrown jungle of modernity."[6] This clearing away should not be imagined as elimination; a weed-eater is not an herbicide. There are two reasons for this: First, both Enlightenment modernity and postmodern thinking share an interest in truth. Second, were we to imagine replacing a modern-patronage ministry model with a postmodern-plural ministry model, we would simply be reenacting an erasure of difference and a condescending "intimate domination" that the practical theology at Beneficent Church is calling into question.[7]

Regarding the first reason, modernity and postmodern thought share a common interest in truth, according to Mobley. What does truth have to do with the story of redevelopment at Beneficent Church? Well, as it turns out, quite a lot. The big bang that gave birth to Beneficent Church was a conflict over the "true" church. Who had the right to claim the name First Congregational Church of Providence? Snow's party or Cotton's party? Who had the right to claim a founding date of 1720 and thus continuity with the congregation's origin? Who broke up with whom? Each party appealed to a different notion of truth in arguing for their status as "true" church. Cotton and the Old Lights appealed to reasoned faith and established authority to legitimate their truth claims. Snow and the New Lights appealed to conversion experience and individual testimony—what Jonathan Edwards called "experimental religion"—to legitimate their truth claims. Both groups appealed to Scripture.

Remember, all these people were operating in a context of modern Enlightenment understandings of truth: truth as transcendent, unchanging, all-pervading, universal light (whether the light of reason, revelation, or some combination thereof),[8] as an undivided, all-encompassing court of appeals that can make "objective" judgments about human affairs free from biases and self-interest. Truth is, as Hegel argued, "the whole."[9] A postmodern thinker might read the story of Beneficent Church and the First Great Awakening, notice the fragmenting true hearts searching for truth, and wonder whether even in a modern religious milieu, postmodern plurality and fragmentation—that is, deconstruction and difference—were in operation. The modern-patronage ministry model, with its unified concept of truth, always already contained within it an *other* postmodern plurality waiting to be recognized (if that is the right word). We consider the generations of Native Americans, African Americans, Chinese Americans, and *others* who on Sunday mornings left their cultural truths at the door of the Beneficent Church meetinghouse, or the poor and working classes who generations ago sat in the "free seats" located in the balcony of the Beneficent Church meetinghouse and looked down during worship on the middle-class and wealthy elites who could afford to purchase pews on the floor.

A few weeks ago, at our last deacons' meeting, our presiding deacon led a Bible study on Psalm 96. The psalm ends with the declaration that God "will judge the world with righteousness, and the peoples with his truth." The presiding deacon simply invited the deacons to respond to the psalm. I noted that this word *truth* was important to our ministry, since Beneficent Church's relational covenant invites us to speak the truth in love. Immediately the deacons began interrogating *truth*. One person linked truth to power and argued that truth is often used in self-serving ways—for example, to impose one's will on someone else.[10] Another responded that truth is plural: there are many truths, depending on your perspective. Later in the conversation, she also observed that truth changes and evolves over time. Knowing her personal story of coming out as a lesbian after many years of being married to a man, I understood her to be speaking out of her personal experience of truth. Responding to the interplay of *truth* and *love*, another responded that sometimes he hides the truth so as not to hurt unnecessarily someone else's feelings. He created an image of truth as delayed or deferred. Truth deferred, truth marked by difference: postmodern themes all. Yet there before us, as a past promise of our future, is Scripture declaring an ancient, divine truth—the one truth of the one God—with the right and the power to judge "the peoples." Suddenly the tables are turned, and Scripture invites all of us to read our modern unities and postmodern pluralities *otherwise*: to question our questions and doubt our doubts. To deconstruct deconstruction.[11]

Just as we are coming to terms with the dark sides of modernity, we also need to deconstruct postmodern deconstruction itself. Whereas practitioners of the modern-patronage ministry model in the United States tend to uncritically accept white middle-class American values as unambiguously Christian values, thereby either marginalizing or assimilating other cultural perspectives, practitioners of a postmodern-plural ministry model run the danger of losing all sense of focus and direction. We continually walk the creative edge along the margin of the "absolute" and the "dissolute."[12] As Derrida writes, "Pure unity or pure multiplicity—when there is only totality or unity and when there is only multiplicity or dissociation—is a synonym for death."[13] The postmodern-plural ministry model is still a model for doing *religion*— that is, a binding back; a reconnection to root, leaf, and stem; an institutional preserving and passing on of gifts, (re)traditions, and (mutating) spiritual DNA. It's a becoming truth for a becoming church.

The second reason that the clearing away of postmodern deconstruction is not elimination has to do with domination. Deconstruction is a strategy for noticing and calling into question the privileging of the one over the many, the same over the different, the eternal over the temporal, the universal over the particular, the theoretical over the practical, intelligible over the sensible, unity over plurality, presence over absence, light over dark, mind over matter, denominational academy over local church, men over women, white middle-class assumptions about what constitutes a good church over other perspectives.[14] Postmodern thinkers have shown how these binaries create totalizing systems—sometimes called "dominologies"—that erase differences.[15] Dominologies do this in two ways: one is by marginalizing and potentially annihilating the excluded other (for example, male-dominated institutions silencing or disenfranchising women). Or a second way is by appropriating the other as simply a deficient or idealized expression of the same (women are an "irrational" version of men or they are men's "better half"). In theology, this appropriation could take the form of suspicion of a religious practice as compromising the philosophical "objectivity" of theology or a reversal of such: for example, liberation theology that makes the praxis of base communities the norm for doing theology. In either case, we remain caught in an either-or logic that deconstruction tries to open up in order to imagine and construct new ways of writing, thinking, and relating in the world. To imagine the postmodern as somehow replacing modernity would mean falling into the same trap of a dominating ideology. Rather, postmodern thought is a strategy for opening up new possibilities for creativity and justice in an overgrown system of Western thought that is slowly suffocating itself.

For this reason, Keller takes pains to argue that a theology of becoming is not intended to replace traditional theologies of being. An understanding of

God as creating from the Deep is not intended to wipe away more familiar understandings of God as creating out of nothing. She writes, "Deconstruction, as its founder has always been at pains to protest, is not the demolition but the destabilization of founding certainties, a 'trembling' proper to a transition between epochs, 'operating necessarily from the inside.'"[16] In a similar way, the postmodern-plural ministry model outlined in this study is not intended to replace the modern-patronage ministry model. It is not a new system imposed from the outside. The model approaches institutional decline as an adaptive challenge in which one role of leadership is to give the work back to the people by empowering marginalized voices and protecting differing perspectives. The folks at Beneficent for whom this approach offers exciting new possibilities for creativity and justice do not intend to take over the church, despite the fears of some longtimers for whom new postmodern-plural answers to questions of purpose and identity seem strange, distasteful, and perhaps even immoral.[17] The shift, rather, is that the modern-patronage model is not the *only* and unquestioned model from which the church might operate. The call is for the modern-patronage ministry model—its language, cultural markers, music, assumptions, and approaches—to take its place as one of a number of options available to the church as it constructs and lives out of new answers to old questions of purpose and identity.

This nondominant theological understanding of purpose and identity also means that we will refrain from wiping the slate clean when it comes to our past, in all its glory and failure. This would make a theology of becoming yet another dominology. As a church, we will no longer labor under the dangerous innocence of claiming we come from nowhere and that what we offer is something fresh and clean and perfect—whether as pastors engaging in redevelopment work with congregations or as congregations prophetically engaging our communities. Keller writes,

> In human form this means that we no longer create as though from an original void. Pastorally, therapeutically, politically: we find ourselves in some densely textured flux, some difficult mix of indeterminacy and constraint. We may feel shame before the chaos in our lives, families, sexualities, movements, ethnicities, drafts, projects. Or we may read this difficult milieu for its freshly emerging order. If we do not try to control what seems out of control, if we rather brood on the fluid face, the *eschaton* between what is too chaotic and what is too limiting, we will discern the specific possibility of the transition. In the inescapable limitation lies the creative *edge*.[18]

Redevelopment is not a time for unacknowledged shame. Rather, redevelopment is a time for courage. It is a time for facing the chaos of our lives and our congregations. As leaders face the chaos of their own situations, their histories, their limitations with courage and without shame—as leaders bring their lives *to light*—they gain the credibility and the power to "influence the community to face its problems."[19] This is the heart work of leadership. This is the Sinai encounter without which no redevelopment can take place. By attending to the chaos instead of fighting or denying it—surprisingly, miraculously—order (perhaps in the form of a renewed covenant or a regulated incoherence?) has the possibility to "irrupt from within" it.[20]

WHERE DO WE GO FROM HERE?

"In the inescapable limitation lies the creative edge." Keller's creative edge lies between the *absolute* of modernity's absolute knowledge, with its tendencies toward totalizing secular and religious analogs, and the *dissolute* of a caricatured postmodernity in which Derrida's "bottomless chessboard" becomes an endless language game in an infinite abyss for which the players are always already too late.[21] It's a chaotic, endlessly indeterminate mess without reprieve; the dark days; a small group of frightened souls bobbing in an open ocean with no hope of rescue; a series of random seismic shocks; an inescapable toxic cloud. Keller calls the in-between of the absolute and the dissolute the "resolute."[22]

The resolute is "the *eschaton* between what is too chaotic and what is too limiting."[23] *Eschaton* is the Greek word for "end, last in time or place." In Christian theology eschaton denotes the in-breaking of the kingdom of God—that is, the eruption into history of God's vision for creation restored, healed, reconciled, liberated. It is the destination toward which this adventure is aimed, an *other* reality always already operating to disrupt exploitive dominologies and the idols of empire.

Throughout the centuries, Christians have debated whether the kingdom of God will be realized here on earth or in a world to come, whether it is a spiritual kingdom available here and now to the enlightened individual soul or a transformed heaven and earth for which a few, many, or all are destined. Modern Enlightenment aspirations for absolute knowledge of universal truth and their Christian analogs have often claimed a triumphant eschaton as inevitable: whether through the victory over sin and death won through Christ's resurrection or through the steady progress of human achievement through science and reason. For marginalized peoples, these visions of victory can be a source of hope; for established power, they become a license to dominate and exploit. A postmodern reading of eschaton—"in human form," as Keller puts it—might call eschaton *possible*: the possibility of the impossible.[24]

Keller identifies theological honesty as a strategy for realizing eschaton as creative edge.[25] This honesty has several dimensions. We need to be honest about Christian history, which is decidedly mixed. While Christians and our churches have done much good in the world, we have also done much evil, which we must continue to confess and repent. At Beneficent, for example, we have recently completed a year-long worship renewal program in which we focused on creating a new model for multicultural worship. In a series of workshops and worship services, we invited leaders of major nondominant cultural groups—Native American, African American, Chinese American, Latino—in our congregation to teach us worship in their cultural traditions. One thing we discovered was how absolutely critical it was for these cultural groups to tell and retell, in the safe and sacred space of public worship, the story of colonization, aided and abetted by Christian missionaries, in which their cultural heritages were lost or forgotten. As we reconstruct cultural traditions together in the context of Christian worship, healing is beginning.

The point is not for Christians to aimlessly, endlessly wander dissolute and depressed over past failures. The point is to recognize that to be a Christian is to, in some sense, always live within the tension of an adaptive challenge—it's to take on a set of ideals before which we have always already fallen short. We will never entirely match our actions with our values. For this simple reason, we should not be surprised when polls find that the word most often used by unchurched people to describe Christianity is "hypocritical."[26] Of course we are hypocritical. How could we not be? Perhaps this is the whole religious project: to hold open the space between what is and what might be. In this light, we might put a qualifier on Heifetz's adaptive change. Adaptive change reduces the gap between stated values and organizational practices, but it doesn't eliminate that gap—at least for congregations. The moment we've arrived is in some sense the moment we've failed. So we are hypocrites, but on our best days we are humble, honest, repenting hypocrites who listen to, learn from, and protect *others*, whether they are culturally other or creative free thinkers, heretics, seekers, interrogators, and prophets.

Keller argues that honest theological discourse should recall St. Paul's words to the Corinthians: "But we have this treasure in clay jars, so that it may be made clear that this extraordinary power belongs to God and does not come from us" (2 Cor. 4:7). The creative edge relates to a creative genius, an unfolding, generative-genetic process that cannot be completely contained. Even as we construct institutions to pass this truth-treasure on from one generation to the next, it always threatens to burst its bounds. It mutates in strange, monstrous, and magnificent ways. For this reason, it's foolish—perhaps dangerous—to imagine our human containers, whether theological systems or ecclesial institutions, as airtight, complete, perfected, or even on the way to some perfect repose in which all differences will be reconciled and all voices harmonized. It seems unlikely that all will be one in any way that corresponds to a modern Enlightenment understanding of truth.[27]

Yet we need some container for this creative genius. We need some safe space in which we can risk the adventure of faith. On the edge of their exodus, in that "midnight of the night" when God gives the final instructions to God's people in preparation for their departure ("At that time when [Pharaoh] sends [you] away, it will be finished" [Exod. 11:1, trans. mine]), God gives them the Passover ritual.[28] One way of understanding the chaos unleashed by the plagues—dark days for Egyptians and Israelites alike—is that they create space for constituting the new community. (Recall Moses's repeated demands that the people be allowed a "three days journey into the wilderness" [Exod. 3:18], in effect putting *space* between God's people and Pharaoh.)[29]

As we come to the Passover account, we transition from narration of events to instruction for a ritual through which this transforming story becomes embedded in the life of the community for generations in perpetuity. Once the space for constituting the new community is created, it must be maintained through paradigmatic ritual. This new ritual emerges from the transformation process itself and becomes the *case* that contains this precious new thing. The example of the Passover shows us that this ritual container is like a "clay jar" made up from things lying around—a meal ritual, the blood from animals to be eaten, flour and water, herbs and doorposts, and neighbors gathered and the question from the child, "What does this service mean?" Passover might be considered a bricolage—a cobbled-together strategy for disrupting domination and a safe enough container for risking freedom.

Creation and resurrection, Passover and Easter, chaos, transformation, death and new life: "Perhaps there is nothing to do but deepen the repetition."[30] For Beneficent Church, the broken vessel to which we entrust our spiritual legacy, the leaky craft in which we sail upon an endless ocean of possibilities, may well be deconstructive-reconstructive itself: "the very experience of the (impossible) possibility of the impossible . . . a condition that deconstruction shares with the gift, the "yes," the "come," decision, testimony . . . and perhaps death."[31] The container for Beneficent's creative genius is simply the process of reinventing itself in the face of God's call.

Imagining and realizing new life at Beneficent Church didn't begin until the congregation faced death, the valley of the shadow of death—the "darkest valley," as some translations of Psalm 23 render the Hebrew. Out of Beneficent Church's dark days, new paradigmatic rituals and spiritual practices continue to emerge: talking circle, sacred conversations, multicultural worship, testimony, and new rituals for prayer, to name a few. But the basic worship order remained unchanged. The church architecture and location has stayed the same so far. In the face of chaos and change, Beneficent Church reinvented itself. The demons of conflict and schism that were in play in 1743 showed their faces again, but this time the congregation stayed together. The broken vessel held somehow, miraculously, impossibly.

Keller's theological honesty could be extended toward an ecclesiological honesty. This honesty might begin with deconstruction's insight that the creation of meaning is always already a process of exclusion. Redeveloping congregations (at least insofar as we are communities of purpose and meaning that ask, "Who are we?" and "How do we do things here?") are always operating on the creative edge of inescapable limits. In the very moment we ask, "Who are we?" we simultaneously construct an *other* called "Who we are not." Likewise, the question "How do we do things here?" generates a set of behaviors we avoid, ones that haunt, disrupt, and sometimes sabotage our achievements.[32] In other words, ecclesiological honesty demands that we make decisions even as we hold judgment in reserve.[33] As the edges of the territory we've been able to map through our study of Beneficent Church come into view, we find ourselves on a fragmented frontier, a continually dividing, roiling, fecund, membranous boundary. What we can glimpse and discern from this vantage is necessarily inconclusive; it is beyond the bounds of any oppressive end, endlessly emerging out of an opening toward the possible. Without conclusion.

So where do we go from here? Over the past few years a debate over mainline decline has been running in the popular media like a background program. In a July 2012 *New York Times* op-ed piece headlined "Can Liberal Christianity Be Saved?" journalist Ross Douthat argued that liberal Christianity has "collapsed," because its doctrines have basically become progressive politics with a little God sprinkled on top.[34] Scholar Diana Butler Bass responded the next day with a *Huffington Post* blog post in which she blasted Douthat for arguing that numerical decline in mainline congregations is a sign of divine displeasure over "liberal" theology. She ended her piece with the question, "Can liberal churches save Christianity?"[35] Ten months later practical theologian Christopher Brittain, in an opinion piece for the Australian Broadcasting Corporation, announced a "plague on both their houses," claiming that both conservative and liberal churches are declining because of "modern individualism." He suggested that "Christians of all persuasions have good reason to distance themselves from the tendency to define churches by the terms of the culture wars."[36]

A lot can be learned from this and other conversations among scholars, journalists, and cultural observers. For example, Douthat is right when he urges "liberal Christianity" to recover "a religious reason for its own existence."[37] But this study would indicate that he's wrong to assume only one "religious reason" exists and that it conforms to his version of orthodoxy. In addition, his longing for a culturally reestablished orthodox Christianity in America just seems like wishful thinking. Butler Bass's defense of mainline congregations is welcome. This book supports her argument that if church folks respect "spiritual-but-not-religious" folks, there's a chance they might become "spiritual *and* religious." But her vision of a "Fourth Great Awakening" in which people "create life-giving community" in "neighborhoods, community gardens, city streets, public transit, parks, cafés, and coffee shops; galleries, museums, and libraries; festivals, fairs, and farmers' markets; rallies and debates; public schools, congregations, and social networks" offers little comfort to struggling congregations, many of whom have known for decades that they are just another option in a highly competitive (now global) spiritual marketplace.[38] Finally, even though "modern individualism" was identified as a threat to religious congregations more than twenty-five years ago by Robert Bellah,[39] Brittain's warning against defining the church in terms of culture wars is well taken. I know Jesus can save liberal churches, but can liberal churches "save" Christianity? Let's first see if we can stop the decline!

At Beneficent Church, we continue to face threats as well as opportunities. We are struggling to complete a strategic plan that will help us set priorities for programming, staffing, fundraising, and infrastructure. We dream of creating a vital student ministry among our neighbors at Johnson and Wales University. We hope to build a national network among multiracial, multicultural, Open and Affirming congregations to share best practices and offer mutual support. We are rebuilding our institutional memory after losing so much over the decades: by writing policies, training staff and lay leaders, and aligning our programs and mission initiatives with the mission, vision, and values of the congregation. We are right at the cusp of a major size transition that will require us to reinvent ourselves again. Will we have the energy? Will we have the resources? Will we be able to change fast enough to meet the needs of our growing church without the whole project going off the rails? Will our overly complex structure and our enormously expensive buildings bring us down in the end? Will the ghosts of Cotton and Snow return to tear us apart once and for all? I hold on to a ray of hope that they won't. God willing.

The prophet Isaiah declares, "The grass withers, the flower fades; but the word of our God will stand forever" (40:8). As you consider your context, take heart. Whereas congregations can be frail and global trends hopelessly beyond our control, the gospel entrusted to us continues to prove its power to change lives, change communities, and even change the world. So love the people. Build the network. Remember that with every yes there is a no. Claim your theology and go deep. Respect differences while opening your heart to unlikely alliances. Get out there, make friends, and invite them to church. Or, if they aren't interested in church, invite them to some other partnership, alliance, or relationship. Open yourself to the possibility not only that your life will be changed but also that you will have the opportunity to bear witness to the life-giving, life-changing power of God at work in the lives of others. Successful and faithful church redevelopment is going to demand every ounce of everything you've got—and then some more. When we give our lives to God without reserve, new life is possible.

Appendix A

Report on the Meet the Ministers Study (2009)

Number of people participating: 80
When: June–September 2009

Comment: The first set of questions we asked people in our Meet the Ministers meetings was "What brought you to Beneficent Church? And what do you like about Beneficent Church?" In general, the people we spoke with had very few affirmations or rarely affirmed what was going on at Beneficent Church at the time (except, of course, for identifying "diversity"). Therefore, in order to have any data whatsoever with which to work, we had to count as affirmations those affirmations of what in the past brought them to Beneficent Church. The items listed are those that were mentioned at least once. For instance, "Hope for the future" was an affirmation of Beneficent Church from one person. The responses are a snapshot of where Beneficent Church was in the first few months of our ministry. If we asked for affirmations today, there might be different responses.

AFFIRMATIONS

(23)   Diversity, ecumenism, economic diversity, Open and Affirming

(19)   Pastoral leadership

(18)   Welcoming, hospitality, friendships, social groups

(15)   Family connections, family feeling

(13)   Mission, social justice, active in the community

(10)   Spontaneous, spirit-filled worship, simple, informal

(8)   Youth programs, children and youth ministry

(7)   Openness to new things

(4)   Location

        Building

        Choir, music program

        Evangelism, outreach, marketing, inviting

(3)   Education, book club, Bible study

        Preaching

(1)   Hope for the future

        Spiritual home

        Exciting, energizing

VISIONS

Comment: The second set of questions we asked was "What visions do you have for the future of Beneficent Church? Or what would you like to see change?" Again, many of the responses were very negative, reflecting the general malaise of Beneficent Church at the time. In order to understand these responses as visions, many of them have been rephrased in positive terms.

(19)   More people, more young people, students, families, programs for students and families

(17)   Inclusive decision-making process; conflict healing; healthy, Christian behavior; honesty; eliminate controlling behavior; no secret meetings; better boundaries; clearly defined roles; relationship

(14)   Mentors, small groups, relationship building

(11)   Connection with the community

(9)   Upbeat music; indigenous, excellent music

(6)   Less stress: all business, no play; people pulling in different directions; not enough celebrating; frustration

(6)   Spiritual connection, spiritual disciplines, transformation

(4)   More welcoming, hospitable, open minded

(3)   More focused, better meetings

Accountability, follow-through, results

Creativity, do new things, reinvention

(2)   More diversity, people of color

Clarify bylaws, structure

Education

Communication clarity, harmony

Down-to-earth preaching

Recognize and thank people

Improve administration

Improve church, pastor, and staff relationships

New worship service

Visioning, identity, distinctiveness

Appendix B

The Grant Yonkman Co-Pastor Ministry Model (2008)

As churches and pastors look for new, creative, and effective models for leadership to address the challenges of the twenty-first century, increasing numbers are trying co-pastoring. Over the years, we [Pastor Nicole Grant Yonkman and I] have learned that churches and pastors have done co-pastoring in a wide variety of ways—some more effective and some less so. We would like to share with you the outline of a model that we have developed over the last five years and that we have found quite effective.

Basic principles

Each co-pastor works out of his or her strengths. The job of a pastor demands an incredibly wide range of skills—public speaking, fundraising, event planning, organizational management, human resources, teaching, leadership training, counseling, crisis management, strategic planning, and the list goes on. No one person can be equally competent in all these areas. As a co-pastor team, our skills are both different and complementary. Co-pastoring allows each of us to focus on those areas of pastoring that we do best, which makes our work on behalf of the church more effective.

By dividing up tasks, together we can cover more ground. Rather than doing everything together, we divide up many of the tasks so that we can get more work done more efficiently. As two people, often we can be in more than one place at a time, and therefore we are able to more easily bring pastoral leadership where it is needed.

We use our time and skills strategically for the benefit of the church. Co-pastoring requires coordination and discipline. While each of us has general areas of responsibility, as specific needs arise we continually ask: Who is best for this job? For example, though one of us might generally be responsible for pastoral care, there may be a circumstance in which a family feels more comfortable with the other co-pastor's style, so that co-pastor will go ahead and do the pastoral care for that family. We find this kind of clear yet flexible style to be most effective. We can work in this way without being defensive or territorial because of the high level of trust in each other we have developed over the years.

Things we generally do together

Worship planning, leadership, preaching
Executive board responsibilities
Staff meetings, supervision

Areas where we divide up responsibilities

Todd: evangelism, pastoral care, stewardship
Nicole: finance, Christian education, administration

Areas where we coordinate our leadership roles

Bible studies, fellowship groups, church events

How we communicate

As co-pastors, we have regular executive staff meetings to coordinate tasks, map out strategy, and ensure that each is informed about important happenings around the church.

When people have specific questions, we make sure that they are directed to the person who is going to have the most helpful information for them.

We remain in continual communication through phone, e-mail, and face-to-face conversation.

Healthy boundaries are a high priority for us as a family. We will ask that the congregation respect our need for family time.

We communicate with the congregation and wider community openly, effectively, and regularly through any and all means at our disposal.

What is the benefit for you?

A broader skill set

Two pairs of eyes bringing their perspectives to each situation give a more accurate view of what's happening around the church and in the community

Two distinct leadership styles that complement each other

More flexibility in how and when pastoral leadership is deployed in church and community life

Appendix C

Relational Covenant

Beneficent Church
A Relational Covenant for Our Community

To guide our communication and offer goals for our relationships

Speaking . . .

We will speak directly to each other using the first person and "I" statements.

We will ask questions for clarification in order to determine if we have understood correctly and ask that others do the same.

We will speak only for ourselves and avoid making generalizations such as "everyone," "they," or "all."

We will encourage everyone to participate and speak for themselves.

The truth . . .

We will be as open and honest as we can with each other while being sensitive to all feelings.

We will accept that there may be multiple perspectives with wisdom based on different persons' interpretations.

We will strive together to understand and speak from factual information, rather than jumping to conclusions based on assumptions or speculation.

We will take time to seek understanding with those we differ with to expand our wisdom and community.

In love . . .

We will speak to each other with respect, seek to understand needs, and avoid reactive responses so we can focus on issues and not cause harm.

We will work to genuinely recognize and affirm the merit in another person's idea or concern before we note its weaknesses.

We will listen to understand one another's point of view, but don't necessarily have to agree.

We will look for opportunities to enable healing for ourselves and for each other.

HONORING THE RELATIONAL COVENANT

"Speaking Directly" (based on Jesus's instructions as found in the Gospel of Matthew, chapter 18)

When someone brings "concerns" to you about another person, this is how you can honor our covenant to "speak directly."

1. Tell the person with the "concern" to "speak directly" to the person about whom they have a "concern."
2. If the person with the concern says, "I'm not comfortable doing that," or "I've tried but they won't listen," say, "I will go with you to that person to 'get the conversation started,' then I will leave and let you two talk."
3. If the person continues to insist on bringing their concern to you instead of speaking directly to the person about whom they have a concern, say something like, "Stop right there. I'm sorry. I love, you, but I will not talk about this concern with you. We have covenanted together to 'speak directly,' and I am going to abide by that covenant."

(Draft from Walking in the Way, with input from Sessions 1 and 2, Fall 2009, and Core Team, January 2010.)

Appendix D

Ministry Partnership Covenant

Ministry Partnership Covenant
January 16, 2011
RPM Voices of Rhode Island and Beneficent Congregational Church

What we share:

A passion for praising God through music

A vision for diversity and inclusivity for all God's children

A desire to create experiences of the holy through gospel music

A creative spirit that is ever changing and moving within us

A belief that we can achieve greater heights together in partnership

What Beneficent Church offers:

A downtown building that acts as a center for community and mission for the city of Providence

A renewed commitment to reach out to the community and partner together in mission

Strong leadership committed to growing a more diverse community at BCC [Beneficent Congregational Church]

A willingness to learn and a desire to stretch beyond our comfort zone so that we can fully embody God's vision for community

What RPM offers:

> Talented and gifted musicians who can effectively teach their skills to others
>
> A cohesive, bonded community of singers who want to share their music with the community
>
> A desire to teach others about gospel music
>
> Strong leadership

As ministry partners we covenant together to:

> Share rehearsal and performance space
>
> Unite our choirs for specific events and worship services
>
> Promote each other's events and expand our reach in the community
>
> Increase participation in BCC and RPM Voices
>
> Learn and grow as we sing and perform gospel music together
>
> Explore the meaning of diversity as we change and grow together

Today we sign this covenant as a symbol of our intention to fulfill our promises to each organization and to one another, relying of God's grace.

_____

Rev. Nicole Grant Yonkman

_____

Dr. Clarice LaVerne Thompson

_____

Deacon Marilyn Washington

_____

Shaunne Thomas

Notes

PREFACE

1. Alfred Korbzyski, *General Semantics Seminar*, transcription, 1995 ed. (Lakeville, CT: Institute of General Semantics, 1995), 58.

2. Gayatri Chakravorty Spivak, preface to *Of Grammatology*, by Jacques Derrida, trans. Gayatri Chakravorty Spivak, corrected ed. (Baltimore: Johns Hopkins University Press, 1997), xiii.

3. The qualitative study and thick description that form the basis of this project are not done from the perspective of a sociologist or anthropologist analyzing a community with which he or she had no previous relationship. Sociologist Gerardo Marti deals with the methodological considerations of the "insider-outsider" problem in an appendix of *A Mosaic of Believers: Diversity and Innovation in a Multiethnic Church*, his study of Mosaic Church in Los Angeles, California, which he did for a PhD program while he was serving on staff there. Marti, who is writing for an academic audience, is sensitive to preserving the distinction between researcher and pastor while doing his study. On the whole, his judgment is that the insider benefits of trust relationships and intuitive understanding of the culture outweigh the risks to the validity of his study. The guidelines he offers to insiders studying their religious culture are ones that I followed in my study, including carefully formulating a key research question before collecting data, clarifying the research topic with prospective respondents, introducing distance in familiar social settings (I did this by asking people to pretend I knew nothing about the church), respecting unexpected responses, and embracing the problematic.

Unlike Marti, I am writing for an audience that includes pastors, lay leaders, students, denominational leaders, and congregational consultants; nevertheless, I found that some critical distance was important for the integrity of this study. My hope is that the reader will find some value in the perspective of a pastor who has "been there" doing redevelopment, who has gotten his hands dirty, and whose smudgy fingerprints are all over these pages. It is an exercise in what I like to call disciplined passion. I am passionate about the work of church redevelopment for reasons that will become clearer in the course of this study. I am unapologetically interested in the success and faithfulness of those engaged in the work, myself included! Nevertheless, I will attempt to direct and discipline this passion by framing it as a conversation in which differing and perhaps even contradictory voices are given a compassionate and adequate hearing. The benefit of this study is that it presents the voices of people who understand the experiences of church redevelopment at a cellular level—that is, people who have felt the feelings, fought the battles, done the work, and are now attempting to tell the tale.

4. One of my parishioners, let's call her Elizabeth, has early onset Parkinson's disease. Once when I was visiting her in her home, she offered me something to drink. When she got up to go to the kitchen, she suddenly had difficulty walking, so she quickly raised her arms and shifted into a sort of side-step shuffle. With each step she bent her arms at the elbow: hands to the chest, hands out to the side like eagle wings. She danced like this across the kitchen to the cupboard where the glasses were. "Sometimes it helps to dance," she explained. For more on dancing and church redevelopment, see Bill Easum, *Dancing with Dinosaurs* (Nashville: Abingdon Press, 1993).

5. Jacques Derrida defines *respect* as willingness to "let be." See Jacques Derrida, *Writing and Difference*, trans. Alan Bass (Chicago: University of Chicago Press, 1978), 141.

6. Catherine Keller, *Face of the Deep: A Theology of Becoming* (London: Routledge, 2003), 230.

7. John D. Caputo, "Jacques Derrida (1930–2004)," *Cross Currents* 55, no. 4 (Winter 2005–2006). See http://www.crosscurrents.org/caputo200506.htm.

8. Jacques Derrida, interview, Society for Biblical Literature, Toronto, Canada, 2002. Audio recording, http://www.youtube.com/watch?v=MG_nyd45czM. For more on Derrida and prayer, visit https://www.youtube.com/watch?v=MG_nyd45czM.

9. Derrida, *Writing and Difference*, 92.

10. "The undeconstructible is the subject matter of pure and unconditional affirmation—'viens, oui, oui' (come, yes, yes)—something unimaginable and inconceivable by the current standards of imagining and conceiving. The undeconstructible is the stuff of a desire beyond desire, of a desire to affirm that goes beyond a desire to possess, the desire of something for which we can live without reserve." Caputo, "Jacques Derrida," *Cross Currents*, http://www.crosscurrents.org/caputo200506.htm. And "Deconstruction is a blessing for religion, its positive salvation, keeping it open to constant reinvention." Caputo, *Deconstruction in a Nutshell: A Conversation with Jacques Derrida* (New York: Fordham University Press, 1997), 159.

11. John Phillips and Chrissie Tan, "Derrida and Deconstruction," webpage, http://courses.nus.edu.sg/course/elljwp/deconstruction.htm.

12. Jacques Derrida, "Structure, Sign, and Play in the Discourse of the Human Sciences," in *Writing and Difference*, 278–94.

13. Gary Jackson, *Fire When Ready Pottery*, http://firewhenreadypottery.com/2009/03/. When I wrote the artist to ask what makes this particular piece a bricolage and not a mosaic, he responded that the pieces composing a mosaic are generally made from the same material, whereas a bricolage such as this one is "similar but uses a wider variety of materials in the same piece. Frequently mirrors are added as well as other unusual pieces." E-mail message to author, July 28, 2013.

14. Diana Butler Bass, *The Practicing Congregation* (Herndon, VA: Alban Institute, 2004), 42.

15. "Open and Affirming (ONA) is the United Church of Christ's (UCC) designation for congregations, campus ministries, and other bodies in the UCC which make a public covenant of welcome into their full life and ministry to persons of all sexual orientations, gender identities, and gender expressions." See http://www.ucc.org/lgbt/ona.html.

16. See also Mary Louise Gifford, *The Turnaround Church: Inspiration and Tools for Life-Sustaining Change* (Herndon, VA: Alban Institute, 2009).

INTRODUCTION

1. Don S. Browning, *A Fundamental Practical Theology: Descriptive and Strategic Proposals* (Minneapolis: Fortress Press, 1991), 7.

2. Our mission statement, which was adopted at our annual congregational meeting in June 2013, reads, "Through the power of the Spirit, Beneficent Church creates meaningful connections to God and one another and promotes justice, peace, and healing in our local and global communities. We are a Christ-centered, Open and Affirming, racially, culturally, and socio-economically diverse congregation."

3. Mark C. Taylor, "What Derrida Really Meant," *New York Times*, October 14, 2004.

4. Karl Barth, *The Epistle to the Romans* (Oxford: Oxford University Press, 1968), 452.

5. For more background into the practical theological method used for this study, see Browning, *A Fundamental Practical Theology*.

6. Denis Goulet, introduction to *Education for a Critical Consciousness*, by Paulo Freire (London: Continuum, 1974), ix.

7. Anthony Robinson, *Transforming Congregational Culture* (Grand Rapids, MI: William B. Eerdmans, 2003), 25.

8. Darrell L. Guder, *The Continuing Conversion of the Church* (Grand Rapids, MI: William B. Eerdmans, 2000).

9. The distinction between unity and uniformity is important for church redevelopment. See, for example, William M. Easum, *Sacred Cows Make Gourmet Burgers: Ministry Anytime, Anywhere, by Anyone* (Nashville: Abingdon Press, 1995), 36.

10. For theological discussions of empire, see such thinkers as John Dominic Crossan, Marcus Borg, and Brian McLaren, who read the Gospels as subversive critiques of the Roman Empire.

11. Gregory Mobley, conversation with the author, Newton Centre, Massachusetts, May 12, 2011.

12. Alice Mann, *Can Our Church Live? Redeveloping Congregations in Decline* (Herndon, VA: Alban Institute, 1999), 1–12.

13. Mann, *Can Our Church Live?*, 9. For other accounts of the formative questions of mission and identity, see Penny Edgell Becker, *Congregations in Conflict: Cultural Models of Local Religious Life* (Cambridge: Cambridge University Press, 1999), 1–25; for the formative questions of identity and purpose, see Gil Rendle, *Journey in the Wilderness: New Life for Mainline Churches* (Nashville: Abingdon Press, 2010), 33–58.

14. Mann, *Can Our Church Live?*, 11.

15. Ibid.

16. Ibid.

17. Ibid., 1.

18. Browning, *Fundamental Practical Theology*, 6.

19. For an excellent critique of the mainline decline metanarrative, see Becker, *Congregations in Conflict*, 206–36. She argues that the "problem" of mainline decline has meant primarily a loss of jobs, status, and power for a relatively small number of religious elites, and that, viewed from a sociological perspective, the shifts associated with mainline decline look more like a mix of both institutional losses and institutional gains.

20. Barry A. Kosmin and Ariela Keysar, *American Religious Identification Survey 2008* (Hartford, CT: Trinity College, 2009), 2.

21. The use of parentheses for *(re)reading* is meant to indicate that in the context of redevelopment every reading is a reading again. Because of the changing nature of a congregation and

its mission field, church leaders need to be continually reading and rereading the situation. For example, Beneficent Church today is a very different congregation from what it was in 2009. This means that Beneficent's leaders continue to go through the processes of reading the context that are described in this chapter.

1. (RE)READING A REDEVELOPMENT CONTEXT

1. All the quotations in the following narrative come from a facsimile of volume 1 of the Beneficent Church Records 1743–1830, the originals of which are archived at the Congregational Library in Boston, Massachusetts. Josiah Cotton was the great-grandson of the famous Boston Congregational minister, John Cotton. For more on a Beneficent view of Josiah Cotton, see Arthur E. Wilson, *Weybosset Bridge* (Boston: Pilgrim Press, 1947), 47–57.

2. Edward B. Hall, *Discourses Comprising a History of the First Congregational Church in Providence* (Providence: Knowles, Vose, & Co., 1836), 13.

3. Is Beneficent Church the only congregation with this self-deconstructing DNA? Sociologist Gerardo Marti quotes Derrida in the epigraph to his forthcoming book, *The Deconstructed Church: Understanding Emerging Christianity* (Oxford: Oxford University Press, 2014): "Christianity is the only mad religion; which is, perhaps, the explanation for its survival—it deconstructs itself and survives by deconstructing itself."

4. Hall, *Discourses Comprising a History*, 15.

5. All the quotations in this paragraph are taken from Hall, *Discourses Comprising a History*, 13–20.

6. Ibid., 13–17.

7. Ibid., 17.

8. William M. Easum, *Sacred Cows Make Gourmet Burgers: Ministry Anytime, Anywhere, by Anyone* (Nashville: Abingdon Press, 1995), 39–47.

9. Stacy-ann Ramdial, PhD candidate in biochemistry at Brown University, personal e-mail message to author, September 19, 2012.

10. Brian McLaren (lecture, Woodbury Leadership Workshop, Andover Newton Theological School, Newton Centre, Massachusetts, February 14, 2010).

11. Alice Mann, *Can Our Church Live? Redeveloping Congregations in Decline* (Herndon, VA: Alban Institute, 1999), 11.

12. For Jesus's description of this process, see Mark 13.

13. Easum, *Sacred Cows Make Gourmet Burgers*, 19.

14. Robert Quinn, *Deep Change: Discovering the Leader Within* (San Francisco: Jossey-Bass, 1996), 3.

15. Easum, *Sacred Cows Make Gourmet Burgers*, 19. See also Edwin H. Friedman, *A Failure of Nerve: Leadership in the Age of the Quick Fix*, ed. Margaret M. Treadwell and Edward W. Beal (New York: Church Publishing, 2007), 194.

16. For example, Easum, theologian Catherine Keller, and educator Margaret J. Wheatley.

17. Easum, *Sacred Cows Make Gourmet Burgers*, 32.

18. Edwin Friedman, *Generation to Generation: Family Process in Church and Synagogue* (New York: Guilford Press, 1985), 226.

19. Penny Edgell Becker, *Congregations in Conflict: Cultural Models of Local Religious Life* (Cambridge: Cambridge University Press, 1999), 139.

20. The table is my own summary of ideas found in chapters 3–6 of *Congregations in Conflict*.

21. Becker, *Congregations in Conflict*, 4.

22. Ibid.

23. See Ronald A. Heifetz, *Leadership without Easy Answers* (Cambridge, MA: Harvard University Press, 1994).

24. Becker, *Congregations in Conflict*, 4.

25. I see some analogy here to Heifetz's notion of "formal" authority. See Heifetz, *Leadership without Easy Answers*, 13.

26. Becker, *Congregations in Conflict*, 158.

27. Ibid., 160.

28. Ibid.

29. John Russell Bartlett, ed., *Records of the State of Rhode Island and Providence Plantations in New England*, vol. 10, *1784–1792*, 128.

30. Yochanan Muffs, *Love and Joy: Law, Language, and Religion in Ancient Israel* (New York: Jewish Theological Seminary in America, 1992), 9.

31. Everett Fox, *The Five Books of Moses* (New York: Schocken Press, 1995), 440.

32. Hall, *Discourses Comprising a History*, 18.

33. Ibid., 19.

34. Cyrus O'Neill, e-mail message to author, October 18, 2012.

35. Hall, *Discourses Comprising a History*, 18.

36. For conversion as cloning, see Friedman, *Generation to Generation*, 226.

37. Jacques Derrida, *Of Grammatology*, trans. Gayatri Chakravorty Spivak, corrected ed. (Baltimore: Johns Hopkins University Press, 1997), 24.

2. SHARING LEADERSHIP

1. Edwin H. Friedman, *A Failure of Nerve: Leadership in the Age of the Quick Fix*, ed. Margaret M. Treadwell and Edward W. Beal (New York: Church Publishing, 2007), 54.

2. Ronald A. Heifetz, *Leadership without Easy Answers* (Cambridge, MA: Belknap Press, 1994), 36–40.

3. For a more detailed discussion of emotional triangles, see Edwin H. Friedman, *Generation to Generation: Family Process in Church and Synagogue* (New York: Guilford Press, 1985), 36–39.

4. Friedman, *Generation to Generation*, 23.

5. Friedman, *Failure of Nerve*, 14.

6. Heifetz, *Leadership without Easy Answers*, 109.

7. Ibid., 14.

8. Ibid., 76.

9. Ibid., 128.

10. Friedman, *Generation to Generation*, 232.

11. Ibid., 226.

12. Ibid., 233.

13. Heifetz, *Leadership without Easy Answers*, 7.

14. Friedman, *Failure of Nerve*, 11.

15. Friedman, *Generation to Generation*, 230.

16. Friedman, *Failure of Nerve*, 188.

17. For more on this metaphor for church redevelopment, see Thomas Bandy's classic, *Moving Off the Map: A Field Guide to Changing the Congregation* (Nashville: Abingdon Press, 1998).

18. I recognize the complicated irony of juxtaposing readings of the *Amistad* story, the story of American independence, and the Age of Discovery. I let it stand as a memorial to the complex historical context in which American congregations minister.

19. Friedman, *Failure of Nerve*, 14.

20. Robert Quinn, *Deep Change: Discovering the Leader Within* (San Francisco: Jossey-Bass, 1996), 3.

3. CONFLICT AND CONVERSATION

1. Further confirming this reading is a report dated July 9, 2008, from the pastoral search committee, titled "Financial Administration and the Participation of the Pastor." The report identifies "two camps" in the congregation with the terms "money" and "mission." This report further argues that "the minister have significant and voting participation in the financial discussion and administration of the financial resources of the church."

2. *Beneficent Congregational Society (Providence, RI) Charter, By-Laws and List of Members* (1993), 2.

3. Since that time, the minister who led the conflict at Beneficent has taken a call to serve a church in another state, though he officially remains a member of Beneficent.

4. Ronald A. Heifetz, *Leadership without Easy Answers* (Cambridge, MA: Belknap Press, 1994), 118–19.

5. For more on the connection between congregational decline and the failure of stewardship education, see Robert Wuthnow, *Crisis in the Churches: Spiritual Malaise, Fiscal Woe* (Oxford: Oxford University Press, 1997).

6. Heifetz, *Leadership without Easy Answers*, 188.

7. Ibid.

8. Ibid., 56.

9. Ibid., 83.

10. Penny Edgell Becker, *Congregations in Conflict: Cultural Models of Local Religious Life* (Cambridge: Cambridge University Press, 1999), 179.

11. Conversation with the author, Providence, Rhode Island, January 2011.

12. Stephen Pattison, *Shame: Theory, Therapy, Theology* (Cambridge: Cambridge University Press, 2000), 155.

13. Douglas John Hall, "An Awkward Church," booklet 5, *Theology and Worship Occasional Papers* (Louisville, KY: Presbyterian Church, USA, 1993), http://www.presbyterianmission.org/ministries/theologyandworship/theological-issues/.

14. Pattison, *Shame*, 131.

15. Earl Thompson, "Michael Lewis on Shame" (lecture, Andover Newton Theological School, Newton Centre, Massachusetts, September 30, 2009).

16. Earl Thompson, "Thomas Scheff and Suzanne Retzinger on Shame and Genuine Pride and the Social Bond" (lecture, Andover Newton Theological School, Newton Centre, Massachusetts, September 30, 2009).

17. Pattison, *Shame*, 163.

18. Ibid., 81.

19. Ibid., 94.

20. One of the keys for redevelopment at Beneficent Church has been reclaiming the church's early identity as a Great Awakening, New Light, community church. This aspect of Beneficent's identity resonates much more readily with Beneficent's current ministry context, which no longer includes Aldriches and Rockefellers but instead is a very diverse downtown urban community. A anecdote about a recent event illustrates that some in leadership still imagine Beneficent Church's identity primarily in terms of the wealthy elite of the city. Beneficent recently had its property—including its silver—appraised for insurance purposes. When the appraiser told a church leader that the silver in Beneficent's vault was not sterling but merely silver plate, she was shocked and denied that such a thing could be possible. In her mind, Beneficent is or should be a "sterling silver" church. In reality, it appears that Beneficent is more of a "silver plate" church. As magnificent and storied as Beneficent has become, at its heart, the church is an anti-establishment (or at least not quite establishment), Great Awakening, New Light, Spirit-led movement-turned-institution located on the not-as-nice side of town on the campus of a non–Ivy League school—Johnson and Wales University—and its communion set is silver plate. And that's okay. In fact, that's wonderful. Beneficent is a place where state officials sit next to homeless people who rub elbows with physics professors who shake hands with blue bloods who share coffee with folks from China who have been living in the United States for three weeks. Beneficent Church sometimes casts an envious eye at richer churches across the river. But its future lies in embracing a gift those churches, for the most part, do not have: social diversity.

4. SHIFTING POWER

1. William M. Easum, *Sacred Cows Make Gourmet Burgers: Ministry Anytime, Anywhere, by Anyone* (Nashville: Abingdon Press, 1995), 9.

2. Penny Edgell Becker, *Congregations in Conflict: Cultural Models of Local Religious Life* (Cambridge: Cambridge University Press, 1999), 182.

3. The quotations in this paragraph are from Ronald A. Heifetz, *Leadership without Easy Answers* (Cambridge, MA: Belknap Press, 1994), 104, 106.

4. Ibid., 107.

5. Edwin H. Friedman, *A Failure of Nerve: Leadership in the Age of the Quick Fix*, ed. Margaret M. Treadwell and Edward W. Beal (New York: Church Publishing, 2007), 11.

6. Heifetz, *Leadership without Easy Answers*, 107.

7. Ibid., 183–206.

8. For more on a theology of self-organizing complexity, see Catherine Keller, *Face of the Deep* (New York: Routledge, 1993), 117. For more on a theology of cocreativity, see Keller, *Face of the Deep*, 218.

9. Darrell L. Guder, *The Continuing Conversion of the Church* (Grand Rapids, MI: William B. Eerdmans, 2000), 9.

10. See Anthony B. Robinson, *Transforming Congregational Culture* (Grand Rapids, MI: William B. Eerdmans, 2003).

11. Edward B. Hall, *Discourses Comprising a History of the First Congregational Church in Providence* (Providence: Knowles, Vose, & Co., 1836), 5.

12. Douglas John Hall puts it this way: "We must distinguish the Christian message from the operative assumption, values, and pursuits of our host society, and more particularly those segments of our society with which, as so-called 'mainstream' churches, we have been identified. And, since most denominations in question are bound up with middle-class, Caucasian, 'liberal' element of our society, what we shall have to learn is that the Christian gospel is not a stained-glass version of the world view of that same social stratum." From "An Awkward Church," booklet 5, *Theology and Worship Occasional Papers* (Louisville, KY: Presbyterian Church, USA, 1993).

13. Guder, *Continuing Conversion of the Church*, 17.

14. Ibid.

15. Ibid., 63, 59.

16. Ibid., 19–21.

17. Becker, *Congregations in Conflict*, 182.

5. EXTENDING WELCOME

1. Gerardo Marti, *Worship across the Racial Divide: Religious Music and the Multiracial Congregation* (Oxford: Oxford University Press, 2012).

2. Mark C. Taylor, "What Derrida Really Meant," *New York Times*, October 14, 2004.

3. Jacques Derrida, *The Gift of Death*, trans. David Wills (Chicago: University of Chicago Press, 2008), 83.

4. "The Other resembles God," Derrida quoting Levinas, in Jacques Derrida, *Writing and Difference*, trans. Alan Bass (Chicago: University of Chicago Press, 1978), 108.

5. John D. Caputo, ed., *Deconstruction in a Nutshell: A Conversation with Jacques Derrida* (New York: Fordham University Press, 1997), 109.

6. Catherine Keller, *Face of the Deep: A Theology of Becoming* (London: Routledge, 2003), xvii, 230.

7. Leonardo Boff and Clodovis Boff, *Introducing Liberation Theology*, trans. Paul Burns (Maryknoll, NY: Orbis Books, 1989), 3.

8. Keller, *Face of the Deep*, 19–23.

9. Enrique Dussel, *Philosophy of Liberation*, trans. Aquilina Martinez and Christine Morkovsky (Maryknoll, NY: Orbis Books, 1985), 43.

10. Derrida writes, "This concept of writing designates the place of unease, of the regulated incoherence within conceptuality." See *Of Grammatology*, trans. Gayatri Chakravorty Spivak, corrected ed. (Baltimore: Johns Hopkins University Press, 1997). Derrida's concept of writing is more than just putting pen to paper; it is also the structure of reality. Is there something to be learned here about the structure of the congregation and its practical theology? "Regulated incoherence" sounds like a description of impossible hospitality that can only be transformed into a momentary coherence by a miracle of the spirit.

11. Caputo, *Deconstruction in a Nutshell*, 107.

12. Ibid.

13. Ibid., 110.

14. Ibid., 106.

15. Jacques Derrida, *On the Name* (Stanford, CA: Stanford University Press, 2003), 43.

16. Jacques Derrida, *Gift of Death*, 122.

17. Derrida writes, "The relationship with the other and the relationship with death are one and the same." *Of Grammatology*, 187. No wonder congregations have such a difficult time with this kind of impossible hospitality! The paradox of declining congregations is that while they are actively dying, they are simultaneously expending enormous amounts of energy to avoid facing death, which, if and when it happens, opens the space for new life. As Jesus said, "Those who lose their life for my sake, and for the sake of the gospel, will save it" (Mark 8:35). Or, as theologian Dietrich Bonhoeffer put it, "When Christ calls a man, he bids him come and die." Bonhoeffer, *The Cost of Discipleship* (New York: Touchstone, 1959), 89. No wonder a common reaction by established power to redevelopment is "You ruined my church." No wonder redevelopment asks of its leaders and followers so much sacrifice.

18. Keller, *Face of the Deep*, 231.

19. Richard Kearney, "Jacques Derrida: Deconstruction and the Other," in *Debates in Continental Philosophy* (New York: Fordham University Press, 2004), 140.

20. Hans-Georg Gadamer, "Destruktion and Deconstruction," trans. Geoff Waite and Richard Palmer, in *Dialogue and Deconstruction: The Gadamer-Derrida Encounter*, ed. Diane P. Michelfelder and Richard E. Palmer (Albany: State University of New York Press, 1989), 110.

21. Derrida, *On the Name*, 43.

22. Rebecca Chopp, "Theology and the Poetics of Testimony," *Criterion* 36, no. 1 (Winter 1998): 2, 8, 7.

23. Gadamer, "Destruktion and Deconstruction," 110.

24. Eric H. F. Law, *The Wolf Shall Dwell with the Lamb: A Spirituality for Leadership in a Multicultural Community* (St. Louis: Chalice Press, 1993), 14.

25. Ibid., 13–27.

6. BECOMING CHURCH

1. Recall both Pattison's process of "integrating" shame and Retzinger and Scheff's process of "acknowledging" shame, described in chapter 3.

2. Ronald A. Heifetz, *Leadership without Easy Answers* (Cambridge, MA: Belknap Press, 1994), 227.

3. Andrew, Beneficent Church interview respondent, Providence, Rhode Island, May 2011.

4. Ronald A. Heifetz and Martin Linsky, *Leadership on the Line: Staying Alive through the Dangers of Leading* (Boston: Harvard Business School Press, 2002), 229. Heifetz and Linsky write, "That's it! That's the message. That's what we learned about sacred heart—the willingness to feel everything, everything, to hold it all without letting go of your work."

5. Catherine Keller, *On the Mystery: Discerning Divinity in Process* (Minneapolis: Fortress Press, 2008), 138.

6. In "Deconstruction and the Other," Jacques Derrida argues that Judaism and Christianity represent an otherness that was never "completely eradicated by Western metaphysics." *Debates in Continental Philosophy* (New York: Fordham University Press, 2004), 148. In a similar vein, theologian David Tracy writes, "The postmodern turn toward the mystics has yielded one of the most surprising developments in contemporary philosophical and theological thought: the amazing return of religion as the most feared other of Enlightenment modernity." Tracy, "Fragments: The Spiritual Situation of Our Times," in *God, the Gift, and Postmodernism*, ed. John D. Caputo (Bloomington: Indiana University Press, 1999), 176.

7. The biblical claim that the word (*logos*) became flesh and dwelled among us (John 1:14) could be considered a radical deconstruction of Western metaphysics.

8. Catherine Keller, *Face of the Deep: A Theology of Becoming* (New York: Routledge, 2003), xv.

9. Ibid., 180.

10. Ibid., 81.

11. "For North American Christians who are serious about re-forming the church so that it may become a more faithful bearer of divine judgment and mercy in our social context, there is no alternative to a disciplined, prolonged, and above all critical work of theology." Douglas John Hall, "An Awkward Church," booklet 5, *Theology and Worship Occasional Papers* (Louisville, KY: Presbyterian Church, USA, 1993), 15. For further reading, see Anthony Robinson, *What's Theology Got to Do with It? Convictions, Vitality, and the Church* (Herndon, VA: Alban Institute, 2006).

12. This is the values gap of Heifetz's adaptive challenge. It is also the nonsite of deconstruction—a place that is no place—from which the congregation can appear as other to itself.

13. *Mrs. Miniver* (1942), directed by William Wyler, won six Academy Awards, including Best Picture. In his book *Bad Religion: How We Became a Nation of Heretics*, journalist Ross Douthat documents the rise and decline of what he understands as "orthodox" Christianity in America, embodied successively by mainline Protestant denominations, Roman Catholicism, and evangelicalism. Watching *Mrs. Miniver*, I imagined it to be an example of Christianity's cultural dominance, the loss of which Douthat mourns throughout his book. As someone born in 1970 (and a generational contemporary of Douthat, by the way), I found the experience of watching *Mrs. Miniver* a strange mixture of nostalgia and alienation. How wonderful it must have been to lead a church that benefited from all the privileges and support of a dominant culture! How completely foreign that image is to my experience of leading churches! *Mrs. Miniver* is a powerful image of the established church's role as chaplain to power.

14. Pastor and denominational leader Richard Hamm, in his book *Recreating the Church: Leadership for the Postmodern Age* (St. Louis, MO: Chalice Press, 2007), connects mid-twentieth-century shifts in mainline Protestant denominational structures to the American experience of World War II. He argues that the World War II generation attributed their victory over Hitler to better organization. They "'saved the world' by getting organized" and restructured their congregations and denominations for the "Christian century" along these same lines "just in time to be obsolete" for younger generations.

15. Recall Jesus's prioritizing of action over words in the parable of the two brothers from chapter 2. Also see biblical texts such as Matthew 7:17–21: "In the same way, every good tree bears good fruit, but the bad tree bears bad fruit. A good tree cannot bear bad fruit, nor can a bad tree bear good fruit. Every tree that does not bear good fruit is cut down and thrown into the fire. Thus you will know them by their fruits. Not everyone who says to me, 'Lord, Lord,' will enter the kingdom of heaven, but only the one who does the will of my Father in heaven."

16. Woven like a thread through the many-colored and multitextured voices of this study (or perhaps like the grout of a mosaic) is theologian Don S. Browning's model of fundamental practical theology, which borrows the Aristotelian concept of phronesis—"practical wisdom"—to argue that all practice is "theory-laden." That is, human activity is always already infused with notions, most often unconscious and unexamined, about how the world operates and what is of ultimate value. See Browning, *A Fundamental Practical Theology: Descriptive and Strategic Proposals* (Minneapolis: Fortress Press, 1991), 6–7, and David Tracy, "The Foundations of Practical Theology," in *Practical Theology*, ed. Don S. Browning (San Francisco: Harper & Row, 1983), 61, 81.

17. James Gardiner Vose, *Sketches of Congregationalism in Rhode Island* (New York: Silver, Burdett & Co., 1894), 75–76.

18. Hall, "An Awkward Church," 7.

19. Richard Kearney, "Jacques Derrida: Deconstruction and the Other," in *Debates in Continental Philosophy: Conversations with Contemporary Thinkers* (New York: Fordham University Press, 2004), 144.

20. Heifetz, *Leadership without Easy Answers*, 116, 106, 119–20.

21. I think the movie Tim is referring to is *Where Eagles Dare* (1968). Though the details of the movie don't quite match Tim's memory, there is definitely a climactic bridge explosion that allows the heroes to escape the Nazis.

22. For a biblical example, recall Moses's protests to God's call from the burning bush.

23. Keller, *Face of the Deep*, 139.

24. Lest I give the impression that Keller's theology of becoming has hardened into some final conclusion, I offer an example of what is perhaps a bit of countertestimony to the "mutual influence" and loving "lure" of *ex profundis*: recall that it is God who hardens Pharaoh's heart in the Exodus narratives. Catherine Keller, *On the Mystery: Discerning Divinity in Process* (Minneapolis, MN: Fortress Press, 2008), 112. In one telling verse, God boasts of hardening the Egyptians' hearts simply that "he" might demonstrate "his" ability to destroy them. In this "text of terror" (referring to Phyllis Trible's 1984 book of the same name), God demonstrates a undomesticated otherness and a frightening freedom (Exod. 10:1ff).

25. Keller, *Face of the Deep*, 214.

26. Brian McLaren, *Church on the Other Side: Exploring the Radical Future of the Local Congregation* (Grand Rapids, MI: Zondervan, 2006), 16.

27. Heifetz, *Leadership without Easy Answers*, 21.

28. Stephen Pattison, *Shame: Theory, Therapy, Theology* (Cambridge: Cambridge University Press, 2000), 36.

29. Keller, *Face of the Deep*, 229.

30. In the commentary accompanying his translation of Exodus, Everett Fox points out the centrality of the Sinai encounter. He notes that the encounter is the "textual center" of Exodus and that Sinai is at the "geographic center" of the wanderings (Fox, *The Five Books of Moses*, 359). Israel's relationship with God did not start at Sinai, and it does not end there, but there is something paradigmatic about the experience that makes it a helpful place from which we can reach through the story back to Moses's birth and forward to the entrance into Canaan. John Collins argues that in later biblical literature—such as Isaiah (see 59:9–11)—creation and the exodus are considered alike, if not identical. See John Collins, *Jews, Christians, and the Theology of the Hebrew Scriptures*, ed. Alice Ogden Bellis and Joel S. Kaminsky (Atlanta: Society of Biblical Literature, 2000), 259. The Bible begins with creation. Beginning at Sinai, we find ourselves in the center of God's creative encounter with God's people.

31. Keller, *Face of the Deep*, 230.

32. This might seem like a puzzling and contradictory aspect of redevelopment: How does one stop the bleeding while unblocking the flow? Once again, Keller gives us a theological clue. She writes that a theology of becoming resolutely oscillates between the absolute and the dissolute. Theologically, the absolute tries to answer all questions, close all gaps, perfect all mistakes, control all outcomes, and eliminate all uncertainties. Like an emergency room doctor, it intervenes with authority to rescue the hopelessly broken. There are moments in redevelopment—especially early on—when leaders have to intervene with authority to stop the bleeding and prevent total dissolution into a chaotic conflict of individual claims. Keller suggests that, oscillating between the decisive intervention of the absolute and apathetic relativism of the dissolute, Christians make a humble but resolute engagement with the world—creatively call-

ing order out of chaos while recognizing that all human attempts to make meaning inevitably give rise to an excluded other whose call will turn the tables on us once again. This oscillation between the familiar and unfamiliar—who we are and who are called to become—is the flow of the Spirit. "Such a process of discernment demands a disciplined spontaneity, retaining always its edge of uncertainty." Keller, *On the Mystery*, 160. Does this sound a bit like sacred conversation?

33. Hall, "An Awkward Church."

34. Ibid.

35. Theologian Johann Baptist Metz argues for churches claiming and celebrating this "slightly out-of-stepness." His term is "productive noncontemporaneity." In fact, given the Derridean deconstruction of the "presence of the present," noncontemporaneity may actually be a symptom of an allegiance to truth. Echoing Hegel (*Phenomenology of Spirit*), Metz calls Christian faith to "tarry with" or "linger over" "images, concepts, and practices" that modern people find "irredeemably out of date." See Johann Baptist Metz, *Faith in History and Society: Toward a Fundament Practical Theology*, trans. J. Matthew Ashley (New York: Crossroad, 2007), 2.

36. Mark C. Taylor, *Erring: A Postmodern A/Theology* (Chicago: University of Chicago Press, 1984), 5.

37. Rebecca Chopp, "Theology and the Poetics of Testimony," *Criterion* 36, no. 1 (Winter 1998): 8.

38. Taylor, *Erring*, 14.

39. Ibid., 17.

40. "'Tis the Gift to be Simple," eighteenth-century Shaker song.

WITHOUT CONCLUSION

1. Hans-Georg Gadamer, "Reply to Jacques Derrida," trans. Richard Palmer and Diane Michelfelder, in *Dialogue and Deconstruction*, ed. Richard Palmer and Diane Michelfelder (Albany: State University of New York Press, 1989), 57.

2. Edwin H. Friedman, *A Failure of Nerve: Leadership in the Age of the Quick Fix*, ed. Margaret M. Threadwell and Edward W. Beal (New York: Church Publishing, 2007), 40.

3. Penny Edgell Becker, *Congregations in Conflict: Cultural Models of Local Religious Life* (Cambridge: Cambridge University Press, 1999), 207.

4. Ronald A. Heifetz, *Leadership without Easy Answers* (Cambridge, MA: Harvard University Press, 1994), 66, 199–20.

5. See Becker's discussion of "primary objective" and the limits of organizational identity in *Congregations in Conflict*, 9.

6. Greg Mobley, conversation with the author, Newton Centre, Massachusetts, May 12, 2011.

7. Catherine Keller, *Face of the Deep: A Theology of Becoming* (London: Routledge, 2003), 90. Keller argues that this is an intimacy without reciprocity that characterizes the Christology, for example, of theologian Karl Barth.

8. Derrida traces the metaphor of truth as light, and knowing the truth as seeing the light, back to Plato. For this reason, he calls Western metaphysics "photology." See Jacques Derrida, *Writing and Difference* (Chicago: University of Chicago Press, 1978), 27. This same metaphor can be found as a thread throughout the Bible, from Genesis 1:3 ("Let there be light") to stories

of Jesus's healing blindness to Revelation 21:23 ("And the city has no need of sun or moon to shine on it, for the glory of God is its light, and its lamp is the Lamb").

9. G. W. F. Hegel, *Phenomenology of Spirit*, trans. A. V. Miller (Oxford: Oxford University Press, 1977), 11.

10. Though I have no reason to think that this person had studied postmodern thought or read Foucault, it is interesting to note that this is precisely the argument that Foucault makes (as did Nietzsche before him).

11. Biblical scholar Jon Levenson, on the deconstructive power of biblical texts, says that the fortunate thing about them is "the nasty habit of the Biblical texts themselves to survive all their modern (and premodern) retellings." From Alice Ogden Bellis and Joel S. Kaminsky, eds., *Jews, Christians, and the Theology of the Hebrew Scriptures* (Atlanta: Society of Biblical Literature, 2000), 264.

12. Catherine Keller, *On the Mystery: Discerning Divinity in Process* (Minneapolis: Fortress Press, 2008), 173.

13. John D. Caputo, ed., *Deconstruction in a Nutshell: A Conversation with Jacques Derrida* (New York: Fordham University Press, 1997), 106.

14. Becker writes that "to call [her congregational] models 'institutional' indicates that they are taken for granted and unarticulated unless challenged." *Congregations in Conflict*, 17. In Beneficent's case, answers to the questions about who we are and the way we do things here weren't understood as representing a particular cultural perspective. The established church identity and practice was simply "normal," "regular," or, most often, "traditional." Deconstruction asks, "Whose tradition?" and "Why yours?"

15. Keller, *Face of the Deep*, xvii, 230.

16. Ibid., 6.

17. For example, for a very small number of longtimers at Beneficent Church, non-Western worship music—particularly if it uses instrumentation other than an organ or piano—to which they are not accustomed is not simply "different" or music that they do not "prefer"; instead, they refer to the music in such degrading terms as "entertainment." Unfortunately, this is an indictment that I have heard regularly throughout my ministry career from longtime church members from a variety of congregations.

18. Keller, *Face of the Deep*, 226.

19. Heifetz, *Leadership without Easy Answers*, 14.

20. Keller, *Face of the Deep*, 190.

21. Jacques Derrida, "Différance," in *Deconstruction in Context: Literature and Philosophy*, ed. Mark C. Taylor (Chicago: University of Chicago Press, 1986), 414.

22. Keller, *On the Mystery*, 173.

23. Keller, *Face of the Deep*, 226.

24. Theologian Jürgen Moltmann writes, "Hope becomes a passion for what is possible." *Theology of Hope: On the Ground and Implications of a Christian Eschatology* (New York: Harper & Row, 1967), 20.

25. Keller, *On the Mystery*, 8.

26. David Kinnamon and Gabe Lyons, *Unchristian: What a New Generation Really Thinks about Christianity and Why It Matters* (Grand Rapids, MI: Baker Books, 2007), 41.

27. In Mobley's view, some results of the modern ontotheological project are "beautiful edifices of logic and palaces for the status quo." Conversation with the author, November 2, 2010, Andover Newton Theological School, Newton Centre, Masschusetts.

28. Keller argues that Genesis needs to be read "in proximity" to Exodus. In other words, creation and liberation correspond. For Keller, justice involves not only liberation from oppres-

sion but also somehow finding and making a home among exiles in the wilderness. *Face of the Deep*, 191.

29. *Différance* is spacing and difference. God institutes Passover that "you might know that the Lord makes a distinction between Egypt and Israel" (Exod. 11:7).

30. Keller, *Face of the Deep*, 230.

31. Jacques Derrida, *On the Name* (Stanford, CA: Stanford University Press, 2003), 43.

32. Recall Friedman's insight that the more well differentiated leaders become, the more sabotage is generated. The key to effective leadership is recognizing sabotage as in some sense self-generated and responding with the appropriate combination of compassion and resolve.

33. Creation *ex profundis* is an act of grace. *Ex profundis* grace is different from *ex nihilo* grace. *Ex nihilo* grace assumes a binary relation of dominance—for example, neo-orthodox theologian Karl Barth's "position of subsequence," in which the creation "follows" in good order its loving, yet dominating, Creator. In the *ex nihilo* storyline, grace is not the act of creation itself, but rather *follows* the fall of creation. *Saving grace* is the act of God to rescue us from the mess we have made of creation through our participation in sin. *Ex profundis* grace also rescues, but it rescues the Deep from the danger of "eternal undecidability." Without the decision, there would be no difference, and therefore there would be "no thing"—just everything in a state of potentiality. For Keller, the sheer fact that there is something and not nothing—"this non-linear might-not-have-been"—is grace. *Face of the Deep*, 180.

34. Ross Douthat, "Can Liberal Christianity Be Saved?" *New York Times*, July 14, 2012.

35. Diana Butler Bass, "Can Christianity Be Saved? A Response to Ross Douthat," *Huffington Post*, July 15, 2012, http://www.huffingtonpost.com/diana-butler-bass/can-christianity-be-saved_1_b_1674807.html.

36. Christopher Brittain, "A Plague on Both Their Houses: The Real Story of Growth and Decline in Liberal and Conservative Churches," *ABC Religion and Ethics*, May 8, 2013, http://www.abc.net.au/religion/articles/2013/05/08/3754700.htm.

37. Douthat, "Can Liberal Christianity Be Saved?"

38. Diana Butler Bass, *Christianity after Religion: The End of the Church and the Birth of a New Spiritual Awakening* (New York: HarperOne, 2012), 263.

39. See Robert Bellah et al., *Habits of the Heart: Individualism and Commitment in American Life* (Berkeley: University of California Press, 1985).

Bibliography

Bandy, Thomas G. *Moving Off the Map: A Field Guide to Changing the Congregation.* Nashville: Abingdon Press, 1998.

———. *Kicking Habits: Welcome Relief for Addicted Churches.* Upgraded ed. Nashville: Abingdon Press, 2001.

Bass, Diana Butler. *The Practicing Congregation: Imagining a New Old Church.* Herndon, VA: Alban Institute, 2004.

———. *Christianity after Religion: The End of Church and the Birth of a New Spiritual Awakening.* New York: HarperOne, 2012.

Becker, Penny Edgell. *Congregations in Conflict: Cultural Models of Local Religious Life.* Cambridge: Cambridge University Press, 1999.

Bellah, Robert, et al. *Habits of the Heart: Individualism and Commitment in American Life.* Berkeley: University of California Press, 1985.

Boff, Leonardo, and Clodovis Boff. *Introducing Liberation Theology.* Translated by Paul Burns. Maryknoll, NY: Orbis Books, 1987.

Browning, Don S. *A Fundamental Practical Theology: Descriptive and Strategic Proposals.* Minneapolis: Fortress Press, 1991.

———. "Congregational Studies as Practical Theology." In *American Congregations*, vol. 2, *New Perspectives on the Study of Congregations*, edited by James P. Wind and James W. Lewis, 192–220. Chicago: University of Chicago Press, 1994.

Chopp, Rebecca. "Theology and the Poetics of Testimony." *Criterion* 36, no. 1 (Winter 1998).

Collins, John J. *Jews, Christians, and the Theology of the Hebrew Scriptures.* Edited by Alice Ogden Bellis and Joel S. Kaminsky. Atlanta: Society of Biblical Literature, 2000.

Derrida, Jacques. *Writing and Difference.* Translated by Alan Bass. London: Routledge, 1966.

———. "Différance." In *Speech and Phenomenon and Other Essays in Husserl's Theory of Signs*, translated by David B. Allison, 129–60. Evanston, IL: Northwestern University Press, 1973.

———. *On the Name.* Edited by Thomas Dutoit. Translated by David Wood, John P. Leavey Jr., and Ian McLeod. Stanford, CA: Stanford University Press, 1995.

———. *Deconstruction in a Nutshell: A Conversation with Jacques Derrida.* Edited by John D. Caputo. New York: Fordham University Press, 1997.

――――. *Of Grammatology*. Translated by Gayatri Chakravorty Spivak. Corrected ed. Baltimore: Johns Hopkins University Press, 1997.

――――. *The Gift of Death and Literature in Secret*. 2nd ed. Translated by David Wills. Chicago: University of Chicago Press, 2008.

Douthat, Ross. *Bad Religion: How We Became a Nation of Heretics*. New York: Free Press, 2012.

Dussel, Enrique. *Philosophy of Liberation*. Translated by Aquilina Martinez and Christine Morkovsky. Maryknoll, NY: Orbis Books, 1985.

Easum, William M. *Sacred Cows Make Gourmet Burgers: Ministry Anytime, Anywhere, by Anyone*. Nashville: Abingdon Press, 1995.

Edwards, Korie L. *The Elusive Dream: The Power of Race in Interracial Churches*. Oxford: Oxford University Press, 2008.

Foucault, Michel. *Power/Knowledge: Selected Interviews and Other Writings, 1972–1977*. Edited by Colin Gordon. Translated by Colin Gordon, Leo Marshall, John Mepham, and Kate Soper. New York: Vintage Books, 1980.

Fox, Everett. *The Five Books of Moses*. New York: Schocken Press, 1995.

Friedman, Edwin H. *A Failure of Nerve: Leadership in the Age of the Quick Fix*. Edited by Margaret M. Threadwell and Edward W. Beal. New York: Church Publishing, 2007.

――――. *Generation to Generation: Family Process in Church and Synagogue*. New York: Guilford Press, 1985.

Gadamer, Hans-Georg. "*Destruktion* and Deconstruction." Translated by Geoff Waite and Richard Palmer. In *Dialogue and Deconstruction: The Gadamer-Derrida Encounter*, edited by Diane P. Michelfelder and Richard E. Palmer. Albany: State University of New York Press, 1989.

Gifford, Mary Louise. *The Turnaround Church: Inspiration and Tools for Life-Sustaining Change*. Herndon, VA: Alban Institute, 2009.

Guder, Darrell L. *The Continuing Conversion of the Church*. Grand Rapids, MI: William B. Eerdmans, 2000.

Hall, Douglas John. "An Awkward Church." Booklet 5, *Theology and Worship Occasional Papers* series. Louisville, KY: Presbyterian Church, USA, 1993. Prepared for Religion Online by Ted and Winnie Brock, http://www.religion-online.org/showbook.asp?title=415.

Hamm, Richard L. *Recreating the Church: Leadership for the Postmodern Age*. St. Louis: Chalice Press, 2007.

Hegel, Georg Wilhelm Friedrich, J. N. Findlay, and Arnold V. Miller. *Hegel's Phenomenology of Spirit*. Oxford: Oxford University Press, 1977.

Heifetz, Ronald A. *Leadership without Easy Answers*. Cambridge, MA: Harvard University Press, 1994.

――――. *Leadership on the Line: Staying Alive through the Dangers of Leading*. Boston: Harvard Business School Press, 2002.

Jameson, Frederic. *Postmodernism, or, the Cultural Logic of Late Capitalism*. Durham, NC: Duke University Press, 1991.

Kearney, Richard. "Jacques Derrida: Deconstruction and the Other." In *Debates in Continental Philosophy: Conversations with Contemporary Thinkers*, 139–56. New York: Fordham University Press, 2004.

Keller, Catherine. *Face of the Deep: A Theology of Becoming*. London: Routledge, 2003.

――――. *On the Mystery: Discerning Divinity in Process*. Minneapolis: Fortress Press, 2008.

Kinnaman, David, and Gabe Lyons. *Unchristian: What a New Generation Really Thinks about Christianity . . . and Why It Matters*. Grand Rapids, MI: Baker Books, 2007.

Law, Eric H. F. *The Wolf Shall Dwell with the Lamb: A Spirituality for Leadership in a Multicultural Community*. St. Louis: Chalice Press, 1993.

Lederach, John Paul. *The Little Book of Conflict Transformation*. Intercourse, PA: Good Books, 2003.

Lewis, Michael. *Shame: The Exposed Self*. New York: Free Press, 1992.

Mann, Alice. *Can This Church Live? Redeveloping Churches in Decline*. Herndon, VA: Alban Institute, 1999.

Marti, Gerardo. *A Mosaic of Believers: Diversity and Innovation in a Multiethnic Church*. Bloomington: Indiana University Press, 2005.

———. *Worship across the Racial Divide: Religious Music and the Multiracial Congregation*. Oxford: Oxford University Press, 2012.

McLaren, Brian D. *Church on the Other Side: Doing Ministry in the Postmodern Matrix*. Grand Rapids, MI: Zondervan, 2000.

———. *More Ready Than You Realize: Evangelism as Dance in the Postmodern Matrix*. Grand Rapids, MI: Zondervan, 2002.

———. *A Generous Orthodoxy: Why I Am a Missional, Evangelical, Post/Protestant, Liberal/ Conservative . . . Unfinished Christian*. Grand Rapids, MI: Zondervan, 2004.

Metz, Johann Baptist. *Faith in History and Society: Toward a Practical Fundamental Theology*. New York: Crossroad, 1977.

Moltmann, Jürgen. *Theology of Hope: On the Ground and the Implications of a Christian Eschatology*. Translated by James W. Leitch. New York: Harper & Row, 1967.

Muffs, Yochanan. *Love and Joy: Law, Language, and Religion in Ancient Israel*. New York: Jewish Theological Seminary in America, 1992.

Pattison, Stephen. *Shame: Theory, Therapy, Theology*. Cambridge: Cambridge University Press, 2000.

Quinn, Robert E. *Deep Change: Discovering the Leader Within*. San Francisco: Jossey-Bass, 1996.

Rendle, Gil. *Leading Change in the Congregation: Spiritual and Organizational Tools for Leaders*. Herndon, VA: Alban Institute, 1998.

———. *Journey in the Wilderness: New Life for Mainline Churches*. Nashville: Abingdon Press, 2010.

Robinson, Anthony B. *Transforming Congregational Culture*. Grand Rapids, MI: William B. Eerdmans, 2003.

———. *What's Theology Got to Do with It? Convictions, Vitality, and the Church*. Herndon, VA: Alban Institute, 2006.

———. *Leadership for Vital Congregations*. Cleveland: Pilgrim Press, 2006.

Taylor, Mark C. *Erring: A Postmodern A/Theology*. Chicago: University of Chicago Press, 1984.

———, ed. *Deconstruction in Context: Literature and Philosophy*. Chicago: University of Chicago Press, 1986.

Tracy, David. "The Foundations of Practical Theology." In *Practical Theology*, edited by Don S. Browning, 61–81. San Francisco: Harper & Row, 1983.

———. "Fragments: The Spiritual Situation of Our Times." In *God, the Gift, and Postmodernism*, edited by John D. Caputo, 170–84. Bloomington: Indiana University Press, 1999.

Vose, James Gardiner. *Sketches of Congregationalism in Rhode Island*. New York: Silver, Burdett, & Co., 1894.

Wilson, Arthur E. *Weybosset Bridge*. Boston: Pilgrim Press, 1947.

Wuthnow, Robert. *The Crisis in the Churches: Spiritual Malaise, Fiscal Woe*. New York: Oxford University Press, 1997.

CPSIA information can be obtained at www.ICGtesting.com
Printed in the USA
BVOW07s1118310714

361106BV00001B/2/P